NORTH END SOULS 3

For The Gentry.

Best wishes,

ISBN: 978-1-8380604-2-8

 Published by Fulwood End Media. Printed in the EU. www.northendsouls.com

PAINTED LOVE

L*EEMING OUT.* The words jumped off the bedsheet in painted letters two feet tall. And as the teenage terrace warrior admired his artwork on the kitchen floor, he was rock-solid sure of one thing: *'That'll show 'em, eh?'*

That night, the flat-capped Kop raised a rare cheer as *'LEEMING OUT'* was unfurled in all its grotty glory.

The Lancashire Evening Post captured the scene for posterity (the picture still pops up every now and then) and its rain-spattered tones catch the mid-80's re-election era perfectly. In a word, grim.

A couple of steps along was another hand-scrawled bedsheet declaring: *'The Board have killed PNE'.* Not long before, we'd seen the classic *'Booth Out, Board Out, Half the Bloody Team Out'* banner in the Pavilion Paddock. This might not have been a vintage time for North End, but it was the golden era of Dulux paint splashed across Woolworth's bedding.

These, my friends, were the darkest days Preston North End had ever seen - and not just because the floodlights weren't lined up properly.

To no-one's great surprise, on the night of the Kop banners, North End got beat 2-1 by Cambridge and the crowd (if you can call it that) was a mighty 2,840.

The loudest (only?) chant was '*Sack the Board'* and a few dozen hardy souls staged a post-match sit-in on Lowthorpe Road. It didn't last long, but to be fair it was a bit nippy, the chippy was closing and they had to catch the last bus home.

The revolution can wait, the Number 11 to Longridge won't.

Of course, the fact that Keith Leeming and his fellow directors were shovelling in a small fortune just to keep the club on life support was beside the point.

The fans had paid a quid to get in and they were going to let those bar stewards know they weren't standing for it any more.

Mercifully, of course, the club wasn't dead after all . . . just resting.

More mercifully still, Chairman Leeming took no notice of the terrace grumbles. If he and his fellow directors hadn't dug deep, North End really would have been pushing up the daisies.

As it was, Brian Kidd quit and Jonathan Clark did what he could. John McGrath arrived and the rest, as they say, is history.

As time passes though, it's a history that's fading before our eyes in black and white. But in my book, it deserves to be remembered.

Delving back into those days to write the North End Souls series is sometimes painful, sometimes joyous, occasionally cathartic, but always absolutely fascinating.

This third volume includes half a dozen people who have managed the club over the past 40 years and lived to tell the tale.

From Tommy Booth's reluctant reign in the 1980s to Darren Ferguson's mistimed spell in charge and the Graham Westley whirlwind *(which eventually reaped his Deepdale career)*, their personal perspectives offer a unique insight into what it's really like to sit in the hot seat.

Familiar themes pop up throughout; broken promises, missed opportunities and the lack of those most precious commodities . . . time and money.

This set of stories also includes a chapter from a former chairman, with Bryan Gray outlining the most dramatic period of change the club has ever seen during the BAXI revolution.

As always, there are great players to tell their tales too, from Mick Rathbone's laugh-out-loud anecdotes to Ricky Heppolette's nights with George Best, and Jermaine Beckford talking us through *that* day at Wembley.

Each chapter has been brought about in the shadow of Covid, made all the harsher for North End fans by our absence from Deepdale for 17 long months. Interviews that would normally have been carried out overlooking the pitch have instead been done via Zoom, Teams or FaceTime.

But they are none the worse for it and, if nothing else, I now know what a lot of ex-footballer's spare bedrooms, kitchens and gardens look like.

A lot like yours and mine, I suspect, and yet again the people involved were an absolute pleasure to talk to, offering their time, their memories and their emotions freely for the sake of this book.

'Are you sure you want me in this?' asked one true PNE legend, 'I don't think anyone will remember me.'

They do and they will - long after all of us have been and gone.

Reading these words tells us that while the people involved may not have got everything right, they understand what Preston North End means.

Even those who were not successful at the club speak genuinely about their pride at having been at Deepdale - and the disappointment when their time was up.

So if these books play a small part in passing on that passion for PNE to generations young and old then it will all have been worthwhile.

Because what comes through loud and clear is that so many of the players, managers and (sometimes) chairmen share our feelings for the club. If not, well, they're missing the point, aren't they?

Which brings us neatly back to *'LEEMING OUT'*.

I wonder whatever happened to that daft young lad . . .

Keith Harrison, Author

IAN BRYSON: HEART ON MY SLEEVE

Pride - that's the first word that comes to mind when I'm asked about Preston North End. Not just because of the 'Proud Preston' motto, but because it's something that everyone who's ever pulled on that famous Lilywhites shirt feels, too.

It's a familiar theme to all the stories in this book and I know from my work as a club ambassador these days that it's a genuine emotion for all the ex-North End players.

One of my duties is to invite a couple of former players to be guests at games and, without fail, they can't wait to come back to Deepdale.

There's something about the club that makes you feel part of the family.

I experienced it when I first walked through the door in 1993 and it's still the same today; everyone's friendly, the fans are fantastic and it's somewhere you love to be associated with.

I'll be honest, when I arrived, I knew about Sir Tom Finney, but I probably didn't know as much about the club as I should have done.

I'd grown up on a dairy farm in Ayrshire and my early years in the game were spent as a full-time farmer and part-time footballer.

Obviously, it was quite a rural upbringing, but me and a pal - big Alan McInally - played for Ayr United's youth teams in our teenage years.

I was let go at 18 and started playing for a local side before Kilmarnock came in for me and offered me a part-time contract.

One of the players I always looked up to was Davie Cooper at Rangers (who sadly passed away many years ago) but my first game was in a friendly against Celtic, which was a massive thing for me.

It turned out to be quite an introduction to the levels required as I was playing left wing up against the Celtic full-back Danny McGrain. Older readers won't need telling how tough an afternoon that was - even in a friendly!

A few years later I moved down to England with Sheffield United in 1988. I was 25 by that point and it was my first taste of full-time football so it was another big challenge.

In my first game, we played Brentford and this time I was up against Keith Curle - so my debuts didn't get any easier as time went on (!). The Blades were in the Third Division at the time but Dave Bassett got people like Tony Agana and Brian Deane in and we went up through the leagues to the old First Division.

I had a couple of seasons in the top flight with the Blades so I was a bit surprised - and definitely disappointed - when the club was prepared to let me go in the summer of 1993.

I went to Barnsley under Viv Anderson and Danny Wilson for a brief spell, but it didn't really work out there and after a few months I got a call from Gary Peters who was John Beck's assistant at Preston at the time.

I knew of John's playing style having come up against that great Cambridge team he put together. It was a really tough task playing against them - the ball never stopped moving and they were on you constantly with players like Dion Dublin leading the charge.

North End were flying in the Fourth Division at that point, so I'd gone from playing in the top level to being in the bottom tier in less than 12 months, which was a bit of a turnaround to say the least.

But Preston were a good club and I thought John Beck would do well.

He was a great coach, even if some of his methods were 'unconventional', and he had put together a very strong team.

Preston had always had a reputation for picking up Scottish players and there were some great lads from across the border during my time; David Moyes, Ray Sharp, Kevin Magee, Mike Conroy and one or two others.

The team spirit was unbelievable and the game I'll never forget is the Torquay play-off at Deepdale. Everything about that night was incredible and for anyone who was there, that match summed up the magic of Deepdale.

Yes, it was a bit decrepit by that point and the plastic pitch was on its last legs, but the crowd, the atmosphere - the stadium just took on a 'will to win' of its own that night.

I'll never forget it, not just for the drama of the game, but also for the fact that it's the only time I've cried with joy at the end.

I'm normally a level-headed kind of guy, but that night was just so emotional, it really got to me. The other thing about it was that it meant I was going to fulfil a childhood dream of playing at Wembley.

I'd missed out at Sheffield United when we reached the FA Cup semi-final the previous year through injury, so to have the chance to play there with North End was a massive thing.

My family had travelled down in numbers for the game and they'd backed me to score first. So when I got the opener, they had even more reason to celebrate!

I'd have taken a scruffy goal to be honest, but to get an overhead kick at the end where the Preston fans were was the stuff of dreams, it really was.

In a 17-year career, I think that was the only time I ever tried one, so I've got a 100 per cent success record with overhead kicks.

Unfortunately, I think we were still celebrating when Wycombe went down the other end and equalised. To be fair, they were a good side and they deserved to win that day.

After John left and Gary made Moyesie his assistant, I was probably the next in line in terms of experience for the captaincy and it was a tremendous honour to lead the team out.

The lads made my job so much easier because there were so many top professionals in the squad and I didn't really need to do very much, if I'm honest.

Everywhere you looked in the team there were leaders - Moyesie and Russ Wilcox at the back, Andy Saville and Steve Wilkinson up front, Dean Barrick, Kelham O'Hanlon, just all throughout the team, really.

Everyone knew what the standards were and everyone understood what was required - on and off the pitch.

That season when we won the league was just incredible. The last three games - Leyton Orient away, where we went up, then Hartlepool away where we won the title and finally the Exeter game where we got the trophy.

When you think about it, we had three bites of the cherry with celebrations every week - times like that don't come around very often and there was a real bond between the team and the supporters.

The Exeter game in particular, with the Tom Finney Stand open and everything that was happening at the club, was just a very special occasion.

I'd had great success with Sheffield United but undoubtedly that 1995/96 season stands out for me because of the football we played - we scored more than 100 goals and only lost six games.

Sav and Steve scored for fun up front, while we had loads of goals from midfield too; I had double figures, Simon Davey - another great leader - got double figures, Lee Cartwright chipped in with a few, Graeme Atkinson too, so we were a really good side that year.

Also, it was the only time I ever won anything in my career (!).

At Sheffield United, we went up both times finishing runners-up and at the time you didn't get a medal for that - which was crazy because the play-off winners actually got one.

What's funny looking back is that it doesn't feel like 25 years ago. I'm 58 now and those days still seem like yesterday. BAXI had just come in and it was the first time someone had put together a plan and had the resources to make it happen.

The momentum that grew under Bryan Gray was tangible and you felt the club was really moving forward. It was just such a positive time and with Preston being such a lively football town, it was fantastic to be a part of.

Bryan had the foresight to see what could be achieved and it was the start of something special. When you look at the stadium now, it's absolutely first class in every area and something everyone can take pride in (there's that word again).

I loved playing at Deepdale so when Gary told me I could leave the following year I was shocked, to be honest.

I'd been captain for a couple of years and I expected that I would stay with the club until I retired, then take up some form of coaching role maybe.

I just wanted to be at the club forever, so I was disappointed.

Instead, Gary gave me a free transfer with the rationale that he wanted to bring in younger players.

He thought that if I was still there, I'd probably restrict Kevin Kilbane's development in particular, because although I was right-footed, I mainly played on the left wing and used to like to cut inside.

I had to accept what Gary was saying, even if it wasn't what I wanted, but it was a sad, sad day when I left for the last time, knowing my time was up.

I went to Rochdale where I struggled for a couple of years with injuries, by which time I was 36.

The ironic thing was, I then went to Bamber Bridge and played 57 games on the trot, while doing my coaching badges at the same time.

The sessions were at The Cliff, Manchester United's old training ground and what was great was that David Beckham would always come over and have a chat if he was around. He loved his time at Deepdale and, even though he was an established star by that point, he still took an interest in North End.

It's something that gets in your blood a bit and it was great to come back when Gary asked me to help out with the Centre of Excellence, which I did for a few years and really enjoyed.

As I mentioned above, these days I'm a club ambassador and do hosting on match days in the Invincibles Lounge, doing the type of thing that the great George Ross did for many years.

When we played Swindon at Wembley, we all went down on a coach with George and some other former players and it was just magical - that family spirit at the club shone through and to have such a special day in such great company is something that will live with me forever.

I've still got a passion for football and a passion for Preston especially - I played in a charity game over the summer with a few of the lads and absolutely loved being back out there in a North End shirt.

I still live in the town, my children have grown up here and my grandchildren are here now too, so we've got proper Prestonian roots.

It's a great place with great people and every now and then, someone will recognise me out and about and we'll have a chat about my playing days.

Whether I was good, bad or indifferent in games, I always played with my heart on my sleeve and pride in the badge.

It seems like only yesterday since we won the league in that glorious 1995/96 season, but hopefully this book can take people back to those days.

If you were there, you were lucky - I know I was.

And if you weren't, you can still take pride in what the lads achieved back then in a different era.

Whether you're a supporter or an ex-player, we've all got one thing in common - we're proud of Preston North End.

Enjoy the book.

Ian Bryson

CHAPTER 1

MICK RATHBONE: RATH OF THE GODS

Every now and then, I'm walking across the Flag Market in Preston city centre and I just can't help myself. It may be cold, wet and empty but I stop for a moment, close my eyes and - *boom!* - I'm back in 1996.

The sun is shining, the place is rammed with North End fans and over on the Harris Museum steps Gary Peters is on the mic, singing about that lot with the tower: 'Altogether now . . !'

To have experienced a day like that just once would have been enough.

To have done it again with Moyesie a few years later . . . well, I'm a lucky, lucky lad.

And that's just one of the reasons Preston North End will always have a special place in my heart. I probably can't list all the others, but I'll have a go. So bear with me while I take you through my time as a player under the late, great John McGrath, then as physio under Gary Peters and a certain very keen Scotsman.

They were among the happiest times of a career that began in the glorious 1970s. That was my era and my team growing up was Birmingham City, the mighty royal Blues.

I was a typical working class kid from Sheldon (the posh part of Brum - twinned with Ribbleton, I believe). And I was lucky to have great parents, a brilliant family and to be able to play football every minute of the day.

Kickabouts would last for hours with your mates, then school matches in the week, a game on Saturday morning, break to watch Blues in the afternoon, then two games on a Sunday and start all over again on Monday morning before the school bell rang. I loved it.

And guess what? No-one got burned out. No-one got injured. The only zone we knew was the Twilight Zone on TV and the only transition was when it got dark and you had to go home. We were just kids, playing for enjoyment - not a coaching manual in sight.

You didn't have fancy kit or the latest boots. You wore whatever you could get your feet in - normally whatever your older brother had grown out of.

But all this 'playing for the love of the game' couldn't last and Birmingham had to ruin it all (!) by offering me an apprenticeship at £16-a-week.

I'm sure you can imagine what that was like in the enlightened 1970s, so I won't bore you with the details.

Suffice to say, I did a lot of fetching, carrying, making tea and cleaning baths, toilets, coaches' cars - and boots.

I'll always remember the numbers of the six pairs I had to clean: 14, 16, 29, 32, 39 and 42. They were so ingrained in my mind that years later, I still used them for my Lottery numbers and guess what?

Not so much as a tenner.

I suppose that's a sign of how things went for me at Birmingham - it could have been lucky and brilliant, but it wasn't.

People might be surprised to hear this but I suffered from chronic confidence issues that held me back all the way through my career, really.

And I mean chronic. Even though I was a good player, my lack of confidence would reduce me to a stumbling wreck at times - an absolute nightmare.

I would overthink things and just wish I could have understood back then what I know now: It's only a game. It's a beautiful game, but it's still only a game. Just enjoy it, because if you can't enjoy football, you'll never enjoy anything.

Of course, that's said with the benefit of 40-odd years when both me and the game have moved on dramatically. Back then, my much younger self wasn't helped by the macho culture that used to be around.

Coaches would absolutely tear us apart and I quickly realised we weren't there to play football, we were there to win matches.

At all costs - just win matches.

Despite my lack of confidence, I got selected for England Youths, played for the Birmingham First Team and landed a professional contract.

The manager Willie Bell told me it would be £45-a-week, but I somehow haggled with him on account of being an England Youth.

'OK,' he said, grudgingly: 'You can have an extra fiver - just don't tell the rest of the lads, for God's sake!'

Willie eventually left and was replaced by none other than Sir Alf Ramsey. When he took over, he informed us underlings: 'I don't like the terms 'gaffer' or 'boss' - it smacks of the factory floor. And 'Alf' is far too familiar.

'So if you all call me 'Sir Alf', we'll get along just fine.'

Then, incredibly, the man who won the World Cup started selecting me for matches; Hurst, Peters, Charlton . . . now Rathbone.

I actually got on with him very well, but I was absolutely terrified before games; not of Sir Alf, just the whole thing.

My legs turned to jelly, my pulse started racing, I was sweating - just a right mess. If you think it sounds horrible - try living it for real.

It wasn't nervousness, it was much more than that - actual fear of walking out of THAT door and going out THERE.

Even now, when I hear the opening bars to Mr Blue Sky, it reminds me of that dark place - the tunnel at St Andrews; the baying crowd, the press waiting to carve me up. I swear I would have rather been anywhere else.

It got to the point that I didn't wear shin pads in the hope that if I got injured, I wouldn't have to play.

So it was a painful period (in more ways than one) and, even though I had ability, I was relieved when I was eventually dropped.

However, it's a sign of my naivety that I let the older pros talk me into going to see Sir Alf. They said I should demand a transfer after I was left out of the team.

What followed was pure football theatre. I knocked on his door and he just said: *'Come!'* (Not *'Come in'* like a normal person, just *'Come!'*)

Enter Rathbone, stage left.
Sir Alf, reading a newspaper and barely looking up: *'Yes?'*
Me: 'I want a transfer. I'm fed up with being messed around.'
He glanced at me. No reaction.
Me: 'Don't try to talk me out of it!'
Silence.
Me, starting to gulp: 'Look, my mind's made up! I want to go!'
More silence.
He then slowly folded his newspaper and calmly placed it on the desk.
Sir Alf: '*Well, you can go by all means . . . but who's going to sign you? You're f****** crap.*'
Exit Rathbone, tail between legs!

Unsurprisingly, I stayed with Blues, who weren't exactly inundated with offers for my services.

As time went by though, I grew increasingly disillusioned and by the time I was the ripe old age of 20 I'd had enough.

It reached the point where I had a job lined up with Dyno-Rod and told my latest Birmingham manager, Jim Smith, that I would rather do that than carry on. Now, some of you may know that Jim could be a combustible character (!) so I expected him to hit the roof.

But instead, he put his arm around me, said he understood what I was going through and that he would arrange a loan to get my confidence back. Top man.

And that's how I ended up in Lancashire at Blackburn Rovers for the next eight years. To say it was a different era is an understatement; I roomed with the legendary Simon Garner for eight years and on a Friday night before away games, we'd have a buffet and end up having competitions to see who could eat the most. Then we'd sneak a few cans back to the room and watch telly 'til all hours.

Garns would be there with a beer in his hand and a fag on the go. I used to stay awake until he'd gone to sleep because I was scared of him dropping off and setting the room on fire. (Seriously!)

But despite his unique preparation, Garns was one of the best strikers I've ever seen - and a lot of defenders soon learned that looks can be deceptive.

Me? I've always looked old. Well, older than I am.

One time I was playing for Blackburn against Everton and the TV commentator said: 'There's Trevor Steven and Gary Stevens, teaming up down that side to exploit the veteran full-back Rathbone.'

Veteran?! I was 25.

(And by the way, Gary-flaming-Stevens was actually older than me!)

I loved my time at Rovers though, mainly under the inimitable Bobby Saxton; a proper old-school, tell-it-as-it-is football manager who later joined the staff at Deepdale. One time we were playing a team from down south and Sacko burst into the dressing room before the game with: *'Lads, we're going to slaughter these today - I've just seen one of their lads come in carrying a hair-dryer!'*

Bob was like a father figure to us, but times change and when he left Rovers Don Mackay came in. He was OK, but I was left out of the Full Members' Cup Final at Wembley in the 1986/87 season and that was my signal that it was time to move on.

By that point, Bobby was helping out at Preston, who had just got promoted from the old Fourth Division under John McGrath.

A few teams came in for me, but with Sacko being there, the history of the club, founder members of the league, etc . . .

It could have been all those things, or it could have been they were eight miles from my house. You decide.

Either way, my mind was set - it was Preston North End for me.

My contract was up at Ewood but they'd offered me an extension and, in the pre-Bosman days, that meant the clubs had to go to a Football League tribunal to set the fee. What a bizarre system that was.

The club that wanted you had to say you were so crap you were basically worthless - and the other club (which effectively didn't want you) had to say you were so brilliant you were worth a fortune.

So it turned out that Rovers wanted £60,000 *(seriously!)* and North End offered £5,000 (a bit more like it).

I was in my late 20s and Rovers said I was 'coming into my best years', while Preston said 'his best years are behind him'. Cheers for that!

Me? I wanted the fee to be as low as possible - not that I had any financial interest in it, but if you sign on a free, expectations are much lower. The less pressure the better, please.

On the day in question, I had to go over to the tribunal with John McGrath and PNE chairman Keith Leeming. We arrived at the offices in Lytham and were sent to a waiting room with Don Mackay and Rovers chairman Bill Fox. There had been some acrimony between the clubs and you could cut the atmosphere with a knife. No-one spoke. No small talk, nothing.

I didn't like it, because I loved Rovers and didn't want to leave under a cloud.

Eventually, I was called in on my own to tell the tribunal why I was hardly worth a sausage; I had given Rovers good service, wasn't being paid a fortune and they'd only offered me a one-year extension, etc.

Then it was back out to sit in awkward silence again. Thankfully, Keith gave me the keys to his Jag and I went to wait in the car. I climbed in the back and sat there, praying for a low fee and basically bricking it.

Finally, John and Keith emerged, all stony-faced, and got in the car without saying a word.

Silence, again. More torture.

Eventually, Keith lit up a big cigar and it was a real Hamlet moment *(not Shakespeare, the old TV adverts).*

With a big puff of smoke, he said: 'Never mind John, you can't win them all.'

Oh crap.

That's when Big John turned round and I discovered my true value: 'Twenty f****** grand! Twenty thousand pounds! That's the most I've ever paid for a player! You'd better do the f****** business son.'

Great, no pressure, then. Cheers, gaffer!

But, pressure or not, I loved John. Any North End fans from back then will know what he was like - an unbelievable character.

When I arrived, the great Frank Worthington was still at Deepdale and he was just magical, wasn't he? You'd play passes into him and they would stick like glue. Chest height, head height, knee height, left foot, right foot . . . he'd control them all just the same; smooth, effortless, just sheer class.

I'd play the ball up to him and he'd take the ball in then do two or three keepy-uppies to give me time to overlap.

Then he'd look up and see I hadn't crossed the half way line yet! So he'd just do two or three more keepy-uppies while giving me a smile as I sprinted *(OK, chugged)* past that said: 'Tell me when you're ready, Baz.'

Then, smooth as silk, he'd drop the perfect pass behind the full-back.

There were people marking him, of course, but it got to the stage where they stood off him a bit, rather than look stupid by trying to get it off him.

He was the exact opposite of me in many ways; massively confident and, even though he was pushing 40 at that point, he still had the film star looks, the long flowing hair, the air of cool. He was just a dream footballer and what an entertainer. It's so sad that he passed away recently - he was a brilliant guy.

Later on, I managed him at Halifax and he was still amazing. I couldn't tell you how old he was by then, in fact I never asked - no-one did - he was just ageless.

Even after Frank left Preston, John McGrath had this blackboard in the dressing room for meetings. On it, he split the pitch up into three sections - all marked up very clearly.

In the defending third he wrote: 'No messing about.'

In the middle: 'Win the physical battle.'

And up front it just said: *'Mr Worthington.'*

That was it. Don't give away any chances at the back, work hard in midfield - and up front, use your skill and be creative; imagine you are Frank Worthington.

(That's easier said than done, isn't it?)

But tactically, it was simple and it made perfect sense. And don't forget in an era of 4-4-2, John played three at the back with overlapping wingbacks. So he wasn't a dinosaur; he knew what he was doing.

Down the middle were the 'solicitors' - Allardyce, Atkins and Jones - with me and Dave 'Dusty' Miller bombing up and down out wide.

It was hard work getting up and down all game, but very effective.

To keep us up to date on tactics (and anything else), we had regular team meetings in the old dressing room at Deepdale. And when I say '*regular*', I mean every flipping day. On the very first day I arrived, as I sat down on the wooden bench, I noticed most of the lads were sitting on towels.

I thought: 'That's odd, I wonder why they're doing that?'

Two bum-numbing hours later, I had my answer. The gaffer would come in and say: 'Gentlemen, there are one or two things that have disconcerted me . . .'

And he was off; first came the rollockings - some poor sod was always in the firing line and John was undisputed world champion at handing them out: 'You've let me down, the club, the town . . . *the Mayor!*'

Then would come the praise - often for the lad who got the rollocking last week: 'I'm proud of you. The club's proud of you. *The Mayor's proud of you!'*

Then there'd be the stories; informing, motivating, captivating - he was a force of nature and I'd never heard anything like it.

One time, he ran through the entire team, likening people to a huge fruit salad. Brian Mooney was 'the strawberry' because he was the tastiest and most expensive. Tony Ellis was the cherry on top because he finished things off. Big Sam and Alex Jones were oranges because they added a bit of bite.

And so it went on until he got to me and Warren Joyce.

'You pair,' he said, 'are bananas - nobody's ever going to pay anything for you, but someone has to hold the flaming thing together!'

Everyone was in stitches, but John hadn't finished.

'Right,' he said, 'I've had so much fruit, I've given myself diarrhoea - I'm off for a dump.'

Of course, we were on the old plastic pitch at Deepdale in those days and it was brutal to play on. It was terrible, just like playing on a carpet with rough sand on top of it. The ball never stopped rolling, skidding, running away from you.

And the tackling - *argh!* - even the memories are painful. I had plastic grass burns for four years solid. You'd finish the season and they'd just about heal before - *uh-oh!* - pre-season and they'd start all over again.

We'd play in an all-white kit in those days and I remember looking round the dressing room at half-time once and every single lad had blood pouring from his knees onto his socks. The day after the game, you'd wake up stuck to the sheets in bed; elbows, knees, thighs, inside and outside of your wrists.

I've still got some scars from those days - it was terrible really, but at the time, you just carry on.

I actually made a good start at North End though and remember my first game like it was yesterday. We lost 0-1 at home to Chesterfield and despite the defeat, I was named 'Man of the Match'. Now, these days players who are 'Man of the Match' get Rolex watches, weekends away, top-of-the-range gifts.

What did I get? *£40 worth of bacon.*

Point Number One: Forty quid's worth of bacon in 1987 . . . is a *lot* of bacon.

Point Number Two: I didn't have a freezer.

So I think half of Preston had bacon for tea that week.

There's a bit of a food theme going on here, isn't there? I remember once when Ronnie Hildersley came on as a sub on a Boxing Day defeat and John McGrath laid into him afterwards.

Ronnie was a great player and a lovely lad, but he had - how can I put this? - a 'compact' physique and the gaffer said: 'Hildersley! You were running around like a stuffed flaming turkey!'

In fact, John's pet hate was players over-eating on the day of a game.

Legend has it there was a time where he dropped someone after seeing him have a big breakfast.

He was literally counting the slices of toast the lad was having and when he got to six, he exploded: 'That's it! You've eaten yourself out of the team, you greedy b******!'

The thing is, pre-match meals are a strange ritual; you get up on the day of a game, have breakfast, then sit down at half past eleven to eat again.

You wouldn't do that normally, but that's what we did.

One time, after a bad defeat in London, we all got called in for a team meeting on the Monday. You knew it wasn't going to be pleasant - or quick. This was going to be a proper two-towel job. 'Gentlemen' Big John began, 'Stand up if you had a pre-match meal at the weekend.'

Everyone stood up.

'Remain standing if you also had a cooked breakfast.'

Quick as a flash, everyone sat down . . . apart from too-honest-for-his-own-good Alex Jones.

Oh my God. The poor lad. There he was. Alone and about to take the full force of the gaffer's fury.

*'Jonesy, Jonesy, Jonesy . . . you greedy, greedy b******. The f****** waiter covered more distance than you on Saturday!'*

I work at Everton these days as Head of Rehabilitation for the Under-23s and I'm not sure modern managers are quite the same as John *(well, OK, I am sure!).*

But personally, I've never been a big fan of the rollocking. In my experience, I'd say that for every player who responds to a hammering, there are a hundred who would prefer to sit down and talk it through sensibly.

The saving grace for John McGrath was that his taterings were laced with humour - and you knew deep down he really cared for you.

Also, he signed some brilliant players; his eye for talent was unbelievable.

In the space of one week, Tony Ellis and Brian Mooney arrived and they both turned out to be incredible signings for Preston.

Tony is a great lad and is now the Academy Director at Rochdale (where my son Oliver played until recently). He hasn't changed a bit - still got that Manchester drawl and that bit of swagger about him.

On his first day at Preston though, he had that mullet haircut with a pudding bowl fringe and that was it for me: 'Blimey lads, we've signed Baldrick!'

That first session was on the plastic and, probably due to nerves *(or some old fella calling him Baldrick)*, he kept losing the ball, mis-controlling it, shooting high wide and mighty - he was just having a nightmare.

Would he get sympathy from the manager and an arm around his shoulder on his first day? What do you think?

*'F****** hell, Les!' shouted John McGrath, 'We've dropped a right b*****k here!'*

Of course, 'Baldrick' turned out to have a cunning plan - he was brilliant; top scorer, Player of the Year, just a fantastic talent.

And what can you say about Brian Mooney? If you're too young to have seen him play, you missed a real treat. Just listen to the older fans and know everything they say is true.

I tell the young players at Everton about him even now.

These days, they're having soft tissue massages, doing bike work before kick-off - everything is timed to get them scientifically primed for that first whistle.

Moons? He would sit there reading the programme until about five to three. No warm up. No stretching. Then he'd go out and be the best player on the park.

Dribbles, step-overs, whipped-in crosses, spectacular goals - he was out of this world. Off the pitch, you'd think he was this beautiful, lovely laid-back Irishman - and you'd be right.

But I tell you what, if we lost, he used to go mad; he'd be shouting at himself - furious, because he absolutely hated losing. He was really unlucky because when we sold him to Sunderland, he had a lot of injuries and if it wasn't for those, he could have gone to the very top - a superb player.

The press nicknamed Brian 'The King of the Plastic' and it's true that we developed a style of play that suited us on the astroturf. We didn't really have any proper training ground, so we were practising on Deepdale every day.

What's weird though is that we'd get to the ground on a Saturday afternoon and we'd be standing around watching a game between two local sides who'd rented the pitch out before us.

We had to wait for that to finish before we could go on!

Sometimes the ground would be filling up and there'd be a couple of thousand people watching these lads, who would then go for a shower, walk round the front and pay to come back in to watch us.

Anyway, because we practised on the plastic so much, we became virtually unbeatable at home, but if you put us near any real grass we couldn't cope - our away record was shocking.

Of course, the pitches back then were a world away from what they are now. You'd go to some places and there literally wouldn't be a blade of grass to be seen.

I remember playing up at Carlisle one night in a Freight Rover game and if you wanted to punt the ball long, you had to flick it up before hitting it. Otherwise, the mud was ankle deep and you had no chance.

Every step was like ploughing through treacle.

I work with the young players at Everton and they sometimes get sniffy about surfaces that aren't quite perfect, so I have to tell them: 'In my day, this would have been considered pristine.'

I think there's a lot of talk about how the modern game is faster than when we played, but you've got to look at the conditions we played in. These days, nearly every surface is perfect - if you see one that's a bit muddy, it's a real talking point.

Then there's the tackling that was allowed back then, just two substitutes, no drinks breaks or anything like that, it was a lot less stop-start - we just got on with it. And I'm not talking 100 years back here, this isn't that long ago.

I'm pleased that when I show some of the young lads some clips from those days, they see that there's a lot of mythology about how slow the game was, etc.

You try playing in those games, then come back to me.

Good players then would be good players now. Anyway, I don't want to stray into 'old fart' territory, but you get the picture.

It's funny how some things stick in your mind. I can still remember the day I scored my first North End goal like it was yesterday.

We were away at Bristol City and I'd been talking to my old Blackburn teammate John Bailey before the game.

I was playing at the back in a five and stole in at the far post to put us 1-0 up. My goal celebration was always the same - I pretended to faint in shock.

When I opened my eyes there were maybe one or two that weren't pretending!

I think I only scored four goals, half of them were against Mansfield - so I didn't get many, but I was prolific against the Stags.

I think two of those four goals went in off the bar. That wasn't something I practised, it's just that I nearly missed!

One of those Mansfield goals came in that match where Moons got a smack in the head and was bleeding everywhere. He had to go off and get bandaged up, then came back out like a gunslinger and the crowd roared.

You could almost hear people saying: 'He's going to make them pay now.'

As soon as he got back on, he demanded the ball, beat about half their team and stuck a worldie in the top corner. What a player, what a guy.

People who were there will remember that goal as clear as day. They've probably forgotten that I got the second one.

To be honest, it wasn't really in the same class; I mis-hit it, it took about three deflections and bobbled past the keeper. But they all count!

The goal I got away at Mansfield was much better, a really well-worked effort. It's on YouTube somewhere and again shows that us lot back then could actually play a bit, you know? *(Try not to faint in shock.)*

Before games, all players prepare differently, but given the confidence issues I had earlier in my career, I got into a habit of trying to ease the tension. I'd go into the dressing room and say: 'Bad news boys . . .'

They'd all be like: 'What's happened?'

Me: 'Their team's just turned up. I think the game's going to be on.'

Twenty minutes later, same again: 'Lads! Terrible news.'

'What now?'

'The ref's turned up. We need to face it . . . it's definitely on.'

It sounds daft but little things like that become rituals and to this day, I do it with the Everton lads and it just helps ease the tension. Call it reverse psychology, but it works today like it did back then.

One day, John McGrath got me and Warren Joyce in his office and sat us down as a couple of senior pros.

He knew the last half hour before kick-off was vital and he said to us: 'The dressing room's getting a bit quiet. I need you two to get the lads hyped up before they go out.

'Put on a bit of a show; let them know what it means, how important it is, get them fired up. Remind them who they're doing it for.'

So me and Joycey were a bit confused, but of course, you don't let on, you just say: 'Yes, gaffer. No worries.'

Come Saturday, he came into the dressing room at about 2.30pm and as soon as I saw him, I jumped into action: *'Right! Come on lads! We're winning this today!'*

I started bobbing around the room shouting and geeing everyone up.

John gave me a little nod.

Then I sat down and Warren took over: *'Lads! We've got to win this today! Do it for . . . the fans!'*

A nod from the gaffer - we're on the right track.

Joycey sits down and I'm on again: *'Lads . . .'* (by this point they're wondering what's going on with us two) *'. . . do it for THE BOSS!'*

Boom! Big smile! That was the right answer and suddenly John's standing there, double thumbs up - that's the one! Joycey sees this and suddenly we're at it in stereo: *'Boys! Come on! Let's do it for . . . THE GAFFER!'*

By now we're completely over-the-top: *'Think how good he's been to us!'*

'I'd kill for that guy!'

'I'd die for that guy!'

Mission accomplished, the beaming boss slipped back out of the dressing room and left us creasing up at the madness of it all.

Now, was that reverse psychology? I don't know, but it worked - the dressing room was both hyped up and full of laughter. No nerves, no tension.

And we went out . . . and won.

Don't underestimate the power of laughter and the team spirit it builds. For example, me and Alex Jones used to take turns asking the ref how long was left.

Me: 'Ref, ref! How long??'

Then Jonesy: 'Come on referee - how long left?'

One after the other, shouting out, as soon as he came within range.

This went on for a while before he stopped the game, called us over and said: 'For God's sake, you pair! *We've only been playing five minutes!'*

We finished 16th in my first season, not tearing up many trees, but for a team that had just been promoted, we'd established ourselves quite well and were prepared for the following year.

Mark Patterson came in from Blackburn and was a great addition to the squad; skilful, hard-working and - *how can I put this?* - 'feisty'.

Mark was a lovely lad, a real salt-of-the-earth type but the fans nicknamed him 'Psycho' which says a lot about a guy who was about five foot seven!

With him and Warren Joyce, we had two players who weren't the biggest guys but you would want both of them with you in a battle. Unbelievable competitors and great players too. The following year, Tony Ellis was banging in the goals, Moons was on fire, Jeff Wrightson came in at the back and had a lovely touch, so we were doing well.

It wasn't all plain sailing though. In November, we ran into a Wolves team that was on fire and we were 3-0 down at half-time at Molineux.

Back then, the stadium was a really funny shape, with a hotchpotch of roofing and just one modern stand that was about 30 yards away from the pitch.

But they had two young lads up front who tore us apart.

One was Andy Mutch and he had a guy with a crew-cut alongside him - Steve Bull. What a partnership they were. The ball would get played up, Mutch would flick it on and Bully would just batter his way through and score.

We got in at half-time and were expecting a rocket up our backsides.

Instead, John was really calm.

Basically, all he said was: 'Lads . . . I don't want any 6-0s.'

And he was deadly serious - don't let it get to six.

Ten minutes into the second half, it had got to 5-0 and I was thinking: 'Please God, no . . .'

Final score Wolves 6 PNE 0. I couldn't believe it. I think they romped the league that season - champions by a mile, but it was a lesson for us, that's for sure.

Despite the odd hammering at Wolves, things started to click for us as the season went on and we finished sixth, reaching the play-offs. We drew 1-1 with Port Vale at Deepdale in the first leg and therefore we knew we needed goals at their place in the return.

So it was weird that we had me and Dusty Miller - two full-backs - on the bench. And this was in the days of just two subs.

Don't get me wrong, us pair were delighted because we were on £100 appearance money for being in the 13 - and that was a lot of money in the 1980s.

But a lot of people wondered why he didn't have Tony Philliskirk on the bench. Tony had come in towards the end of that season and done well - scored loads of goals.

However, we had a team meeting in training a few days before the game and John McGrath must have had eyes in the back of his head.

He was talking about something to the squad, but he somehow sensed Tony laughing and joking behind him. It was only a minor thing, but the gaffer turned round, gave him both barrels and that was it - come the day, he wasn't in the 13.

There was no messing about with big John. He'd have a laugh and a joke - but he was deadly serious about winning matches. And when he talked, you listened.

After our play-off campaign, we expected to kick on the following season, but it just didn't happen.

I remember quite early on we had a terrible performance away at Bristol Rovers where we were about 3-0 down after 20 minutes and never in it. There started to be a few grumbles from the crowd - *just a few* - but it was the first time.

Thankfully, Moons hit a hat-trick in our next game, we won 5-0 and things went away for a bit.

But you can feel these things growing; it starts with those few groans, then the odd shout from a voice in the crowd, then a few more - players and managers pretend they don't hear it, but they do.

There starts to be criticism in the local paper or the phone-ins and the only way to turn it around is by winning games. Look, Preston is a fantastic club with very loyal supporters, but you can put your finger in the wind at times and sense that a change is coming at any club.

We hit a bad run at the end of January and with the first defeat, there's people leaving early and a few groans at the end.

Second defeat, raised voices and a few angry shouts.

Third defeat, people gathering round the old tunnel and giving the manager and players some stick at the end.

By the fourth defeat, they're shouting at the chairman and that's that, really.

I've seen it loads of times and it's very hard to stop.

In the end, we had five defeats on the trot and what would have been unthinkable 12 months earlier happened - Big John was sacked.

Everyone was sad to see him go, but there's no denying that the last few weeks had been ugly - a lot of shouting, a lot of tension in the dressing room.

That's what a bad run does for you.

What you need to do is calm down and start enjoying it again and Les Chapman was the perfect guy for that.

He'd been a great assistant to John and they were a really good team together, but now the new boss's first task was to get smiles back on faces again.

He faced a tough challenge though because around that time, the club started selling off a few players. I think Mark Patterson went to Bury and although I was sad to see him go, I was pleased in a way because it meant I knew we'd be getting paid over the next few months.

It sounds selfish, but that was the reality of it at times.

Your mate went, but the club could afford to pay you at the end of the month.

I don't think North End were unique in that regard in the late 1980s - there was nowhere near the amount of money in the game there is now.

Les brought John Thomas back and that gave the fans a lift and also started to look at some of the young lads who might make the step up.

Luckily, there were a few around that time; Lee Ashcroft, Nathan Peel and Martin James, who was a good young full-back.

Obviously, that was my position and up to that point, barring injury, I'd played most games. But it's funny when you get to a certain age and your hunger starts to go. No-one tells you, it just creeps up on you and one day, it hits you. For me, I was out injured for a while and Martin came in at full-back and he was fabulous.

Now, when I was younger, if that had happened, I'd have been desperate to get back, firing on all cylinders and making sure everyone knew I was first choice.

But I remember watching from the stand and not being that bothered.

He was Man of the Match and I was standing up applauding.

I was probably 31 at the time and I remember thinking to myself that it was quite telling that I was enjoying his performance in my position.

The fact that I wasn't thinking *'I'm going to show this kid that shirt's mine!'* tells its own story. He was a fantastic player and another one who PNE sold quite early on when maybe they'd have been better keeping him.

Lee Ashcroft, too - a brilliant player, Preston to his core and a great character to have around. I look in the dictionary for the definition of 'cheeky little sod' and there's just a picture of Ashy. He was sold for big money too and I think Walter Joyce should take enormous credit for developing those young lads at that time.

So there was this generation of young talent coming through and by the 1990/91 season, Steve Senior and Martin had virtually nailed down the full-back positions.

We'd just about stayed up the previous season and were lower mid-table again. I was in and out of the team, but after suffering a few too many injuries, I was no longer an integral part of things.

I'd always thought the term *'his legs have gone'* was a myth until one game at Deepdale I found myself chasing back towards our goal to clear a long punt.

As I raced along the touchline I could hear footsteps gaining on me, stride by stride.

Thankfully, I managed to get to the ball first and whack it out of play.

Suddenly there was a huge groan from the crowd - I looked round and the guy who'd been catching me up was . . . the linesman.

The end was nigh.

One of the things that had hindered me was a number of injuries I'd picked up and the way rehabilitation was done in those days.

I'm not being critical of anyone, but at one point, I had four months out, came back for one training session and was put straight in the team on Saturday.

That just wouldn't happen nowadays; the sports science knowledge has moved on and players are much better protected these days - quite rightly, too.

I remember one time, I damaged a ligament in my knee - an injury that would mean at least six weeks out these days.

Back then with smaller squads there was a 'needs must' attitude. (And with the wages we were on, it was 'needs must' for your appearance money too, to be honest.) So I had a 10-day lay-off, put a big strapping on and just got on with it.

Inevitably, these things catch up with you eventually.

I actually shared my last league start with Brian Mooney; a 2-1 win against Southend was the last game at Deepdale for both of us, although I knew who the fans would miss most.

My time just petered out really amid a flurry of injuries; I'd had a facial injury, broken ribs and a serious knee problem that had required cartilage surgery.

Even though I hadn't fully recovered from that, Preston released me at the end of that campaign. I had a few offers to go to teams in the league below, but I thought 17 years as a professional footballer was enough.

I was no longer the player I was at 21 bombing down the wing with my long hair flowing.

I was now 31, with a bald head and a catalogue of injuries that were rapidly catching up with me.

It was football's version of euthanasia and I accepted it without any great soul-searching - I was more concerned about the exciting chapters ahead.

So I sat back and waited for the offers to roll in for this former football star (!) with no proper qualifications, who'd never done a real day's work in this life.

Surprise, surprise . . . nothing happened.

The phone never rang and suddenly I'd gone from being 'Baz' the footballer with the fans chanting my name (sometimes!) to being plain old Mick from round the corner.

Let me tell you, that's a hard step that so many pros aren't prepared for.

I know I wasn't.

I ended up doing a bit of buying and selling clothes before getting talked into joining a PFA course for ex-pros to learn physiotherapy at Salford University.

One day, as luck would have it, I called in at Halifax Town where John McGrath was now managing.

They were looking for a physio and after having a quick chat about the good old days, John asked if I fancied it.

Ever the confident one, I told him I hadn't finished my studies so I might not be very good.

'No worries,' he said, 'We'll give you a crap wage so you don't feel so bad about it.'

I ended up staying at Halifax for several happy years as physio, then manager for a while, as I continued my physio studies before being made redundant when the money finally ran out at The Shay.

I had no problem with that, it's a great little club and the crowd are absolutely hard core. Anyone can be a Man Utd fan, but those fans choose to support Halifax Town. Fair play to them.

Actually, the timing of my departure worked well as I was coming to the end of my four-year course and it allowed me to concentrate on that.

Now, my life has been punctuated by phone calls that lead to amazing opportunities. They're like double decker buses; if you're desperately waiting for one, they don't come.

If you're not expecting one, it just appears.

That's what's happened throughout my life and, thank God, in early summer 1995 I got on board again.

I was coming to the end of a work placement at Blackburn hospital outpatients' department, which was hard work as you're basically seeing a different patient every 20 minutes.

You're also not being paid and I was just starting to think about what I was going to do after my course finished. I had two young children, no job lined up and I was concerned about the future.

Incredibly, on that very day, a nurse appeared at the door and said: 'Are you Mick Rathbone? There's a phone call for you on reception.'

I didn't think anyone knew I was there, so I was fearing the worst as I picked up the phone. Instead, it was unbelievable.

'Hi, is that Mick? This is Gary Peters at Preston North End.

'I'd like to invite you to come in for an interview to be our new physio. Are you available?'

Errr, yes I am. Morning, noon and night, boss.

So my entire future, the whole course of my life was changed by that 30-second phone call. I'll never forget it.

To this day, I've no idea how Gary heard of me or managed to get in touch, but I was just so grateful. I still am. I was out, now I was back in - and that was such a good feeling.

When I got back to Deepdale, it was a very different place to the one I'd left. BAXI had taken over and after years on the breadline, money was now starting to flow through the club for the first time in decades.

I started the week before the players returned and on my first day, Gary said he wanted me and a senior player to go down to this big local park and sort out the running for the following week.

He was thinking of offering this lad a player-coach role so said the two of us could fix up the sessions together. Rightio, no problem.

So we got there and the first thing we did was a run round the park.

When we finished, the lad said it might be better if the players ran it in the opposite way. 'Yeah, good idea - I'll note that down for next week,' I said.

'No, we should run it ourselves just to see.'

I thought: 'Blimey, he's keen, but OK.'

So we ran it again in the other direction. Then came the sprints; 12 in rapid succession with a one-minute recovery.

So that's what we did, the two of us, getting a sweat on now.

OK, all sorted. Next.

'No,' the guy says, 'A minute recovery is too long. Let's say 50 seconds.'

Right. Noted. Next.

'No,' he said (and by this time I knew what was coming), 'I think we should try it ourselves.'

And on it went like that for several steaming, hot, sweaty, knackering hours until in the end we basically collapsed into the car to head back to Deepdale.

'Blimey,' I said, 'You're keen. Do you see yourself as a coach in the future then?'

The guy looked at me, deadly serious, and replied: 'Baz, by the time I'm 45 I believe I will be LMA Manager of the Year in the Premier League.'

I tried not to laugh and, of course, the fella was wrong.

By the time he was 45, David Moyes had been Manager of the Year THREE times.

So it was great to be back and Gary was putting together a very good Preston side at that level.

They'd just missed out in the play-offs for the past two years, but you could feel a real momentum with the BAXI involvement and plans for the new Tom Finney Stand taking shape. It felt like the start of a journey - and it was.

On the first day the players came in, I went for a run round Moor Park with three of the young lads: Lee Cartwright, Kevin Kilbane and Paul McKenna - not a bad group, who ended up with about 800 PNE appearances between them.

After eight weeks, Gary called me in and said everyone was delighted with me and the club were going to give me a rolling 12-month contract - *an actual contract!* - at £500-a-week.

Compared to what I'd been on at Halifax that was a fortune and the contract gave me the first bit of security since I stopped playing, which meant a hell of a lot to me.

I loved being back and I'll never ever forget the first game of the season at home to Lincoln; the sun was shining and everything was set up perfectly.

The thing I remember most though is the first time I ran on to tend to a player, this great cheer and applause broke out from the North End fans - it was just spine-tingling, a real lump-in-the-throat moment.

I thought they'd have forgotten about me - some of them may have wanted to!

But instead, there was this incredible warm welcome back from the Preston fans . . . it was just amazing.

Thinking about it now gives me goosebumps - and all I'd done was run on!

(It was always nice to get a good reception from my old clubs; one time later on I raced on to look after an Everton player at Ewood and as I made my way back to dug-out, some wag in the crowd shouted: 'Blimey Baz - you never ran that fast when you were playing!')

Thankfully - praise the Lord - the plastic pitch had been torn up at Deepdale and the surface was now a beautiful lush green grass.

Gary had put together a team to match it, with Andy Saville and Steve Wilkinson up front, Graeme Atkinson, Ian Bryson and Simon Davey in midfield and young Kev Kilbane and Lee Cartwright on the wings, Andy Fensome and Dean Barrick as full-backs. What a line-up.

Ryan Kidd, Moyesie and the senior pros marshalled things and Ian Bryson was another big leader on and off the pitch.

But if Brys wasn't moaning about something, you'd have to check his temperature to see if he was OK!

It was just a magical time; I was now a fully-qualified physio at a club that I absolutely loved. The lads were all fantastic, Gary was a great manager, Moyesie was there learning his trade and the club was really moving forward with the BAXI bucks behind them.

We ran away with the league that year - and rightly so. The football the lads played was outstanding at any level and that Sav-Wilkinson partnership was just a thing of beauty, wasn't it?

Preston fans who saw that season will remember it to their dying day.

And it's OK to get misty-eyed and nostalgic for times like that; you've got to relish those seasons and never forget them, because not every year will be like it - not by a long chalk. The open top bus, the Harris Museum, the scenes, the singing, the sunshine - just all of it. Magical.

Again, it's real lump-in-the-throat stuff and you've got to make the most of those days - they'll sustain you through the tough times.

For me, that season showed the true beauty of football and its real rewards. They aren't monetary - no-one was on a fortune - but days like those are absolutely priceless. You could see that no matter what happened, the club was only heading in one direction. And so it proved.

Gary was a very clever manager, but he also did some things that were simple. He'd look at who made the PFA Team of the Year or were players of the year at their clubs and try to sign as many of them as he could.

Over his time, Gary also brought in young players like Jon Macken, Micky Appleton and Colin Murdock, who were all great signings.

We consolidated in the division above before Gary moved into a role with the youth set-up the following year. I think everyone knows how much Preston means to Gary and, for him, the club always came first - he's a top man.

Obviously, Moyesie took over and the rest, as they say, is written into PNE folk lore.

In his first full season, we lost to Gillingham in the play-offs but the gaffer had already put his stamp on things. He carried on the good work that Gary had set up and built on those foundations.

Under the pair of them, good players came in; Sean Gregan, Graham Alexander, Michael Jackson - we were really building a team that could not only win the division we were in but challenge in the Championship also.

Greegs was an unbelievable player and a fantastic guy; I think the fact people in Preston still miss him to this day shows how good he was.

He was big and strong, he could play and was a natural leader of men.

His first game was in the Associate Members Cup (or whatever it was called that year) at Chesterfield and he was centre half.

He came in like he owned the pitch and basically ran the game from defence. Everyone was saying: 'Wow! That lad with the huge backside can play, can't he?'

They weren't wrong.

He also loved a Stella - not the female variety, either - and after games, you knew Greegs would be on it on a Saturday night.

As time moved on, 'recovery' became a buzzword and we started having the lads in on a Sunday morning.

I'd go to Deepdale first, check on any injuries, then race over to Springfields where Moyesie would be putting the lads through a session.

Sometimes, I'd ring David and say: 'Greegs is here, he's not feeling great or whatever.'

If it was a bad injury, the gaffer would be OK with it but other times he'd just say: 'Oh, really? Baz, get him up here - he's running today.'

One morning, we had this guy in who was talking about a training method called SAQ: speed, agility, quickness.

I don't think the lads were keen on it to be honest and, having been out the night before, you can imagine what Greegs thought.

The guy stood up and his first question was: 'Can anyone tell me what SAQ stands for?

'Yes,' says Greegs: *'Stella Artois - Quick!'*

Everyone cracked up and again that power of laughter was a great thing for the squad.

Don't underestimate Sean though, he trained hard and also, he played when he was hurt. Greegs had to be dragged out of that team even if he was injured. It was always just: 'Strap it up will you, Baz? It'll be reet!'

He was so committed to North End, you could see he would throw himself into every challenge, every game and the supporters don't forget that.

I remember us playing Arsenal in the FA Cup and they had Vieira and Petit in midfield. We just went out there like it was any other game around that time: This is Deepdale, this is our home, it's packed with North Enders, we don't care who you are - we aren't going to lie down here.

And we didn't.

Kurt Nogan scored twice early on and we were flying. The stadium was bouncing and the noise was just incredible - what an atmosphere that night.

The thing that killed us I think was their goal just before half time.

After that, David Eyres (another great player) was sent off for taking out Marc Overmars and they beat us 4-2.

No complaints really against a team with World Cup winners in it (but I tell you what, we gave them a game, didn't we?).

What I remember from that night is that I was just really making my way in the game as a physio.

By contrast, the Arsenal physio was Gary Lewin, probably THE top guy in the country, working with England and acknowledged as the best in the business.

After the game, he introduced himself to me, gave me some kind words, wished me all the best in my career and gave me Nelson Vivas' Arsenal shirt.

I've never forgotten that kindness and over the years, Gary and I have become really good friends.

I think most people in football are just working class guys who have done well and most of them never lose that sense of reality.

They know how lucky they are and if they weren't being paid, they'd probably be coming through the turnstiles to watch.

Jordan Pickford, for example at Everton, is a lovely lad who never forgets his time at Preston. I always tell him he's an honorary North Ender now!

Back in the league, we had some unbelievable matches that year - I think we went to Wigan towards the end of the season and took something like 9,000 fans.

We came out of the tunnel and were like: 'Blimey! That's our lot - and it was half the ground!'

I think that was the game Greegs broke a bone in this back - and still tried to carry on playing.

I remember when we went up that second time, we were down at Cambridge on the crucial day and were uncharacteristically awful in a 2-0 defeat. At the end though, we knew we were up and the players were on the pitch, celebrating with the fans.

Everyone was delighted - except one man.

Moyesie was missing. I went back into the dressing room and there he was, pacing up and down, quite agitated, waiting for results to come in.

'Promotion's not enough, Baz' he said, 'I want the title. I'm not celebrating until we've got it.'

We were sat there, David, me and Kelham basically with our heads in our hands, until someone, it might have been the Cambridge kit man, popped his head round the door and said: 'Congratulations lads - Gillingham have drawn at Millwall, you're Champions.'

Well, then it just went crazy! The three of us were just jumping around in a little circle, Champagne flying everywhere, shirts being whirled around, all the noise of: *'Campeones, ole, ole, ole!'*

We raced up the tunnel onto the pitch and this massive roar went up as everyone had heard the news!

It's absolutely spine-tingling to be remembering it now, what a feeling.

And I swear we stopped at every pub on the way back from Cambridge.

We'd just about drag ourselves out of one place, get back on the coach and ten minutes later someone would shout: 'Pull in here! I know a good pub!'

So it took a while to get home and yet when we got back to Deepdale, there were still fans there waiting for us.

We piled off the bus and piled into Squires - and, to be honest, I can't tell you much more after that.

It was just incredible - and at the heart of it was that guy who made me do the running on my first day; just 37 years old and already on his way to making his prediction come true.

A couple of other teams had come in for me over the course of the season, but I never wanted to leave for a second.

There was such a strong bond about the place and now we were rolling our bandwagon one step away from the Premier League.

I tell you what, we all thought we'd give it a go; no fear, let's get up there and see what they're made of - let them worry about us.

We knew we were a good young side, with a brilliant manager, decent financial backing and a big, passionate fanbase right behind us.

Everything was there for us to go on and take that next step.

And we nearly, *nearly* did, didn't we?

All season, we went toe-to-toe with teams that had been at the level for years and we beat them.

One of the worst things that season though was the injury to Steve Basham at Deepdale in a game against Tranmere.

He'd broken his leg in a very bad way. You get those types of injuries very, very rarely but when they happen they are sickening.

It was one of those where the other players were trying to hold Steve down to stop him looking at it. The lad was understandably screaming in agony and as physio, you're right in the middle of it.

I looked at his injured leg and was just trying to figure out how I was going to get him onto a stretcher in that state when there was an unexpected slice of luck.

Rob Edwards, the Preston full-back, ran up, absolutely fuming and shouted: 'Not even a f****** yellow card ref! Not even a yellow?!

'Have you seen his f****** leg? It's hanging by a thread!'

At which point, Steve conveniently fainted.

That made it a lot easier to carry him off the pitch - but it was tragic though, because Bash was a lovely lad and a really good player for Preston. You knew he had a hard road to recovery ahead.

Seeing injuries like that hurts, but as physio, you then go into doing every single thing you can to get the lad fit again and properly rehabilitated, mentally and physically.

It's a big responsibility and, for all the laughing and joking in clubs, you never lose sight of the fact that caring for the players is the absolute top priority.

I think the saddest one at North End was when Ryan Kidd had to retire after suffering a prolapsed disc in his neck.

He had an operation at first and came back good as ever - playing at Cardiff in the play-off final and having a good game on a bad day for us.

But one of the tell-tale signs was pins and needles in his arms and legs and I'd solemnly said to him: 'Kiddo, promise me that you'll tell me if it happens again.'

That was the caveat to letting him come back and play.

I remember him going down in a game and telling me it had happened and straightaway, right there on the pitch, I think we both feared the worst.

When the specialist said he could never play again, well, it was just devastating. We both had tears in our eyes and understandably so.

It's heartbreaking to hear about any player and especially Kiddo, who had worked so hard and was such an all-action player . . . it was a really tough one.

What's good now is that he stayed in the game and is doing a great job as a coach at Blackburn.

North End seem to have spawned a lot of coaches from around that time; Brian Barry-Murphy, Mike Flynn and Tony Ellis are at Rochdale, Warren Joyce has done very well, Graham Alexander and Chris Lucketti, Michael Jackson, Steve

Robinson, Simon Davey's doing well in the USA, Michael Appleton, Gareth Ainsworth - there must have been something in the water!

Obviously, it all built up to us getting in the play-offs where who should we come up against? My old club Birmingham. You couldn't make it up.

People ask me what I can remember about those two games and the answer is . . . *everything*.

Mark Rankine had a hamstring strain for the first leg at St Andrews but he wanted to play. Moyesie wanted him to play - but I said 'no', so it was a really big call.

They were both a bit naffed off with me (to put it mildly!) but I said to Mark: 'Ranks, trust me, you will score the winning goal in the second leg.'

I don't know why I said that because he didn't score many, but I just had this feeling.

Obviously, we lost the first leg down there 1-0 and got out of jail really - it could have been more and I think everyone knew it.

Maybe because that first leg had been so straightforward, the Blues were a bit over-confident for the return at Deepdale.

It's true that Jasper Carrott turned up in their dressing room before the match with a load of Champagne and that didn't go down too well with some of our lads.

My best mate Brian Hickson, a Deepdale legend behind the scenes, fronted Jasper up: 'Bit previous aren't you mate?'

'Nahh, we've got it in the bag!'

'OK. We'll see, mate. *We'll see.*'

Word obviously reached our dressing room and the boys, who were already fired up, just went up another notch.

The night itself . . . well, what can you say? You couldn't make it up.

As a piece of football theatre, it had everything. If you were there, you don't need me to tell you. It's a night that people will talk about for the next 100 years.

What I can say is this; amid all the euphoria of the game, the penalty miss, the last-minute drama - Moyesie was calm and collected; he was always thinking. He never got too high or too low.

Of course, he celebrated when we scored. But within seconds, he was back issuing instructions, calling players over, telling them: 'The job's not finished. I need you to do this, do that.'

Right down to the penalties, where Dave Lucas knew which way to dive, we were prepared as well as any team had ever been for any game.

Meticulous is a long word - but it's too short for that level of preparation.

When Paul McKenna put the winner in . . . well, then Moyesie gave me the biggest hug I've ever had in my life!

It was a feeling of pure joy that we shared - absolutely unbelievable, the magic of football. Fans on the pitch, chairing players off - just *wow*.

Thinking about it now, it's making the hairs on the back of my neck stand up. *(Take a minute now and it'll do the same to you!)*

Of course, afterwards Brian Hickson was in overdrive, popping his head in the Brum dressing room: *'Want any glasses for that Champagne, Jasper?'*

(Funnily enough, when I was a kid at Birmingham, I'd been so in awe of Trevor Francis, I could barely bring myself to speak to him. But I've met him quite a bit down the years and he's a lovely chap. I saw him a couple of years ago and we had a bit of a laugh about that night at Deepdale, so he's finally over it. I think!)

As for us, we went out to Squires (again) and the place was packed with North End fans, people standing on chairs, waving shirts around, just celebrations everywhere.

It felt like the whole town was out that night and suffice to say, I can't remember the details again, just the feeling, both on the night - and the morning after!

We were one step from the Premier League with a team that had started off in League 2 a few years earlier. It was just a snowball that kept rolling and getting bigger as it went - and now we were really knocking on the door.

In the end, the final in Cardiff was just a bridge too far for our inexperienced team. We went to the stadium the night before the game and, I don't know about the players, but I was really nervous.

I actually prefer the Millennium Stadium to Wembley in terms of atmosphere. The size of the place when you're standing at pitch level is genuinely awe-inspiring. It's just cavernous and I was like: '*Woah!*'

Again, being involved was something money can't buy, but we were on a decent bonus of about £20,000 to win it, which was more than I had in the bank at the time (!), so there were all sorts of things hanging on that day.

I remember seeing Colin Hendry before the game and I'd played with him years before at Blackburn. We had a brief chat and as he shook my hand I noticed that it was stone cold dry.

My hand was sweaty . . . and that kind of sums up where the teams were.

They had so much experience in their squad - Col had captained Scotland in the World Cup - and to them, it was just another big game. The surroundings, the atmosphere, the size of the crowd - it was all just second nature to them.

Some of our lads had been playing in front of five or six thousand crowds a few years earlier. We'd made a big thing of it and gone down a couple of days earlier. They came down the night before. It was just another day at the office for them.

And in the end, it was one step beyond us. Nobody's fault, everyone tried and although we didn't play very well, we didn't deserve to get beat 3-0. But in the end that's what the record books show.

(Funnily enough, Michael Ricketts who scored for Bolton that day and later played for North End became my son's agent a few years later and I got to know him really well.)

I think if we'd have gone up, David would have kept us there and we could have been a Bolton or a Blackburn that became established at that level for many years. As it was, we had an event at the hotel after the game, but you could just sense the chapter was coming to a close.

No-one said it, but it felt like the journey had come to an end.

The next day, I had to take Bjarki Gunnlaugsson to see a specialist in Cambridge, so it was back to business straight away and getting ready for the next season when we could do it all again. And we did.

We prepared well again and gave it a real go, but all season it was a question of *when*, not *if*, Dave would go to a big job. He was linked every time someone got the sack, so it wasn't a surprise when he went to Everton the following Spring.

No-one wanted to hold him back from an opportunity he deserved and it's absolutely no surprise that he's gone on to be such a success. But the funny thing is, when he went and Kelham O'Hanlon took over, Kel did a brilliant job.

He'd been David's assistant and people might have wondered about him stepping up on his own, but my God, he grabbed the bull by the horns, stepped out of the shadow and did a hell of a job that season.

Gareth Ainsworth came back on loan and always kept me busy in the treatment room, but he was another one who would run through brick walls for the club. Everything you hear about Gareth is true; he's a lovely lad, very clever - and he loves Preston North End.

We were so unlucky not to make the play-offs again - just a couple of bad away results in the run-in tripped us up, but otherwise, with the extra experience from the year before, we might have shocked one or two people.

As it was we missed out and by the end of that season Jon Macken had gone, Sean Gregan was going and the journey was kind of petering out. It was all set for a new chapter and I knew I wasn't going to be part of it. After much soul-searching I decided to follow David to Everton when the new season began, but it was the South Korea World Cup and we had the longest summer break in years.

So I was still there when Craig Brown arrived and, as everyone says, he was a lovely man. But he was chalk and cheese compared to Moyesie. When I told him we had the injured players in every day he said: 'What? Sundays, too?'

When I said yes, the new boss said: 'Well, we can stop that, Baz. People have families and I don't want them - or you - in on Sundays. If I see anyone here on a Sunday they'll be fined.' So that was that - he was just a very nice man.

I remember the first time I ran on the pitch to sort someone out, I came back off and reported back to Craig that the lad was OK to carry on.

He said: 'Thank you Baz for giving me that information.'

And he wasn't being sarcastic - he was genuinely grateful.

Moyesie would have been like: *'Too f****** right he's staying on!'*

Any injured players had to report to me at Deepdale at 9am to be assessed before being passed fit to train that day.

When Ricardo Fuller came in, he had a bit of trouble with a tight hamstring so he'd report to me at the ground on a Monday and I'd ring Craig at Springies to tell him he wasn't going to be at training. Craig would just go: 'Thank you Baz, I will leave him in your capable hands and look forward to him rejoining the squad tomorrow.'

If I'd have rung Moyesie with the same thing he would have hit the roof: 'You what? He's had all f****** day off yesterday and now he's coming out with this?!' So yes, they were very different characters those two.

Before I left, Craig took the squad up to Scotland for pre-season and we were in St Andrews.

Every night after training, him and Billy Davies would take me and Kelham out into town, where Craig seemed to know everyone - and everyone knew him.

He'd take us into a pub and say to the barman: 'These gentlemen are my guests. Please do not let me turn around at any point and find their glasses are empty.' He would insist he was paying for everything and then say: 'Right, there's only one rule tonight . . . nobody mentions football.'

You could talk about anything; family, world events, the price of bread - just not football. If that had been Moyesie - he would have been the exact opposite; you could ONLY talk about football.

So two very different approaches, but two very successful guys and it just shows that there's more than one approach out there that can work.

It wasn't long after that trip that my own time at Deepdale came to an end and to say it was a wrench was an understatement. I took a lot of time to reach the decision to leave, because the club meant so much to me. People throw the '*L-word'* around, but I genuinely loved the place - I still do.

In the end though, the opportunity was just too great and I headed to Everton with David. My only caveat was that the clubs reached an amicable agreement between themselves over my departure.

I was still under that rolling contract and I said I wouldn't go unless everything was above board and North End were happy with the deal.

They'd been so good to me, I didn't want to leave under a cloud and thankfully, Everton were OK with that.

The lads had a whip round and Colin Murdock presented me with a very nice watch which is one of my favourite possessions to this day, because a big part of my heart still lies at Deepdale (along with flesh and blood from that plastic pitch).

To see the club come so close a few years later under Billy was both a moment of pride and heartbreak, but I still firmly believe North End will reach the Premier League one day. The club is so smart in its dealings; buying low and selling high.

In the wider game, a hell of a lot of teams look at Preston and aspire to be like them. Clubs spend millions and ended up below them year after year.

I spent a short time with Warren Joyce at Wigan when he was manager there and I know the facilities at Euxton are unbelievable. That's a massive step forward for North End and, again, don't underestimate the importance of those facilities in many, many ways.

The stadium, of course, is now fantastic - it's a proper football ground and brilliantly designed. When you see that glow over the Preston skyline at night matches, it's impossible not to get excited isn't it? Deepdale under the lights is a special place.

It's unrecognisable from my playing days apart from one thing - the atmosphere. The supporters are as passionate as ever - they've stuck with their team and they deserve success. There will be people still going to games now who were there in my playing days.

That loyalty will be rewarded one day, I'm sure of it.

The day will come.

And when it does, I'll see you on the Flag Market.

CHAPTER 2

JERMAINE BECKFORD: UNFORGETTABLE

I loved everything about my time at Preston North End - apart from two games. Actually, maybe three . . . who can forget about Colchester United away? (Not me, even though I've tried to blank it out!)

But those odd moments can't overshadow all the good times I had at Deepdale, some amazing away games and, obviously, Wembley.

I loved it all and just wish it could have gone on longer, just like my playing career really, especially as I was a bit of a late starter.

When I was a kid, I was on Chelsea's books and one of the great things about it was catching glimpses of the senior pros after our training.

I remember sneaking over to the first team's pitches and watching Gianfranco Zola climbing up a goalpost and tying a sock to the top corner.

It's not every day you see one of the world's greatest players shinning up a goalpost on his own and I thought: 'What's he doing?'

He jumped down and went to the edge of the box where a load of balls were waiting. Then he spent ages trying to hit the sock with free kicks - over and over again. It was something he'd picked up from Maradona in Napoli apparently and it was kind of mesmerising just watching him, ball after ball, time after time, when nearly everyone else had gone home. And this is one of the top players in the world at that point - nothing to prove to anyone, yet there he was, still putting it in. What a player - and what a classy guy.

Unfortunately for me, I suffered a bad achilles injury and when I was 15, so they let me go. I didn't cry about it. They had so many kids on the books that it was just one of those things. I didn't give up on my dream to be a footballer, I just thought it would take a different path.

I probably didn't realise how different, but being different was always cool with me - you make your own way.

For example, when I was younger, my dad was a Man Utd fan, even though we lived in London. He wanted his kids to be Man Utd too, but I wasn't having that, so me and my brother followed Arsenal.

They had players like Ian Wright *(Wright! Wright!)*, who was an inspiration for me in so many ways, especially coming into the game late and having that unbelievable drive to succeed. (If you're a bit younger reading this and only know him as a TV pundit, look up some old videos online because he was a hell of a player.)

Anyway, when I left school, I got a job with the RAC fitting windscreens and I tell you what . . . I *loved* it!

I had my own little orange van and I loved being out talking to people, especially when you're the RAC man, because everyone's always pleased to see you.

The money wasn't great, but the best thing about it was they gave me a fuel card, so at weekends I could be buzzing about all over London and have my petrol paid for. Simple pleasures, happy days!

I was playing non-league for Wealdstone and scoring a few - OK, a lot - of goals when League clubs started taking a look at me.

First up, Yeovil offered me a deal and I didn't even know where it was. To be honest, I didn't care. A league club wanted me and that was it - I just grabbed a map and set off driving. It was a professional contract and in my mind as soon as I got there, I was signing. It was as simple as that. It's big cider country out there, isn't it? Well, they could have offered to pay me in apples and I would have signed.

But (and it's a big BUT) as I drove along the motorway, my agent rang and told me to turn round - Crystal Palace and Charlton were interested and wanted to offer me trials. Oh, hang on. *Sorry, Yeovil.*

In the end nothing came of those London clubs, although Palace did say they'd let me know. I'm still waiting!

By that point, everything was happening really quickly and I had another trial almost straight away at Watford. That went well and Aidy Boothroyd offered me a deal on the first day there. Trial in the morning, contract in the afternoon - it doesn't get much better than that.

I was just about to sign and rang my agent with the good news when he said: 'That's great . . . but Leeds United have come in for you.'

Argh! Really, as soon as I heard that, my mind was made up to go there, which was a bit awkward as I'd already told Aidy I'd be signing.

Instead I handed in my RAC fuel card, signed for Leeds and never looked back. The only thing was, that was the year they lost in the play-offs - to Watford, of all people.

I'd made a few appearances as a sub, coming on in the last game of the season when North End beat us 2-0 at Deepdale, but then I wasn't even on the bench for the play-off games or the final, which was painful to be honest.

What made it worse was I bumped into Aidy Boothroyd after they beat us at the Millennium Stadium, but he was OK with me to be fair.

It was just one of those *'look at what you could have won'* moments.

Kevin Blackwell was the Leeds manager at the time and I think overall he preferred lads like Richard Cresswell and Rob Hulse to me.

Don't get me wrong - they're both really good players, but I think I was still the 'unproven wildcard' option and he didn't really fancy me in such a big game.

Eventually though, I had a great time at Leeds, especially under Simon Grayson and then Everton under David Moyes and Leicester with Paul Gallagher, Sean St Ledger and Dave Nugent.

At Leeds I'd been with Paul Huntington and Neil Kilkenny, as well as ex-PNE guys like Eddie Lewis, Dave Healy and Cressy.

Then, even when I went to Huddersfield on loan later on, I was with Simon again as manager and guys like Tom Clarke and Calum Woods, so there's always been this Preston connection wherever I've been.

In 2015 I was at Bolton with ex-North Enders Andy Lonergan and Tyrone Mears, as well as Craig Davies, who had been on loan at Deepdale and loved it. Neil Lennon had come in as Bolton manager and I have no problem with him, we still bump into each other now and have chats.

But I wasn't really getting in the team there, so when Simon came in for me at Preston, I was up for it from the start.

He rang me and said: 'Look, I think we're building something really special here and you could be a big part of it.'

In all honesty, I just said: 'For you, anything gaffer.'

I loved working with him so much that I couldn't get to Preston fast enough. He gave me that confidence to try things and not be looking over my shoulder all the time thinking: 'Uh-oh, I'm in trouble now if this doesn't come off.'

He lets you take chances, not play it safe all the time and as a person, he's right up there. I love the guy. Same with Glynn Snodin, Ian Miller and Steve Thompson too, they're guys who know what they're doing and when they speak, you listen, no matter how long you've been in the game for. There was so much respect for them, but it was a two-way thing and you always got that respect back.

When I got to Preston, I saw all these guys who I'd played with before and I looked around thinking: 'Wow, this is a really good squad.'

Big Kev Davies was there too and really, I thought: 'Look at all these players - we should probably be going straight up here.'

Joe Garner was the top man up front. He's another guy I loved and we hit it off straight away - big Preston fan and a tough guy to play against.

Arms and elbows everywhere, bullying people, winning things all the way through, never shutting up!

The thing about Joe is, he's not the biggest guy, but physically? Wow!

His spring to win headers from a standing start was just ridiculous and I think he caught loads of defenders out because they didn't think he could get near balls then - *zip!* - he's beaten them in the air.

We had a great understanding, because I'd see him going up for balls knowing he was going to win them, so I was already on the way to get on the end of the flicks. He must be a nightmare for defenders, but he was an absolute dream to play alongside. I think, physically, you do whatever you can to gain an advantage in games and hope the ref doesn't see it, but you've got to be careful.

One time I was playing at Millwall and we were waiting for a corner at their end, so the crowd were already giving me absolute grief, just because I was near. Big Andy Morrison was marking me and just before it was taken, I stamped on his foot. Then, as he curled up a bit, I elbowed him in the ribs, peeled off, got my header in and scored - *ho ho!* - happy days and a celebration right in front of those lovely fans, who were absolutely pelting me. They'd seen what had gone on, but the ref hadn't. You've got to laugh.

Well, maybe not at Millwall as half the ground wanted to kill me after that. I went to take a throw-in and even the ball boy was like: *'Beckford, you cheatin' 'effin . . !'*

And this was the ball boy! He absolutely hammered me and I just said: 'Oh shut up and give me the ball, son.' Well, that was it. *Uh-oh!* This tide of angry Millwall fans came piling down the stand towards me.

Naturally, I did what any sensible person would do . . . I legged it into the middle of the pitch and left some other poor sod to take the throw.

I can't remember who it was, but later on he was like: *'Oh by the way, thanks for that, Becks!'*

No worries, mate!

Anyway, when I first arrived at Preston, it took me a while to get going. My first game was away at Oldham in the Johnstone's Paint Trophy - and I missed a sitter. If you remember that - *ouch!* If you don't . . . *good!*

It ended 2-2 and was one of those ties that went to penalties so I took no chances with mine - I blasted it straight down the middle.

Neil Etheridge - a really good keeper - was in goal for them but in the end, he missed a penalty and Thorsten Stuckmann, our goalkeeper, got the winner. What a way to start off, eh? To be fair though, at first I really wasn't sharp enough.

I needed games to get up to speed and a lot of people will tell you the same thing; training is good, but there's no substitute for playing matches.

As a player, when you play week-in, week-out, your mind is a little bit more switched on; you're working a little bit quicker than if you're just coming off the bench. It just gets you to that level and makes it easier to play well. So it took me a bit of time to get my feet together, work out where I was supposed to be and how quickly I was supposed to be there.

It was so frustrating at first, because I had this little niggly injury that was annoying and was hampering things.

Then I finally got over that and was just starting to enjoy myself and score a couple of goals when - *bam!* - I had this inner ear infection that came on literally overnight and flat-out nearly finished my career.

I woke up one morning, sat up in bed and as soon as I got up to a 90 degree angle, my whole world started spinning around.

I felt like I was on the tea cups at a theme park and someone had just spun them at a million miles an hour.

I collapsed back onto the bed and felt nauseous, sick, confused - everything you can imagine - it was just horrible. It was diagnosed as labyrinthitis and it gave me this chronic vertigo. If you've ever had anything similar, you'll know how bad it is. For two or three weeks, I wasn't able to get out of bed, that's how serious it was.

I had to crawl on my side to go to the bathroom. Same with showers, I had to crawl in and lie on the floor while my wife turned the water on. It sounds crazy but it was such a horrible, horrible experience.

There was no way I could get out of the house, let alone go to training, so it was a real nightmare. It got to the point where I genuinely thought I was going to have to retire. There was no way I could see that would get me back to any level of normality. Nothing the doctors, chiropractors, acupuncturists or anyone was doing was working and it was so, so scary.

Finally, after about four weeks, my wife Laura researched a homeopathic remedy in the USA.

By that point, I was prepared to try anything, so we got it shipped over and I swear within 24 hours . . . I was fine.

Once I was able to stand up and walk 20 yards, I was like a caged animal set free. I'd been thinking it was all over and now I was back in the game, so yes, I was determined to make every minute count with this new lease of life. I think in my first start back in the team we beat Crewe 5-1 at Deepdale and Joe got four goals, while I got the fifth.

Callum Robinson came on as a sub in that game and you didn't need to be a football genius to see how good he was going to be.

His first-touch control was unbelievable and his movement was different levels, even back then.

There were a few good young lads in the squad who have gone on to great things and, in all honesty, none of them have surprised me.

Jordan Hugill was just starting to be around that season, but even before he found his feet, you looked at his attributes - speed, strength, workrate, attitude - and you thought: 'Yes, that kid's a bit raw, but he's got a great chance.'

Same with Josh Brownhill, who's really developed physically since then and doesn't look out of place in the Premier League.

North End fans don't need me to tell them how good Alan Browne is and he's another one who cares deeply for the club and can do everything; score goals, win headers, tackle, defend, killer passes, just a great footballer and it's no surprise to see him captain at Deepdale these days.

He's also a great guy and, I'm not just saying this, but all of the guys were brilliant in that squad and everyone really got on.

There were no cliques like you sometimes get, no 'big-timers'; you could literally pull out any five names from a lucky dip, put them on a table together and everyone would get on like a house on fire.

Trust me, that's not the same at every club - and it's a big thing. You're going in every day, looking forward to being with your mates, instead of thinking: 'Oh God, I hope I don't get stuck with him today.'

I'm still in contact with all the boys and I spoke to all the young guys when they made big moves in recent years. I told them all the same thing: 'Look, you're going to go through bad times, but use them as motivation for when things are going well. Stay focused and enjoy the ride. It's not a long career so make the most of every minute.'

Winning helps, of course, as does scoring goals - that always puts a smile on my face - so I was like a Cheshire cat that season, going on probably the best scoring streak of my career.

I'm not saying it was down to the standard in League One, it was more about playing in such a good team that was well managed, tactically smart and had very good players.

You've got Daniel Johnson and Paul Gallagher playing through balls for fun, I mean, come on! It was a striker's dream!

I like to think I've got good technique but those two? Different levels.

We played Notts County away towards the end of that season and it was like a masterclass from those pair. I always remember my first goal that night as one of my favourite for North End.

I was being marked by Hayden Mullins who I know quite well. Gally played an unbelievable reverse pass in and as it came in, I heard Hayden say: 'Mine!' Well, it wasn't! I got there first, lifted it over his head with my first touch, totally blindsiding him.

I swear, as the ball was in the air I actually heard him go: 'Oh s***!'

By the time he'd turned round, I'd volleyed it into the back of the net and was away laughing my head off.

Anyway, a couple of minutes later while the game was going on, he walked past me and out of the corner of his mouth said: 'Becks . . . that was a lovely goal.'

Then he just carried on walking! Top class from a top guy.

Really, the third goal that night summed things up. Sam Johnstone launched this big kick and it looked like it was going straight out of play, so all the Notts County fans were giving it the big ironic cheer.

But, as I mentioned earlier, Joe Garner could get to balls other people couldn't so we kind of knew he would keep it in.

He did, DJ picked it up and we played a sweet one-two before I buried it for a 3-1 win. Game over.

At that point, we should have been home and hosed for promotion, but MK Dons were right behind us every step of the way - I think that was the year they had Dele Alli playing for them - and it all came down to . . . Colchester away. Like I mentioned at the top, I can't tell you anything about that day unfortunately, because I've blanked it from my memory.

Just kidding - if only!

It was an absolute nightmare, wasn't it? We were full of confidence going into it, scoring lots of goals and playing really well as a team.

I'm not saying we were over confident, but we definitely jumped the gun a little bit by pre-booking a flight for Las Vegas straight after the game. Yeah, that was a mistake.

We fancied ourselves so much and we were just thinking: 'We're on a roll here, they're not doing so well, we're going to do this, no problem.'

There was nothing that could go wrong but . . . unfortunately for us, it just wasn't our day.

We had great opportunities, their keeper made a couple of good saves, we missed a few brilliant chances that should have definitely nestled in the back of the net and even had that big let-off when they missed a penalty. You think you've got plenty of time and you'll get there in the end, but then they scored and the clock goes 'whoosh!'.

You start snatching at things, the pressure ratchets up - and suddenly it's all over. Absolutely heart-wrenching. We'd flown down there and I'll always remember that a couple of hours later, we were in the same airport as the Colchester boys, who were flying out to Ibiza or somewhere.

The energy between those guys and us said it all. They had their music blaring, dancing about, laughing and joking . . . and we were just sat in silence.

But you know what? There's a part of me that is glad that we didn't go up that day.

Don't get me wrong, I'd have loved it and we'd have had a great celebration, had a longer summer and maybe partied a little bit more.

But everything happens for a reason.

And to come through those play-offs and win at Wembley? That's GOT to be the best experience you can have.

You might not think that at the time, especially as we had two tough opponents, teams that if we're being honest, could easily have beaten us on other days, especially Chesterfield over two legs.

But instead, it was absolute bliss . . . absolute bliss. There's no other way of putting it.

In that first game at Saltergate, I managed to score early on and that set us up well for the whole tie.

I've always been confident and I know I'm going to miss a lot of chances, but I also know I'm also going to score a lot of chances. So don't let the ones you miss affect you - just take each one as it comes. Try not to get too excited before you've hit it and seen where the ball is going.

With that one, the ball came to me and I had a bit of time, so I just thought: 'Right, clean connection, bit of lift . . .'

And as soon as it left my foot I just knew it was going in.

As a striker, you know it's in. The home fans go quiet because they know it's in - and then there's that little half-second delay until the away fans realise it's in.

Now THAT'S a great feeling.

In the second leg at Deepdale, we were quietly confident at 1-0 up and also, for me, I knew a couple of the guys in their team from playing with them in the past, so I knew how to handle them.

I knew what they didn't like to do, so you use that to make them do those things. This defender hates being dragged wide, so I'll pull him all over the place. This guy has no left foot. This guy can be got at.

Especially when you've played with guys, you pick these things up; they tell you about it when you're teammates and then when you move and you're not on the same side anymore it's: 'OK, I remember what you told me!'

They had a couple of chances in that game before I got the first one at a really good time; I was just able to roll the defender and smash it in from about ten yards. Joe then smashed in a brilliant penalty - he was never going to miss was he? - and then the third one, well, that's just one of my favourite goals ever.

Bailey Wright won a great tackle and popped it up to me and as soon as I nipped it through the defender's legs, I looked up and saw Joe Murphy off his line.

I thought: 'Ohhh, I tell you what, it's a long way, but I kind of fancy it from here . . .' *(Plus, I was a little bit tired!)*

I'd played with Joe before and knew he likes to come out a long way, so I just absolutely leathered it, put my laces through it. Just watching the flight of the ball, as soon as it left my foot, I KNEW it was going in.

If you watch it back, there's an angle from the Bill Shankly Kop and I start peeling off to the left, ready to celebrate, *before* the ball has even hit the net.

As soon as it did, *ohhh* . . . it was wild wasn't it? It was a moment of pure relief because the sensible thing would have been to take the ball on - not shoot from there. But it was also wild because I knew - everyone knew - that it cemented our place in the final.

The pictures are fantastic and I just dived into Simon's arms. (It sounds like something from Mills & Boon this, doesn't it? A right bromance!)

But he just brought out the best in me and as I mentioned earlier on, he gave you confidence which for a striker is a massive thing.

Would I have tried that shot under a different manager?

Well . . . maybe. But with Simon, you knew that if it didn't go in, you wouldn't get crucified for trying something off the cuff.

The reaction at the end when the fans piled on the pitch - they're just scenes that stay with you forever; players and supporters celebrating as one - just the way it should be.

As for Wembley itself . . . oh my word. What a day. What. A. Day.

On the coach journey in, Simon had lined up a video for us on the bus. It was every single goal we'd scored that season, every great save that the keepers had made, every tackle that John Welsh made, every block Tom Clarke and Hunty made . . . it got everyone going, but underneath it all was this reinforcement of exactly how good we actually were.

You know you're a good side, because you've gone all through the season and are in the play-off final.

But just to watch it again with fresh eyes on the way to the stadium, to see genuinely how good some of those tackles were, the saves, the goals, everything, we just came off that bus feeling ten feet tall.

Me? I was playing it cool and - this is going to sound big-headed - but I was saying: 'Guys, guys, don't worry . . . I've got this.'

I don't know why I was like that because when I'd played there before, I'd lost! But those defeats are what gives you mental toughness; I knew what it was like to be on the losing side, such a sickening feeling, so I was prepared to go above and beyond.

And that wasn't just me, there were quite a few of the Preston boys who'd had their own play-off stories so we all had this resolve that it wouldn't happen to us again. We knew we were going to have to be in top form because I think Swindon were by far the best footballing side in the league that year. They passed people off the park.

But we also knew they had one or two injury concerns and that they'd gone to extra time in their semi-final, which was about ten days earlier, but maybe it had taken a bit out of them, physically and mentally.

Right from the first whistle, we were at them, trying to turn them and put them under pressure. We knew their captain Nathan Thompson was carrying an injury and he was down to man mark me.

So right at the start, Gally was playing these balls in behind and the very first one, he fouled me.

As we landed on the floor, I actually heard him wince. He let out this big *'argh!'* and I thought: 'Hello! That's interesting, sounds like you're struggling today mate.'

I jogged off into the box and he followed me, but I was putting a little bit of added pressure on him as we waited for the free-kick; twisting, stepping, making sharp movements more than I would normally do - and I could see the guy wasn't right. He's normally a pretty strong boy and a good player, but that day he was clearly off it.

When the cross came in, I just pinned him and popped a left-footed volley in for a pretty straightforward finish really.

Great ball by Gally, as usual, and I tucked it in to give us a dream start.

This is going to sound bad, but as I was running off celebrating, I heard the guy screaming in pain on the floor and I knew he was done for the day, three minutes in. Unfortunately, that's the game and thankfully he recovered over the summer and is OK again now. But for us to have that start was massive for us, especially knowing that North End had lost in all their previous play-offs.

There was a lot of talk about it outside the camp and a lot of pressure that people tried to put on us, but we were looking at it going: 'Yeah, so what? That's the past and today is OUR day.'

What's funny is that I should have scored the second goal too!

Another great ball from Gally - *let's face it, aren't they all?* - and I should really have got my head on it. I was just a little bit too low.

Thankfully, before I had time to think, Hunty popped up with a real striker's finish and I was buzzing for him because he's such a top Preston man. So we were on top, but I still don't think we were overly convinced that we were home and dry even at 2-0, because we knew how good Swindon were.

I think they had a decent chance just before I scored my second and if that had gone in . . . it's a different game.

As it was, Joe got up for another of his unbelievable flicks and it came to me about 25 yards out. I got it back onto my left foot then just thought: 'Right, let's hit this as quick as I can to try and catch the keeper off guard.'

And that's exactly what happened.

Thankfully when it went past him, it landed right in the bottom corner of the net and then again, I ran towards Simon pointing and saying: 'You're the man!'

It was just down to the belief he'd shown in me and at 3-0 all the lads started looking at each other saying: 'OK, now we can start to REALLY believe this is our day.'

But we were all still very cautious, especially as Gally had to go off in that first half and Browney came on.

At half-time, the dressing room was carnage, to be honest with you.

Simon and Snods were trying to calm everyone down, but all the lads still had the adrenaline going and people were shouting and jumping around, very pumped up: 'THIS IS IT, BOYS! THIS IS OUR MOMENT! HEADS IN THE GAME!'

All that sort of stuff is great, but not when the manager is trying to make a point and be heard. It's about finding that balance between a team of pumped up guys and a level-headed manager, who's been there, done it and knows exactly what to say.

That day, the message was: 'Keep doing the simple things and most of all, do not let them get an early goal.' If we'd given them something to build on early in that second half, it would have been a different story.

So our instructions were, keep it tight at the back, hit the channels, nothing silly and play football when we can. Most importantly - keep the ball. If we did that, we knew we were going to win.

And we also knew that they'd have to go for it so we'd get more chances as the game went on.

As it was, quite early on in the half, DJ played another great ball that put me through one-on-one with Wes Foderingham. I took two big touches and tried to place it in the far side, down to his left.

But I must have telegraphed it a little bit too much; if I'd have taken one more touch, it would have made it much more difficult for him and I'd have probably chipped it over him, because I knew Fods liked to commit early.

Of course, he got down to it and, yeah, I let him have that one!

A few minutes later though, that first miss came in handy, when Joe won another scuffle in the middle of the field and put me in one-on-one again.

This time, I did take that extra touch and as I got my head up, I saw the same gap in the far corner.

I thought: 'Go on then, I'll put it a bit wider this time and he's a bit nearer now and place it . . . *yeah, there you go.*'

As soon as it went past him, that was it, man. A Wembley hat-trick, you couldn't write it, could you?

I glanced up and behind the goal, every single Preston fan was going absolutely bonkers. It was one of those goosebump moments, you know?

Frozen in time, I can see it now. It was just incredible.

Celebrating running round the side of the pitch was unbelievable, too.

I was looking at the cameraman, who was a massive North End fan, and he was running with the camera trying to keep it level but he was also going crazy, shouting: *'Yeeeesssssssssss!!!!'*

All around, the lads were going wild, Hunty piled in on top, the fans were going bananas . . . you live for moments like that. Live for them!

Players and fans, we all share exactly the same feelings in that moment. Pure, pure joy. If we could bottle it, we'd be millionaires Rodney!

That's when your mind goes back to Colchester and you think: 'Wow! This was meant to be!'

(Only two other players have scored Wembley hat-tricks in the play-off final and I didn't realise it until the stats guys told me afterwards; Clive Mendonca for Charlton in 1998 and a certain Scott Sinclair for Swansea in 2011. I wonder whatever happened to him?)

Once the final whistle went, it was party time, but I nearly missed the photocall with the lads because I was doing a TV interview, so I just about slid in in time.

But then afterwards, we got back in the changing room, ready to party and - *argh!* - I was selected for the random drug test.

I was fuming, to be honest. It should have been one of the best dressing room parties I'd ever been in and instead I had to spend 40 minutes away from it all with a medical guy, waiting to pee! I was devastated, but what can you do? Someone's gotta do it and, after all, I'd just scored a Wembley hat-trick so it wasn't a bad day overall, was it?

Once we were up, we started talking about signing permanently, as my Bolton contract had now expired. I had a couple of other offers and one in particular that really tempted me - the chance to go to New York City in MLS.

That was around the time they had Andrea Pirlo, Frank Lampard and David Villa playing and it would have been a great adventure.

It was a good offer too, but I'd just been so happy at Deepdale, being back with Simon and Snods and really enjoying my football again. So it sounds a bit funny to say I chose Preston over New York, but I did.

After all, there was no guarantee that I'd have gone out there and had the same chemistry with the boys that I had at Deepdale, so no regrets at all. Most of all, I loved it at North End; I loved the club, had a great relationship with the fans, the manager, everyone.

People talk about Peter Ridsdale but I always got on well with him. We had a very good, professional relationship and he was the sort of guy you could talk to openly about things.

I hadn't been with him at Leeds, but he was always a very sharp operator and I never had any problem with him. Same with the owner. I didn't see much of Trevor Hemmings, but when I did it was all very friendly and I think he cares passionately about the club.

I remember the first time I met him, he'd just had a good day at the races with quite a few winners and he was telling me about them. I said: 'I wish you'd have told me beforehand - I'd have put a few bets on.'

And he replied: 'Yes, but you'd have been after more money if they didn't come in!'

So a new deal was signed and everything was looking good going into that first year in the Championship, but as always things didn't run smoothly.

Out of nowhere in training one day, I just turned and ended up doing my medial ligament, cartilage and also six micro-fractures in my knee.

I went from being on Cloud Nine to being absolutely devastated.

I made a couple of appearances early on but I wasn't right and it was so frustrating having to miss so much of that season while I got back to fitness. You're watching games, desperate to be playing, helping the guys.

And as much as I was around things, it's not the same when you're stuck in the physio department while the guys are on the training field.

I was out for about nine months, which felt like an eternity, but I came back right at the end of that season and managed to get on against Blackburn where there were about 7,000 PNE fans.

We were winning 2-1 at Ewood and I was just thinking: 'Let me get out there and play in front of those fans!'

I made my first start back against Rotherham and scored after six minutes at Deepdale, so that was great to be back in the groove.

That was the game where their keeper got sent off and the centre forward went in goal towards the end - and saved Joe's penalty. Unbelievable save, too to be fair!

I got a couple of goals towards the end of the season, but I think DJ was top scorer that year with eight. I'd like to think that if I'd been out there all year, I might have beaten him to that title - I hope so anyway.

But, as I said before, everything happens for a reason and you've got to be mentally strong, not just in football, but in life.

You take the positives from things; I ended up strengthening other areas of my game, rather than just relying on the speed and power aspects.

As much as I didn't want the injury to happen, it helped bring out new aspects to my game and, no matter how long you've played, you never stop learning.

Having had a frustrating season, I couldn't wait for the next one to start, especially as Simon made one of the best signings Preston have had in recent years. Aiden McGeady was frightening - what a player.

I've been around some 'street footballers' who can juggle the ball and do amazing tricks. But everyone knows they couldn't do them in games with a six-foot defender on their backs. Geads? He could.

I've never seen anyone do the stuff he did in games, he was cut from different cloth. In training, he was just ridiculous - I was glad I was an attacker, so I never really had to try and stop him because he could make very, very good defenders look bang average.

Talk about quick feet, he was like the guy off Riverdance!

Unfortunately, injury struck again and I suffered a hamstring strain early the following season so that was another two months missed.

I got back against Newcastle at Deepdale when we lost 2-1 but a few weeks after that came a real low for me.

You know what I'm talking about don't you? Sheffield Wednesday away, myself and Doyler. What a nightmare.

The funny thing is, me and Eoin are really good mates. It was crazy.

What I will say is this; what happened that day at Hillsborough is something that happens every single day at a club somewhere - it's just that normally there aren't 20,000 people there watching!

Call it ego, testosterone, whatever, we were both just desperate to do well and score goals. The pair of us had been on the bench that day so we were both champing at the bit to get on and do well.

It was right at the end, we were 2-1 down, chasing the game and I remember Eoin had the ball and I was in a great position.

I was like: 'Give me the ball! Come on! Play me in - let me do my job!'

I can't remember it exactly, whether he tried to shoot from an outrageous position or something, but I was a little bit ticked off (!) and said to him: 'Doyler! Pass the flaming ball next time!' (OK, it may have been a bit stronger than that.)

Obviously, he was a bit frustrated as well and it just ended up coming to a head on the pitch, maybe because we were so near each other when the move broke down.

Normally, these things would have happened in the changing room, but it just so happened that we were quite close to each other. If we'd been say 20 yards apart, it would just have been a bit of verbals and that would have been it.

Look, it wasn't a proper fight was it? We had a misunderstanding, but I've seen proper fist fights in training at clubs I've been at and 90 per cent of players will say the same thing. It happens all the time. Unfortunately, for us two, it bubbled over unnecessarily on the pitch, a bit of pushing and shoving, the crowd got involved and the ref pulled out two reds. A nightmare. Embarrassing.

We were both shepherded away down the tunnel separately and immediately after, we were in the changing room just looking at each other; heavy breathing, dirty looks for about 30 seconds. Testosterone!

But then it was like someone flicked a switch and we came to our senses: Oh my God. what have we done?

'Sorry, Doyler.'

'Sorry, Becks.'

We hugged it out and that was it, done and dusted. It was wrong and it was embarrassing, but it was all heat of the moment and then over and done with.

Me and Doyler were fine and we're still fine - we both just wanted to get the team back in the game, but obviously maybe we wanted it a bit too much on that day. I think we're both sensible pros and relatively nice people as well (!) so it was one of those things that should never have happened, but unfortunately, in the heat of battle, it did.

Simon? Yeah, he was furious. I've had some fairly big rollockings off him down the years but that one was definitely up there.

He expected better from both of us and rightly so.

On the plus side, I think the fans got their money back from the fines we had to pay so I hope they don't hold it against us too much now a few years have passed, because I know it's not cheap at Sheffield Wednesday is it?

What made it worse was that when I got back from suspension, we played Leeds at Deepdale and I really wanted to make a good impression.

I came on with about 25 minutes to go and . . . I was off again three minutes later. Another red card. Another nightmare.

To be honest, that was an outrageous decision from the referee. It should have been a red the other way against Kyle Bartley, who was already on a yellow and knew exactly what he was doing when he came through the back of me with his knee right up.

He lunged in from so far away that he was never going to win the ball, but either way, my reaction was unnecessary. I lashed out for a split second and I shouldn't have done it, plain and simple.

To get sent off straight after coming back from a red card suspension? That was more painful than the whack in the back.

It was one of those things, but you live and learn and it hurts me so much every time I see it back because I know it was stupid.

Funnily enough, when we played against Leeds again later on that season, in the warm-up, Kyle came over to me and said: 'Becks, I'm really sorry about what happened in the last game mate, I genuinely don't know what I was thinking.' I accepted his apology and it was fine.

We had a bit of a chat and he said: 'Mate, we're lucky the roles weren't reversed, because if you'd have smashed me like I smashed you, there would have been fists flying.'

That would never have happened though - it's not in my nature!

But it was good for a fellow pro to come over and apologise like that and it's good when something like that's happened but there's that mutual understanding of what really went on.

Obviously, I've got a big connection with Leeds but let me tell you this; whenever I played against them, I wanted to score just like every other game. There was no 'going easy' - I mean, come on!

That's definitely not in my nature. I know they used to sing 'You're Leeds and you know you are!' But I'm telling you, when I had that North End shirt on, I was Preston all the way. Part of me always will be, for sure.

Unfortunately for me though, after that Newcastle sending off, opportunities to start for North End became rarer. Maybe it was understandable.

To be fair, Jordan Hugill was on fire around that time and we would often play one up front, so it was a case of coming off the bench mainly towards the end of games.

I was glad that I was able to play in the last game of the season away at Wolves, even though we lost, because by then it was clear I would be moving on and it was good to be able to say goodbye to the Preston fans, who were always brilliant with me - I couldn't have asked for any more.

I loved it at Deepdale and it gave me everything I wanted at that stage of my career; a good club, winning games, great set of lads, top manager and memories that will live with me forever.

I wish I could have stayed longer but it wasn't to be and at the end of the day, we shook hands and parted on good terms.

I still keep in touch with the lads, still keep an eye out for the results and always want them to do well.

Maybe the best thing is whenever I meet any North End fans, they always say the same thing: 'Do you remember that day at Wembley?'

Remember it? How could I ever forget?

CHAPTER 3

DECLAN RUDD: LIFELINE

Preston North End has been a lifeline for me in more ways than you probably know. On the pitch and off it, the club has been a major part of my life for many years now - and always in a positive sense.

Obviously, I've gone from being a fresh-faced kid to looking like Tom Hanks in Cast Away, but apart from that . . I think I've aged well!

I'm approaching 200 games for the club now and my only regret is that I haven't been here longer.

And, before you ask, no I don't only eat avocado - my vegan days are behind me now and anyway, I'm from Norfolk, land of the Sunday roast dinner (!). I grew up in Diss, about 25 miles outside Norwich and was always quite good at school, but if I'm honest my priorities were football, football and football. Luckily, that was also my best subject, but not in the way you might imagine.

When I first kicked a ball, I was a midfielder and absolutely loved it, becoming captain of my local boy's team. I was only about eight years old but I was playing a couple of years older than my age group when I was scouted by Norwich and invited for a trial.

It was six-a-side and we had no goalkeeper, so had to take it in turns to go in goal, no gloves or anything, just jumping around.

I must have done quite well because at the end of the session, they said I wasn't quite good enough as an outfield player, but they were willing to give me a few months of coaching as a keeper.

From there, the Academy goalkeeping coach Paul Tong took me under his wing, I pulled on some actual gloves for the first time and the rest, as they say, is history.

So I was at Norwich from a very early age at around the time Rob Green was goalkeeper - I used to get to games early just to watch his warm up and see if I could learn anything from it.

A few years later, we had a great run in the FA Youth Cup, beating Louis Moult's Stoke when I saved three in a penalty shoot-out and then topped it off by scoring the winner from the spot. (I don't score many, so come on, let me have my moment!)

We then beat Everton, where I saved another three penalties, but got knocked out in the semi-final by eventual winners Manchester City at the Etihad. They had Ben Mee, Daniel Sturridge and Kieran Trippier playing, so while it was a shame, it was a good experience at that age. We had a decent side to be fair, with Korey Smith, who's now at Swansea, George Francomb, who's at Crawley, and two or three others who've made a career in the game.

Me? I made my debut for Norwich quite young; I'd just turned 18 and Paul Lambert had just come in as manager when we were down in League 1. He refreshed the senior group and started to put a few young lads including me on the bench, probably just to get a taste of things.

I was absolutely loving getting that insight, but then Fraser Forster got sent off at Gillingham and suddenly I was on for my debut - I had no chance to be nervous, it was just get the gloves on and get out there.

First task - face a penalty.

First touch - picking the ball out of the net.

Welcome to the Football League!

Thankfully, Darrel Russell, who later came to Preston, got a last-minute equaliser so at least I didn't start with a defeat.

Now Fraser's always been a fantastic keeper, but around that time he was a bit clumsy and somehow got sent off three times that season. So I ended up playing about half a dozen games at a time when Norwich had very good players like Grant Holt, Chris Martin and Wes Hoolahan in the team.

The other keeper in the squad was Jed Steer, who's gone on to have a good career too, so there was a lot of quality around and I was very lucky that Paul Lambert took a chance on me. We went on a real charge under Paul, coming up from League 1 to the Premier League with two successive promotions.

I got my first taste of the Prem when John Ruddy gave away a spot kick and got a red card at Stamford Bridge.

First task - face a Frank Lampard penalty.

First touch . . . you can guess the rest.

Welcome to the Premier League.

It was one of the hardest shots I've ever faced - it absolutely flew into the back of the net.

The following week I made my Prem debut in 2011 against West Brom at Carrow Road. That was that for a while though and by 2013, Chris Hughton had taken over and basically told me I wasn't ready to play at that level. I was still only 21 and he wanted me to go out and learn my trade a bit more.

At that time, there was only one team willing to give me a chance - Preston North End. I'd been on the bench for Norwich at Deepdale a couple of seasons earlier, so I'd seen the stadium and been very impressed. At the time, North End were in the Championship and it seemed strange to see them now down at the wrong end of League 1 - they just seemed too big to be there, especially given the history of the club and its standing in English football.

Either way, I was happy to be on board - although first days at any new job are always awkward aren't they? Trust me, it's the same for footballers.

But as soon as I arrived, the first person that came up to me was this lively Australian kid who made me a coffee and showed me around without being asked.

I didn't really know who he was at that point, but me and Bailey Wright became such big pals he was an usher at my wedding later on. He had so much confidence that I thought he must be a big member of the squad, when in fact he was still just breaking through into the team himself.

I knew straight away that he was the type of person I'd keep in my life no matter what, because people like that are very rare. I know Bails left a few years later, but everyone will tell you what a great guy he is.

As for everything that is said about Graham Westley, he gave me a chance and I'll always be grateful for that. He put his neck on the line to sign me and took me on the premise that I would be first choice, which was a big thing for me, as that had never been the case at Norwich.

Of course when I arrived, he put me on the bench for the first two games so I thought: 'Oh great, what's going on here?'

And then when I did make my debut against Yeovil, he got sacked the morning after - so it was an interesting start (!).

To be fair, Graham brought in quite a few of the lads who have been top players for North End in recent years and I'll always have a good word for him. I think he had a tough task, cutting the wage bill and maybe getting rid of one or two big egos as the club was rebuilding things, which is never easy.

On the other hand, we were losing a lot of games and I know quite a lot of the supporters were pleased when he went - that's football, I suppose. It can be a brutal business.

When Simon Grayson came in, everything just seemed to turn around really quickly. Almost since that day, the club has been moving in the right direction and it's been a great success story.

Previously, Graham was a very intense guy and like all managers, he had a certain way of doing things. He had you training exactly the way you play on a Saturday afternoon, so it was shin pads, full-on tackles and everyone getting stuck in, no half-measures.

Now, that can be a very successful method, especially in terms of getting you ready for match days. But with the amount of games we were playing, I think over time that approach took a lot out of the lads and in the end it caught up with the group.

Getting Simon in was a breath of fresh air; he's a completely different character, he doesn't create any conflict and he likes it to be a nice steady ship. He wants it to be an enjoyable place and he raised morale for sure.

You normally get a lift off the back of a new manager, but he had the knack of keeping that going throughout his time at the club.

I was first choice for the rest of that season and it was a great learning curve for me, to be playing regularly in a team with some really top, experienced players; John Welsh, Paul Huntington, Joe Garner - big characters who set the tone.

Those lads (and Tom Clarke later on) weren't exactly ranters and ravers, but they were leaders in the way they played the game, the standards they set and their sheer will to win.

They put their bodies on the line every single time and to have a defence that would stop so many shots even reaching me was an absolute dream. Simon really tightened things up at the back and we kept eight clean sheets towards the end of that first season to pull away from any fears of relegation and set ourselves up for the following year.

You could sense that it was becoming a really tight-knit squad so I was delighted when Simon and Peter Ridsdale asked Norwich if I could come back on a season-long loan for 2013/14.

Norwich had gone back up to the Premier League and were happy to have me around the club, but the reality was I wasn't likely to play much, if at all. I knew the only way to improve was to keep playing and I'd seen how Simon had turned things around, so I was really keen to be a part of it again.

When I got back, I went straight into training and one of the biggest things for any player is to feel wanted - that's exactly how I felt at Deepdale. Peter and Simon had made it clear how much they wanted me to come back and that always gives you confidence.

For the first loan, I'd been staying at Farington Lodge, which was a lovely place, but it becomes a grind after a while.

So I knew when I came back, I wanted somewhere of my own to move into. I couldn't face the thought of ten months in a hotel.

Some people might think it sounds great, but it's just not enjoyable in the long term - look what it did to Alan Partridge!

Thankfully, the club sorted me out with a nice place up in Longridge, a lovely barn conversion and my wife and I were really happy up there; it's a great little town packed with North End fans.

Simon not only put together a great coaching staff, he also had a fantastic eye for a player. He signed Clarkey on a free transfer that summer and he was an absolute warrior for the team.

One of his first games was against Blackpool and everyone knows what happened next. To be part of that night was incredible - I can only imagine what it must have been like to score the winning goal.

It sounds weird that one game in the League Cup was such a big thing, but obviously, it was much, much more than that - it was one of the most intense experiences of my career.

I'd played in the Premier League a couple of times, but you could tell the meaning of that game against Blackpool from the minute the tie was announced.

The noise when we scored was unbelievable and to go in front so late on, all I was thinking was: 'You've got three minutes to keep the ball out of this net - don't do anything stupid, Dec!'

I had all those Blackpool fans behind me in silence and the rest of the stadium bouncing, so I was just desperate to get to the end.

When the final whistle went, the fans piled on the pitch and it was pandemonium.

A few days later, we had a team meeting and the lads took great delight in showing a clip of me on the big screen.

When the final whistle went, the crowd piled on and moments later these police horses appeared over my shoulder - I just took one look, put my head down and legged it as fast as I could. (I'm a goalkeeper - get me out of here!)

Obviously, Tom's gone down in history after that night, but I don't think it's just because he scored that goal - it's down to everything else he brought to the team, because he's an outstanding professional, a top man.

Back in the league, Simon had us so organised and well drilled, we always felt confident about picking up points wherever we went.

I'm not sure whether we were catching people by surprise, having struggled the year before, but we had a great season and probably should have had automatic promotion.

Wolves were in there that season and were streets ahead of everyone, along with Brentford who were starting to put together a very good side.

Apart from a couple of cup ties, I played every game as we reached the play-offs and the first game against Rotherham is probably remembered for just one magical reason.

Joe Garner's volley was outrageous, wasn't it?

I had to pinch myself at first because I was thinking: 'Wait, Joe can't strike a ball like that!' But of course, he did and it was an absolute wonder strike - unbelievable.

What sticks with me though was how unlucky we were in the second leg at their place. We hit the bar twice, their keeper let one through his hands, it hit the woodwork and bounced straight back to him . . . it was just one of those games where the gods seemed to be against us.

Meanwhile, everything they did was hitting the back of the net and it was just really frustrating to be so close, but fall just short.

At the final whistle, the Preston fans were singing my name and, I'll be honest, I got very emotional. I ended up in tears in the dressing room because the season was over and I was absolutely gutted; we weren't going up and that might have been my last game for Preston.

I didn't want it to end - certainly not like that.

I'd loved being back at Deepdale and that night was a real sickener.

It was my first taste of being a regular for a full season and I think I played 55 games overall.

Once I got my head round our play-off disappointment, I was so grateful to the club because it was a massive step forward in my career and set me up going forward. North End wanted me back again on a permanent transfer, but as it turned out, that didn't happen - I would spend the next couple of years away from Deepdale.

It's a decision that I regret, but also one that I'm glad I made. I know that sounds weird, but bear with me. Chris Hughton had just been sacked at Norwich and my old youth team coach, Neil Adams, got the job as first team boss.

They'd just been relegated to the Championship and he rang me to say I was part of his plans. I would be Number Two to John Ruddy and as a lifelong Norwich fan who'd been at the club since I was eight years old, that was a massive thing for me to hear.

I was still only young and had been given a new contract at Norwich, where all my family were, whereas Preston was four hours away from them. But I was really torn. After the year I'd had at Deepdale, Preston had become a big pull for me; Simon, the players, the club, the people, the supporters - everyone had made me feel such a big part of things.

In the end I stayed in Norfolk and really, it was a decision I made with my heart, not my head. I couldn't walk away from my hometown club - the team I supported - when there was still such an opportunity to play for them.

It was a gamble and it paid off to a large degree.

Unfortunately Neil Adams left, but a new manager came in who led us to promotion that year - a guy called Alex Neil. You may have heard of him (!). And from there I ended playing 11 games in the Premier League the following season - so there were pluses and minuses about turning Preston down.

On the one hand, it gave me a chance at the highest level, but on the other I regret it because I could have had an even longer association with North End and been part of that promotion season under Simon.

The funny thing was, Norwich were in the Championship play-off final the day after North End played Swindon at Wembley.

We were staying in the Hilton Hotel right next to the stadium, so I could see all the PNE fans outside and I was desperate to join in and go to the game.

I asked our goalkeeping coach if I could nip across to the stadium, but understandably, with the biggest game in the club's recent history the following day, he didn't want anything to distract us from the preparation.

So I was gutted and I ended up watching it on TV in my room, near enough to join in with the cheers when the goals went in.

I was absolutely delighted for the lads and obviously we won our own game the following day, so that was a wonderful weekend all round.

Alex had come in at Norwich that February and done wonders; we had a great squad, but he stuck his foot up a few people's backsides and really got us going. When we went up, he put me in the team and we had some great results - including winning away at Manchester United.

It's an incredible standard up there though that you probably don't fully appreciate until you've played in it.

I remember we played Tottenham at White Hart Lane and Erik Lamela cut in from the right hand side and hit this 'rabona' shot that flew past me.

I dived but as I was going through the air I was thinking: 'I can't believe he's just done that!' If it hadn't hit the bar and bounced away, it's a goal you'd have seen a thousand times by now.

I was in the first team from December to February, but in the end, the team was struggling, my performances weren't good enough and I was dropped. That was the start of a really tough time in my life.

People, especially men, don't tend to talk about things like mental health, but I have no problem doing so and if you're struggling at any point, I hope you can get some support to help you out.

Because, trust me, it can happen to anyone.

There was nothing too severe going on in my life, but these things come up when you least expect them.

We'd just had our first child, I was in the team at Norwich and was thinking: 'Life's great.'

Then suddenly I was out of the team and told by Alex that I wasn't wanted at Norwich, which was a big blow.

I had to find a loan club and ended up going to Charlton, which was a very low point in my life and my career - it wasn't enjoyable at all and the club was in an absolute mess.

In all honesty, I was still hung up on what had happened at Norwich and that was affecting my performances, which I know weren't good enough. It was a really tough period for me in many ways and when the season at Charlton ended I was left wondering where things would go from there. I hadn't enjoyed Charlton and the manager at Norwich had told me I wasn't good enough.

And then came the lifeline from Preston - again.

Two years after turning them down, they still wanted to take me on a permanent transfer. It was the best news I could have asked for. It meant so much to me and I dread to think where my career might have gone if it wasn't for this club. As soon as I heard about it, in my head I'd signed - I couldn't get back to Deepdale fast enough.

But even though there was this great news, if I thought that was the end of my problems, I was wrong. You can't just flick a switch with mental health, it doesn't work like that. Even when I was back at a place I loved, it took me probably a year to 18 months to get properly back on track.

Almost as soon as I came back, I was injured and out for about six months. Then when I did get in, I wasn't performing - I was all over the place at times.

I just felt a bit lethargic and things were a bit hazy - it's hard to explain.

I hadn't got to grips with my mental health situation and like a lot of people, I tried to ignore it, which wasn't helping at all, because if it's not addressed, it just gets worse. I was always down, always fed up, always negative - just not an enjoyable person to be with.

I had a fantastic wife and a good career, but it doesn't make you exempt. I had a baby on the way and a beautiful two-year-old daughter, but it was getting to the stage where sometimes I didn't even want to play with my child at home. In the end, it reached a point where my wife quite rightly pulled me to one side.

By that time, it was obvious I was struggling and she said: 'You need to sort yourself out and get help. It's beyond the point of excuses now, there's clearly an issue - go and talk to someone about it.'

It might sound strange, but that was one of the best conversations we could have had - it changed both our lives for the better.

I literally rang the PFA there and then and within two hours I'd got an appointment to see someone a couple of days later from Sporting Chance, which was set up by Tony Adams to support athletes.

From then on, every day has been better and better - it turned my life around. It's a journey that I'm glad happened, because it made me value what life really is about. Thankfully, people are starting to get a bit more open about mental health and that's brilliant because talking about it is really is the only way you can start to overcome it - take it from me.

Obviously, it's not all been plain sailing and I remember from Day One when I came back to Preston in 2017, things didn't go as planned.

The night before we were due to report back for pre-season training, me and my wife went to see Adele at Wembley (she was brilliant, by the way). We drove up to Preston after the concert, got into the hotel and I was up early the next day.

I couldn't wait to get going so I thought I'd get in early, but as I drove into the training ground, I saw Simon Grayson driving out. He gave me a wave and I thought: 'He must be nipping to the ground - he'll be back in a minute.'

A while later when everyone had turned up, Peter Ridsdale came in and told us Simon had gone to Sunderland and he wasn't coming back.

I thought: 'Well, that's a great start. I wonder who'll take over?'

Three days later, I had my answer - it was the manager who said he didn't want me and that I didn't have a future at Norwich.

Hello again, gaffer. Fantastic.

From then on it was a battle to prove myself to Alex Neil, to change his mind and win him over by showing I was good enough.

Thankfully, over time I won that battle, established myself at Preston and we had a great relationship for the rest of his time at the club.

In a strange way, I'm pleased he said that I wasn't wanted at Norwich, because it gave me a new fire and determination to prove people wrong.

When I was fit again, I came back into the side for the FA Cup game at Wycombe, which was a great performance by the lads, and then I was starting most games for the rest of that season. I was taken out for a week or two a couple of times, but Alex always came back to me when I was needed. We finished just outside the play-offs but I knew I still had a lot of work to do to get to the levels that I wanted and to show the standards I was capable of.

My confidence was growing and as time went by, my relationship with the gaffer was getting stronger and stronger. He's a demanding guy, but all top managers are and everyone knows what's required.

Pre-seasons were tough but enjoyable and going into the 2018/19 campaign we started off with a home game against QPR in the sunshine at Deepdale. It was one of those days that football was made for - a good crowd, everyone optimistic and two decent sides going at it.

Alan Browne put us in front with a great header but right towards the end of injury time, I made a save I'm really proud of.

A free kick came into the box at speed and as it bounced around, their lad connected with it really well from about six yards out.

I managed to get a hand to it to turn it behind for a corner - pure reflex, but it's a good moment that I remember (I also remember the bad moments, by the way!).

What was funny was that when the corner came in it went out for a goal kick, by which time there must only have been seconds left.

I was doing all the usual tricks to wind down the clock and thought: 'I'm just going to put this into the stand to waste a bit more time.'

So I leathered it and it literally landed at the gaffer's feet on the sideline, where he volleyed it back onto the pitch and went absolutely ballistic at me for kicking it out. Thankfully, as QPR took the throw, the final whistle went - game over, three points. We had a laugh about it in the dressing room later and the gaffer just said: 'I'm sorry. I don't know what happened there, I lost it for a minute.'

No problem - that's what it's like in games and that intensity can be a really good energy.

It's funny because I probably don't remember as much as I should; the big games and the important saves are the ones that stand out.

I remember when we played Leeds at their place and drew 1-1, I made a stop from Eddie Nketiah that kept us in front, right in front of their fans and things like that give you great belief.

The annoying thing was that their goal right at the end was deflected into the top corner. (Deflections like that are infuriating but there's not much you can do with them unfortunately.)

Another save I remember was where we were winning 1-0 at home against Huddersfield when Pearo got robbed in midfield, they broke on us and it was a one-on-one with the striker. I quite like those situations because the pressure is all on the guy with the ball.

As it was, I made a save and it's another case where the importance of it makes it memorable - it made a difference to the result.

Sometimes you make a great save but if you get hammered 5-0, it doesn't mean as much - people tend to forget about those.

There's always competition at a club like Preston. At the start, Thorsten Stuckmann was there and he'd been Player of the Season a couple of years earlier and was a very good goalkeeper. Later on, Chris Maxwell was around, so you could never rest on your laurels. We hit a bad run early on in that 2018/19 season and after a 3-0 defeat at Leeds I was taken out of the team.

When you get called in for that conversation with the manager, you tend to know what's coming. I certainly did, but it's still something you never want to hear. I was out for about eight games and then came back in when Chris was suspended. Again, that spell on the sidelines relit my fire, because I was just so desperate to get back out there.

Things that seem negative at the time can turn out to be positives in the long run. You either let it affect you or you think: 'Right, I've got to work twice as hard, do twice as much work in the gym, I've got to eat twice as well - I've got to do whatever it takes to show that I'm good enough.'

That's what I did and from that moment, I've never looked back. And it's a good job really, especially as another promising goalkeeper had emerged.

Chris got sent off at Ipswich for two yellow cards and, being a Norwich lad, I couldn't wait to get on.

As soon as the red card came out, I started to get stripped but the gaffer said: 'I'm sorry Dec - we've used all three subs!'

I was gutted and I looked out to see Gally pulling the gloves on with about half an hour left. When that happens in a game of professional football, you fear the worst. But then he started making these wonder saves, coming for crosses and generally being brilliant.

I thought: 'Is there anything this guy can't do? I'm still going to be on the bench next week and he'll be starting as keeper!'

Afterwards, Gally was telling us how he was a keeper as a kid and I was thinking: 'Yep - and I was a midfielder, but I couldn't do what you do!'

Thankfully, the next week Gally was back in midfield, I was in goal and ever since then I've gone from strength to strength, mentally and physically.

I've recently hit the dreaded age of 30 where everything you eat tends to stay with you as body fat a bit longer. As people probably know, I was a vegan for about 18 months, but the upshot of that was that I lost a lot of muscle.

A game that sticks out was when we played Bristol City at home and I got bullied on two crosses in the first half. I came for one and got nowhere near it because I was getting blocked and wasn't strong enough to do anything about it. Thankfully we got back into the game for a draw, but that day changed the way I looked at things.

Since then, I've put on 12 kilos of muscle and I feel all the better for it. I look back at pictures of me in that period and, being honest, I just didn't look well.

I heard the 'vegan' chants from the fans and didn't know what to think at first; are they taking the mickey or is it a term of endearment?

Thankfully it was the latter (I hope!) and it's always nice to hear your name sung by the supporters - it shows you must be doing something right. It sends a tingle down your spine every time and it's always a special feeling. There have been times elsewhere where I've had songs sung about me that didn't make me tingle (!) but at Preston it's always been positive and you really can feed off that.

It's one of the reasons I love it here so much, there's a great rapport with the crowd and you can tell they're a decent bunch, never any trouble.

For the record, my pre-match meal is avocado on toast, followed by an avocado smoothie and avocado ice cream, all served in avocado-coloured bowls.

Just kidding, of course!

It's actually a bowl of porridge (nothing too heavy and, if you want the science, it has a slow energy release). If I went to a restaurant, I'm a roast chicken dinner man. I'd have it seven days a week, breakfast, lunch and tea if I could (apologies to any vegans out there!).

Not sure that would be the best match preparation though and the porridge works much better, especially as I normally cover around seven kilometres during a game, as I always try to keep on the move.

It's a funny position being the goalkeeper, because you've got to concentrate for 90 minutes, never knowing when you might be called into action. Two days after a match, you can still be mentally exhausted from it.

But if you let your concentration slip even for a moment, you can be punished, as I know only too well.

OK, it's time: Let's talk about Birmingham and that great finish that beat me from near the half-way line . . !

Yes, it was the clanger of clangers, but that's the deal if you're a goalkeeper - if I'd stayed in midfield all those years ago I wouldn't have to worry about it! Instead, you are constantly on the edge of failure - a whisker away from being the hero or the villain.

There's no-one between you and the goal so if you make a mess of things, no-one's going to bale you out. That's just the way it is and you couldn't make much of a bigger mess than I did in that game.

To this day . . . I can't explain it.

It was probably down to concentration because it's a ball that I've picked up 10,000 times in my career - and if I do it another 10,000 times, it wouldn't happen again.

I've watched it over and over and it hurts more every time. What made it worse was that we were 0-0 at half-time and the gaffer had said: 'Get through the next 20 minutes without conceding and then we'll go from there.' Five minutes later, I've let the softest goal ever go past me and I've now got to stand in front of 20,000 Brummies hammering me every time the ball came near: 'Dodgy keeper! Aahhh!'

We went on to lose 3-0 and I just held my hands up to the fans and my team-mates that day. But as I mentioned earlier, you can take a massive negative like that and turn it into a positive.

For me, I looked at it and thought: 'Well, it can't get any worse than that, can it?' It's the biggest mistake I'll ever make and it's done now.

I'm still playing football, it didn't ruin my career and if anything it's inspired me to be a better player. I've still got a beautiful family, a good life and at the end of the day . . . it's a mistake in a game of football.

I'm really sorry about it, but there's nothing you can do, other than to keep it in perspective and not let it crush you.

Playing football, like life, is one big learning curve and things like that are building blocks for where I am now as a player and a person. I'd be a liar if I said something like that will never happen again, because you just don't know. But I'd like to think I've come a long way from then.

The next game was away at Nottingham Forest and the gaffer pulled me to one side beforehand. He said: 'Dec, I'm keeping faith with you - just put the other day behind you.'

I remember telling him I wouldn't let him down and that was the day we won 1-0 at the City Ground when Moulty scored.

They really put us under pressure at the end and in the last minute I made a good save right in the top corner to keep us in front.

When the final whistle went the gaffer ran onto the pitch, headed straight for me with a big smile on his face and just said: 'It's a funny old game Dec, isn't it?'

The pair of us burst out laughing, but he's right - and those two games summed up the life of a goalkeeper - villain one week, hero the next.

As a team, we faded away towards the end of that season, but it's a myth that players switch off if they think the season is over and they're not going up or down. No-one goes out thinking like that.

A more likely explanation is that we've been punching above our weight for the past few years and haven't really got a squad of players that has been there and done it at the business end of the season.

We've got one or two, but overall it's the type of club that gives opportunities to players on the way up, which a lot of clubs don't.

A lot of places go back to the same old names that have been at the same old clubs, but North End is not like that.

They give chances to lads who have proved that they deserve their shot. The recruitment is very rarely wrong and most lads that come in do a good job, no big names and no big-timers.

That's how the club's been run since I've been here and it's got a very good reputation within the game for that.

Perfect examples of that are Callum Robinson, Jordan Hugill, Ben Pearson, Ben Davies, Alan Browne . . . all these good young lads who were given a chance and have developed into top, top players.

They had the talent, but you need the right environment to develop and that's what there is at Preston. It's part of our identity and while some people might criticise that approach, I think the majority would say it's the right way forward and also that it's been successful in recent years.

Football is cyclical and teams develop over time, then get refreshed and come again. I think that's what we will see at Preston and hopefully we can put everything together at the right time to push for promotion.

It's hard to judge the long-term impact of the pandemic on clubs, but I do know that North End is a very well-run club and very stable compared to some other teams.

It's not somewhere where managers get sacked every six months, or they're signing loads of players every summer.

It's stable, it's sensible and it's a very good place to play football - I think most people in the game would acknowledge that, especially when you look at the trouble some other clubs have found themselves in.

There's a real family spirit and everyone feels part of it; players, the people who work in the offices and the coaching staff, too.

Coming into the 2019/20 season, there was interest in me from West Ham, but I never came close to leaving - it was something that was made bigger by the press than it actually was.

I've never once looked away from Deepdale since I've been back - when you find something this good in this game, you want to hold onto it as long as you can. I owe so much to North End, not just because they gave me a chance, but for lots of other reasons too.

We started that season like a house on fire, but it's strange sometimes how little things can knock your momentum.

For us, it came in the last minute of the game against West Brom at Deepdale when there was an outrageous penalty decision given against us.

With that incident, there was contact - but only because their player stuck his leg out and basically kicked my thigh!

Say what you like about officials, but something like that is not down to the ref, it's down to the player who basically cheated us out of a point.

And if I'm honest, there have been times where I've totally cleared players out and not even had a free-kick given, so it's swings and roundabouts, I suppose. You don't think like that at the time though and I was absolutely fuming.

Of course, when the pandemic struck, it became the strangest season any of us had ever been involved with.

At the start of the first lockdown, I was ill for a while and in bed for about three weeks, so I lost a bit of fitness, but after that, we were doing sessions on Strava, recording them and sending them into the fitness coach.

In fact, it worked quite well for me because when I came back, I'd put on quite a bit of muscle and felt a lot stronger than before.

I'm sure it was a tough time for everyone reading this, so again, you have to look for positives. For me, that was the chance to spend every day with my family for three months, which doesn't happen very often when you're a footballer, so I made the most of that.

When things got going again, well . . . it was rubbish without the fans.

When there's no-one there you don't get that sense of occasion.

If you gave me the choice of an empty stadium or those 20,000 Brummies giving me stick, I'd take the crowd any time.

Normally you go onto a pitch and there's thousands of people who have paid to come and watch you, it puts you under a bit of pressure - but it's a good pressure that brings out the best.

When people are watching remotely on the internet or whatever, it takes something away for players and supporters.

I don't think any of the lads like it, because we all feed off the support that the Preston fans give us. Football isn't football without the fans there.

Even the big games, cup finals and Champions League, or whatever, they all lost that sense of occasion in an empty stadium and I think there's a lesson there for people to acknowledge and appreciate the role the fans have. I loved the fact that when we played our first away game at Norwich the following season, there were Preston fans who'd booked into the hotel in the corner - that was a great effort.

Later on in the season, Gally moved into more of a coaching role and he is a massive influence in the dressing room.

Everyone has so much respect for him as a person, as a player and for what he's achieved in his career. He's been phenomenal for Preston but some of the best players don't know how to get things across to other players when they step up into coaching.

Gally does and he's brilliant to work with; he has a warmth to match his intelligence and I've no doubt he will be a success as a coach.

The big issue we have is how to replace him on the pitch, because he's been such a big influence on the team for so many years.

Same with Hunts, he's another one who sets the example with how he trains, prepares and does everything the right way. You look at true professionals like that and it's no surprise why they've had long careers at a good level - it's genuinely been a privilege to be at the club at the same time as them.

Agonisingly, I suffered a bad injury midway through the 2020/21 season. It was the week leading up to the FA Cup game at Wycombe in January and we'd been at it in training for an hour.

It was my last rep of the set; I came out to make a block and just got my leg stuck in the ground, completely twisted.

My cartilage popped out between two bones and went in behind the knee cap. It locked my knee up and basically made a real mess of things.

Saying it quickly like that doesn't quite get across how painful it was.

In the past, I've done my cruciate, I've ruptured my ankle, broken my jaw, so I've had a few injuries . . . but this? This was excruciating. I was screaming on the pitch in so much pain - it was by far the worst injury I've ever had. I couldn't move my leg for about five weeks and I was on really strong painkillers, liquid morphine and things, it was so bad.

It's hard to describe really, not just the physical pain but also the frustration of sitting out games and seeing the lads struggle to get results.

Daniel Iversen came in and was absolutely brilliant, but unfortunately Alex lost his job and that was a really sad day.

The club has a lot to thank him for, not just in terms of results, but also in the way he developed so many players into assets. He was a hard taskmaster, a very good coach and superb in getting players performing to their full potential with no stone left unturned in terms of preparation.

Unfortunately though, in football, every horse runs its course and you see that with the very best in the world.

In time I'm sure people will look back on the work he did at North End and appreciate the progress the club made while he was here.

Frankie McAvoy did a great job when he took over and he's a lovely, knowledgeable guy; you won't find anyone with a bad word to say about him and he's just so genuine in everything that he does. He wears his heart on his sleeve and is one of life's good guys.

For me, I just want to get back to my best and play as many games as possible for the club. I want to inspire young people to become goalkeepers (it's a great position, honest!) and I want to give the people of the city something to look forward to every weekend.

We're in the entertainment business and we've got to make sure that supporters enjoy coming to the games and get their money's worth.

The longer I can do that the better, and my only regret is that I've not been able to play even more games for the club up to now.

It's hard to explain just how much the club means to me, but I hope I've set it out to some extent here. You don't go through those experiences without developing a real bond and my feelings for the club run deep.

It's not all been plain sailing, but I'll always be grateful that my footballing journey brought me to Deepdale. It's like one of those on-off relationships that was always destined to happen in the end.

When I was starting out and needed experience, Preston were there for me.

When I was told I wasn't wanted elsewhere, Preston were there for me.

When I've needed support, Preston have always been there for me.

I want to be here for North End for as long as possible.

CHAPTER 4

TOMMY BOOTH: IT WASN'T ME

I only played for two clubs in my career and I'm proud to say they were Manchester City and Preston North End. The fact that I went on to manage PNE is something I never expected to happen when Tommy Docherty took me to Deepdale in 1981.

I'm a Manchester lad and I'd spent my entire career at City, beginning as a schoolboy centre forward, but quickly being moved back to centre half. I started out under two football legends in Joe Mercer and Malcolm Allison - so if they said I was a centre half, I bowed to their superior knowledge!

At first I was only on amateur terms as I was doing an engineering apprenticeship at the time and training with City a couple of nights a week. I don't think the young lads do that any more (!), but for me, it was good to have a trade - or at least a back-up plan.

Thankfully, as it turned out, I didn't need one.

City were First Division champions when I made my debut as a 17-year-old and in that first 1968/69 season, I scored one goal - in the FA Cup semi-final, to give us a 1-0 win over Everton and send us to Wembley.

Future PNE striker Neil Young famously got the winner and over the following year we won both the League Cup and the European Cup Winners Cup. By the time I was 21, I was also playing nearly every game in the league for City, so it's fair to say I hit the ground running.

The seventies era at Maine Road had the likes of Colin Bell, Dennis Tueart, Joe Corrigan, Mike Summerbee, Francis Lee - names that are legends to this day. We won the League Cup again in 1976 and missed out on the league title by just one point the following year. That was 'classic City' at the time. Tony Book was the manager then but by 1981, John Bond had taken charge as City had another run to the FA Cup Final.

I'd scored the winner in the quarter final, but was injured for the semi.

City won without me, but John Bond told me I'd definitely be playing in the final against Spurs at Wembley.

So we were all suited and booted down in London for the Cup Final - a huge thing - and the manager decided to tell us the team the night before.

As he rattled through the names, I couldn't believe it - I wasn't picked, not even on the bench.

I don't know what had happened to change his mind, but he'd never spoken to me about it. It was just like that; I was out - and I was heartbroken.

I didn't even go to the game. I just got on a train the next morning and came home. So that was the parting of the ways for me with City.

I was sad - really sad - because I was a City supporter and I'd had so many highs with them. I loved the club and I still do.

Preston fans reading this will know what I mean when I say it was 'my club', my hometown team, a massive part of my life. But I just didn't see eye-to-eye with John Bond and it was time to leave, even though it was a big, big wrench for me to go.

So I was on the lookout for a new club and Tommy Docherty had just gone to Preston. Nobby Stiles had been there before him and North End had just slipped into the Third Division.

So it was a big step for me, having been in the First Division throughout my career and just missed out on playing in the FA Cup Final a few months earlier to playing in the Third Division.

It's like going from the Premier League to League 1 nowadays.

But The Doc was The Doc wasn't he?

He had this charisma about him and he could sell you anything.

The way he talked it was like North End were on a par with City and with him in charge, they would be overtaking them soon.

It sounds daft, especially when you see how things turned out, but when he spoke to you, he had all these big plans and you just believed he would do it. It was a case of 'when' we get promoted, not 'if', with The Doc.

He made you feel ten feet tall and you always wanted to go out and do well for him. He was a smashing fella and it's so sad that he's recently passed away.

Anyway, I think the fee was about £30,000 and I joined North End in October 1981 at the same time as another City lad, Gary Buckley.

I'd played at Deepdale a few years earlier for City and thought it was a good stadium for the time; lots of big terracing on the old Kop, decent crowds.

It was a good club and I signed expecting that we would bounce straight back up to the Second Division and then take it from there.

After all, you don't sign for any club thinking 'this is going to be a struggle'.

I looked at North End and thought we'd be OK, we'd do well.

Obviously, at 31, I was one of the more experienced players and within two or three days, Tommy was asking me to take some training sessions.

I'd never really done it before, but I had no problem with it and it was a way of passing on my experience to some of the younger lads.

In all honesty, we hardly ever saw The Doc until the games came around. You'd see him the day before for a team talk and then on match days - that's the way he was; he had other people doing training and stuff while he was more of an overseer.

He was such a motivator though. Earlier in my career, I'd nearly signed for Brian Clough at Derby and The Doc was similar to Cloughie.

They both just had this presence about them that's hard to explain.

Tommy would give little pointers and tips though - he was a proper football man. Training was mainly at Willow Farm and I remember the pitches and facilities up there being very good.

We also had some astroturf pitches at the back of the old Town End and a bit of a gym in the Pavilion Stand so I think for the time, the training was good. There were some good players around too.

Alex Bruce was up front and had a great season and I played at the back with Don O'Riordan, a lovely Irish player who was never flustered in defence.

I think those two played every single game that season and there was also a decent local lad, Andy McAteer, coming through at full back too.

There had been a bit of a turnaround in players when The Doc arrived though and by late autumn results just weren't coming.

I think we got beat at home to Brentford and I got a call from The Doc at home saying he thought he was about to be fired. I couldn't believe it. I said: 'Hold on boss, things aren't that bad, we'll be able to turn it round.'

I tried to reassure him because he'd only been there a few months and I genuinely thought he would get us going sooner rather than later.

But I think he knew it was coming and he was asking me to look after the players, do this, do that - basically trying to prepare me for when he'd gone. He'd been a player at North End, was big pals with Sir Tom Finney and really cared for the place. He said that if they offered me the job I should take it, as it was a great club.

As it was, that didn't happen at the time - when they sacked The Doc the directors brought Gordon Lee in and I had no problem with that.

I'd never fancied being a manager and I was glad they'd brought in someone as experienced as Gordon, who'd been in charge at Everton and Newcastle.

Now, anyone from that era will know that he was almost the exact opposite of Tommy Doc; very quiet and thoughtful. He was also tough though.

In his first team meeting, he made it clear to all us lads who The Doc had brought in that we had to prove ourselves to him now - no-one was going to get in on reputation.

He laid the law down pretty strongly and I thought: 'OK, fair enough.'

After that, it was a case of doing it on the pitch and, to be fair, he played me most games, as we eventually finished mid-table in that 1981/82 season. I don't think it was what anyone had expected at the start and it was a bit of a reality check about the division we were now in.

It was a tough league and you'd have to battle to get out of it.

That turned out to be painfully true didn't it?

If you'd have told anyone it would be 20 years before Preston were back at Second Division/Championship level, I don't think they would have believed you! But of course, that's what happened.

I'd got injured at Fulham towards the end of that season and I think it was just wear and tear in the knee from the amount of games I'd been playing. There was only one sub in those days and defenders didn't tend to come off unless they were injured.

Quite often, the sub wouldn't get on at all - for either team. The starting eleven finished most games and again, that takes a toll on your body after a while. I had an operation on my knee but I just knew it wasn't right after that. Truth be told, I still struggle slightly with it now, but at the time, I played on the following season.

Really, you've got to be 100 per cent fit to play, but I was getting through games even though I wasn't quite right. I'd always been good positionally and used my experience to get the job done.

I came back mid-season and then had a run towards the end of the year when we only lost one of our last eleven games to finish mid-table again.

People talk about the ambition of the club, but I think at the time everyone really wanted promotion - they just didn't have the money to throw at it.

It was just a case of getting your best eleven out there and hoping it all comes together; you get lucky with injuries, signings pay off, results go your way.

Everything has to click and if you look at the number of times teams get promoted, it doesn't happen that often.

So I don't think anyone was doing cartwheels about Preston being mid-table, but it kind of summed up where we were. You finish where you deserve to finish.

The experienced Alan Gowling had come in and done well, Steve Elliott had broken into the side and scored goals, Don was still at the back, so we'd done OK.

The following season, Brucie was released, Don was sold and although we brought players in, results just didn't come.

Dave Jones, who went on to be a decent manager, was at the back with me but at one point we lost eight on the trot and Gordon Lee went soon after that.

We were fourth from bottom when Alan Kelly, a club legend, stepped in and results picked up straight away. We put four past Port Vale at Deepdale and then beat Scunthorpe 5-1 away, with Steve Elliott getting a hat-trick against a defence that included cricket legend Ian Botham (!).

So things improved, but I think by then there wasn't much money going around and things were going to be difficult for whoever took over.

It was free transfers mainly - very hard to actually buy anyone, because the club was very short of money. By that point, the club had sold Willow Farm off for housing and we were training opposite the old Courtaulds factory with its giant chimneys towering above us. So I think Alan did as good a job as anyone could expect in the circumstances.

I don't think that was unique to Preston in the 1980s - I think a lot of clubs were in the same boat, just trying to keep their heads above water.

Attendances had dropped massively since the 1970s and the game wasn't anything like it is today in terms of TV money, sponsorship and hospitality. It was a million miles away.

The main income was fans coming through the turnstiles, so when crowds dropped off, clubs were always going to be affected.

Often, there were no overnight stays before matches any more; we'd go down on the day even if it was somewhere down south.

So you'd have an early start and be stretching your legs at a service station before playing the game and then back on the bus up north.

We're not talking glamorous here, you know? But that's the way it was.

The state of the pitches was unbelievable at the time and I remember us going down to play Wimbledon's Crazy Gang at their old ground, Plough Lane. Well, it was the right name because the pitch definitely looked like it had been ploughed, I can tell you.

I remember at one game it was so muddy that the ref stopped the game and got the groundsman and a few volunteers to do the lines again before we could carry on - in a league game. Unbelievable, really.

Deepdale though, was always a great pitch - absolutely beautiful compared to some of the ones we played on.

The ground itself still had that 'grand' feeling about it from Sir Tom's days and while it was sad to see it with just a few thousand on, you've got to remember that was par for the course with a lot of clubs back then.

So we finished 16th again under Alan Kelly and I think by that stage, the club was happy with that, given the finances and the circumstances.

I don't think anyone could - or would - have predicted what was to come over the next couple of seasons; we seemed a steady Third Division club.

We actually started the following year really well, winning four of our first five games.

In that run, we beat Hull City and featured on Match of the Day, which was a real rarity back then. They only used to show three games and for us to be on was quite a big thing.

What was brilliant was that we beat Hull, who were a decent side, with two absolute screamers. Jonathan Clark got the first and then Mark Jones - Dave's younger brother - put one in the top corner from about 30 yards out. It was an absolute cracker - up for Goal of the Month - and really, we were flying at that stage.

What sums things up though was that despite a couple of decent away results, when we got back to Deepdale for the next game, there were only just over 3,000 on as we lost 3-0 at home to Rotherham.

That defeat was a turning point really.

The next game, we went down to Plymouth and scored four at Home Park. The only problem was . . . they scored six.

We were winning 4-3, then Jon Clark got sent off and they scored three in the last ten minutes. A crazy game and the start of another bad losing run. I was injured a couple of weeks into that bad streak again and that was it for me as a player, really.

I'd been on antibiotics and injections just to get me through games, but the doctors said the more I played on it, the worse it was going to get.

They were sticking this big needle in just below the patella, because every time I kicked the ball, this pain shot up my leg.

I got back for a win at Deepdale on my last home appearance, but my last game overall was away at Millwall where we got beat 3-0 at the old Den. I'd had the injection and thought it was fantastic, no pain in the game at all. I thought: 'Brilliant - I'm cured.'

But then I woke up in the middle of the night and I was in absolute agony. The painkilling injection had worn off and I tell you what . . . it didn't half hurt. I just thought: 'That's it. Enough.'

I was still going in for physio and trying to get fit, but in my heart, I knew it would probably never happen. So I'd been out of the team for quite a while when Alan eventually resigned in February 1984.

It was sad because he was a North End legend and he was Preston through and through. He always tried to do things the right way and was a good man, but I think it was a near impossible task at that point - as I was about to find out. I'd never really been one of those players who wanted to stay in football after they finished playing. Some lads will go anywhere and do anything to stay in the game and good luck to them.

Dave Jones, for example, had always been the type of guy who had the makings of a manager when he was playing.

Me? I'd never really fancied it.

So when the club asked me to take over after Alan went, I was surprised and a bit unsure. But I thought I owed it to them in a way as they'd always been good to me.

I still had a couple of years left on my contract, I wasn't playing and I was on decent money (relatively-speaking), so it made sense for them. I said I'd give it a go, but deep down, I think I always knew it wasn't really my thing.

I hadn't minded putting a few training sessions on previously, but picking the team and all that pressure and responsibility didn't sit well with me at all. I didn't enjoy it. It just wasn't me.

But I honestly look back now and think: 'Well, I did what I could.'

Fairly early on, I was lucky in that I spotted a couple of decent young lads playing for Sheffield United in a reserve game.

The reserves were in the Central League back then and it was a competitive league with a mix of first team players and young lads coming through.

That day, Sheffield United had Gary Brazil and Bob Atkins playing and straight away I liked the look of both of them.

Gary was nippy and skilful up front while big Bob was calm and had a lovely touch in defence (the Preston fans later nicknamed him 'Skilful Bob' and you could see why).

In those days, I had to put a request in to the board and they did all the negotiating over fees and whatnot, but I think we got the pair for about £25,000 - a great bit of business. We also got John Platt in, who was a good goalkeeper, so we were wheeling and dealing a bit.

Even though we were having a hard time, Preston was still a club to look up to and players wanted to come to Deepdale. But whatever we did, whoever we signed, it didn't transmit into results and we just seemed destined to go down that year. We'd have a couple of good results followed by three or four defeats and when you get on a losing run like that, confidence goes and it's hard to stop.

There was no lack of effort from players or management; we tried everything - different players, preparation, formations.

Everyone was trying their best, but again, the table doesn't lie.

We lost at home to Wigan in our last home game and that was a killer. It left us needing to win at York and hope other results went our way.

We went there and Ian Stevens - a good young player from the youth team - got us the goal in a 1-0 win, but it wasn't enough sadly.

The fans had been brilliant that day and it was really, really sad to see the club relegated. If they were angry, I could understand it. Preston shouldn't have been in the Fourth Division.

It was the first time they'd been that low in their history and we were all gutted. Everyone was numb from it all really, a little bit in shock.

You'd look around at Deepdale and wonder how we got there but I don't think it was just that season, it had been coming for a while sadly.

I thought about resigning, but I wanted to do what I could to get the club back on the right track. I still had time on my contract and the club were happy for me to carry on so I thought I'd give it another go. I was learning and I thought it would get better as time went on.

The bottom line is though, I just wasn't cut out to be a manager.

Even in the Fourth Division, we still couldn't get a decent run of results going. We'd have flashes where we'd win 4-0 at home one week then lose 6-0 away the next. Even if we got a win, I couldn't really enjoy it because my mind would be straight on to the next game.

We'd win a couple, then lose three or four on the trot.

We were relying on the same eleven or twelve players and when you looked at them, they were all decent lads, good players in their own right, but we just couldn't get it together consistently.

I brought Brian Kidd in to help with the coaching and Kiddo was brilliant; really ahead of his time with his methods and everything he was trying to do.

We brought John Thomas in, Wayne Foster too; good players who went on to have great careers and you'd think: 'Right, we've got a chance now.'

But then you'd work hard all week on things and then see it go wrong on a Saturday afternoon and it was all so frustrating, depressing really.

You feel it 24 hours a day. It weighs on you. People say being a football manager is the loneliest job in the world and they're right. It got to the point where I was driving into work, dreading it - and that's no way to carry on.

Obviously, things were really bad on the financial side. I've no idea how many people were on the board, but there seemed to be a lot of directors knocking about.

To top it off, the club had done a deal with the council, who now owned the ground, and in November the floodlights were condemned.

We couldn't afford to fix them so we had to play a game against Scunthorpe on a Tuesday afternoon, 2pm kick-off. I mean, come on, in the Football League . . . how bad is that?

I'd tried to bring a couple of players in who I thought would do a good job for us, but by that stage there really was no money around and the board said no.

We ended up bringing Mel Tottoh in for that Scunthorpe game. He was a good local league player, but he'd been at work in the morning and played for us in the Football League in the afternoon. That sums things up.

You end up doubting yourself and in the end, I had to say enough is enough, for the good of the club and for me.

The fans were having a bit of a go, but I've no problem with that. They are the people who make the game and they want their team to win - it's as simple as that.

They have their say and if you're losing, they're not happy. It's the same at any club. They'd always been great to me as a player and I understood their frustration.

There was a lot that they didn't know about what was going on behind the scenes, there was probably a lot I didn't know about too.

But even if the fans had known, would it have made any difference?

They want wins, not sob stories.

The thing is, to be a successful manager you've got to be someone who doesn't give a toss what the fans think and what they say.

Someone like The Doc couldn't care less. He just did his thing.

I wasn't that way inclined. I took it to heart and I felt bad about it. The pressure was immense and in the end it became too much.

I think the club were thinking of making a change anyway, so it was all quite amicable given the circumstances. I'd still got a couple of years left on my contract and the club couldn't afford to pay it off all in one go so we reached an agreement that worked well for both parties.

I knew the financial situation and didn't want to add to the worries on that score. I was just sad that I'd not been able to turn things round.

But I've got to be honest, I was a bit relieved that I wasn't in charge any more. Someone else could take it on. Obviously, they asked Kiddo to take over and he came to me to ask if that was OK.

I had no problem with that at all, as he was a great bloke, a great coach and I really thought he'd do well. However, when you see how it went for Brian when he was in charge, it shows how deep the problems were.

He's gone on to be one of the top coaches in world football - still working in the Premier League now - and even he couldn't turn things around that season.

Jonathan Clark then took over and things picked up for a while, but when you look back, it's almost as if the club was destined to hit rock bottom that year.

Anything that could go wrong, did go wrong.

And it had felt like that for a while.

Thankfully, there was no relegation at the time, it was just a case of being re-elected by the Football League, who definitely didn't want to lose Preston North End. Clubs wanted gate money and Preston always took good numbers away, even when things were really bad. At some of those Fourth Division games, there'd be more away fans than home supporters when PNE turned up.

In hindsight, although it was painful and a terrible time, maybe in a weird way the club needed to hit rock bottom to shake it up and start to recover, which it did over the following seasons thankfully.

It's such a good club, with such a great history and - I'm not just saying this - fantastic fans; really passionate, proper football supporters.

I don't look back with any regrets. I tried everything I could and I now know that management wasn't for me; I wasn't cut out for it and I didn't enjoy it.

Thankfully, others came in at Preston and put the club back in a decent position - it's got its pride back these days that's for sure and is very highly regarded in football circles.

Deepdale of course is now unrecognisable from my day and what a brilliant stadium it is - it makes me proud to think that I once played out there for PNE.

These days, I'm involved on the corporate side at the Etihad, but I always look for the Preston results and it's great to see them doing well again. As I mentioned back at the start, City and North End were my only teams and they still are.

Let's face it, if you're only going to play for two clubs in your entire career - make them good ones.

CHAPTER 5

JONATHAN CLARK: GIVING EVERYTHING

I signed for Preston North End thinking it was a club that would go places. Well, it did . . . just not in the direction I had hoped for.

Even though they were in the old Third Division, they still had a world famous manager, a solid fanbase and a great stadium.

What could possibly go wrong? Well, we'll come to that.

If you don't know the story, you might want to strap in and fix yourself a stiff drink.

If you do know the story . . . *make it a large one.*

But to start at the beginning, even though I was born and brought up in the rugby heartland of South Wales, football came to me very early in life.

After my first game for the school under-11s, the guy in charge of the opposition took me to one side and said: 'I'm retired now, but I've scouted for teams for years - and if you don't make it as a professional, I've no idea about football.'

I was only nine or ten, playing in the year above my age group and I didn't really think anything of it. Playing football for a living was a dream, but it all seemed like a world away - I was just having a game with my mates. I'm a Swansea lad and had a great childhood. I was one of five children and we were a typical working class family, complete with an outside toilet. (A bit nippy in winter, but it never did me any harm.)

My mum and dad were brilliant parents, they worked hard and gave us everything they could.

Really, I think my football career came from having three older brothers - I was always kicking about with them and learning from them, even though they were all mainly good rugby players.

I didn't know it at the time, but there was a Manchester United scout in Swansea and from a very young age he'd told my dad: 'As soon as he's old enough, we'll get him up to Old Trafford.'

In fact, I found out later that when I was 10 or 11 they'd already said they'd offer me an apprenticeship at 16, then a professional contract at 17. I've still got the letter somewhere.

My Dad was brilliant. He gave me an ethos that stayed with me throughout my career: 'Give your best in every game you play - that's all you can ever do.' That stuck with me for life.

Growing up, I knew something was going on because we'd get all sorts of people turning up at our house; Spurs boss Bill Nicholson came to see me. Malcolm Allison popped round from Crystal Palace, Bobby Robson from

Ipswich, John Charles - all these top, football men would be coming to our house in Swansea. (God knows what they thought about the outside loo.) This was in the days before the internet and I'd be asking my parents some daft questions: 'Who's John Charles?'

Big John was working for Swansea at that time and Dad would say: 'Son, he's one of the greatest players ever to kick a ball.'

It got to the point where we'd been invited to go to every First Division club and there was even a piece on me in the Daily Mirror claiming I was wanted by all 92 clubs in England. So I was exceptional as a young player, probably classed as the best in Britain at that stage, which was a big thing to take in when I look back now.

Thankfully, my family kept my feet on the ground and the knowledge that there was a deal in place with Man Utd meant I wasn't nervous about the future - I knew where I was going when I left school.

Despite me choosing United, I'll always remember Bobby Robson sent me a lovely hand-written letter wishing me all the best in my career and telling me he would follow my progress with interest. As many people have said down the years, Sir Bobby really was a class act.

Speaking of which, I used to play against future PNE star Stevie Doyle as a kid in the inter-town games. He was a year older than me and was from nearby Port Talbot - a fantastic player. You didn't want to be up against him, but you would certainly want him in your team.

Happily, we played on the same side for Wales as kids along with the likes of Eddie Niedzwiecki and one or two others who made professional careers. So it was a fairy tale upbringing really, built around family and football.

In the summer holidays at the age of 13, I'd go up to Manchester for six weeks and be talking to the likes of Denis Law, Bobby Charlton and other United greats. I'd been a Chelsea fan as a lad and they came in for me too, along with Liverpool, Arsenal, loads of others. But as soon as I went to Old Trafford and saw the Stretford End in full voice, George Best playing, the whole atmosphere . . . well, that was it - all I wanted to do was play for Wales and United.

There was a time when I went up there as a teenager and Bestie was training with us kids. He'd had some falling out with the club and was barred from the First Team for a while. We couldn't believe it.

There he was; this world famous superstar and he was really nice to us young lads, he'd always have a chat.

I found that throughout my career, the best players - the REAL greats - were often the nicest people.

Bobby Robson, Bestie, Tom Finney, Bobby Charlton - these people were so good, they never needed to brag. If anything, they played their achievements down.

Anyway, with George, you'd talk to him and even though he was older than us, he just seemed quiet and shy. You'd think: 'Wow, he's just a normal bloke.'

Then you'd pick up the newspaper the next day and the headline would be: *'George Best drank Champagne fountain and slept with Miss World last night.'*

It was hard to tally up the quiet guy you'd see around the training ground with the character you read about in the press.

Just getting to train with him was unbelievable though and a few years later, I played against him in David Nish's testimonial. By that point, I was a young man at my physical peak and Bestie was coming to the end of his career, many Miss Worlds and Champagne fountains later. But even then, when you tried to get near him - he was gone. It was like catching mist. You'd turn round and there was no catching him, even at the end - a truly, truly great player.

Happily for me, when the time came, United were true to their word. I signed as an apprentice at 16 straight from school and as soon as I turned 17, in November 1975, I was on a professional contract.

Tommy Docherty was in charge and a couple of days before my 18th birthday, I found myself coming on for Colin Waldron against Sunderland in front of 42,000, alongside the likes of Steve Coppell, Lou Macari and Gordon Hill.

It was a dream come true, but it didn't go great for me on the night, if I'm honest. I made a mistake that led to a goal in a 3-3 draw *(you can leave that bit out if you like!).*

But you've got to make that first step and I was hoping that would be the first of many appearances. Unfortunately, that was as good as it got for me at United. The Doc had been the manager when I started and he was great with young players. I thought he was brilliant, which is a good job, because I signed for him three times. If he liked you, he would always give you a chance.

If he didn't, then he didn't want you at the club. Simple as that.

Black and white, no middle ground. You were either in with him, or you were out. When he was sacked by United, he went to Derby and not long after that, they came in with a bid for me.

Dave Sexton had taken over at Old Trafford and given me a new contract, but I just didn't feel I was getting an opportunity, so in the end, I followed The Doc to Derby. They were also in the First Division, so I felt it was a good move. He used to drive me down there to training because I hadn't passed my test, so I got to know him well. Just listening to him talking about his career and his playing days at Preston was a privilege in itself.

He'd played with and managed some all-time greats. But for The Doc, there was only one player he idolised - Tom Finney.

He would wax lyrical about Sir Tom all day and all night; how he could do things no other player could ever do, his skill, his speed, his strength, his accuracy - there was nothing Tom Finney couldn't do in The Doc's eyes. Not only did he say Tom was the best player he'd ever seen, he thought he was the greatest player the WORLD had ever seen.

People might mention other greats down the years, but he would just say: 'I'm telling you now - Tom Finney was better.'

For The Doc, there was no question about it.

At Derby, he gave me a chance in the First Team which was great, because this was still the era of one substitute, so getting game time and developing as a player was vital.

These days, young lads can go on the bench and be given a taste for the last ten minutes when there's nothing on the game and that's a good way of easing them into it. Back then, teams didn't have that luxury so young players had to learn quickly on the job. I played at Highbury, Stamford Bridge, all the big grounds of the day. I remember defending a corner in front of the Anfield Kop and you literally couldn't hear your teammate shouting a few feet away. That wall of noise and the crowd surging down towards you in waves was incredible.

But it was a good education - you learn that you've just got to get on with it. Unfortunately, Derby got relegated a couple of years after I joined and The Doc was on his travels again.

I'd played 50-odd games in midfield for them when I got the call to link up with him once more - this time at Deepdale. North End had just been relegated under Nobby Stiles and were in the Third Division.

I had a couple of other teams come in for me and had talks with Burnley manager Brian Miller, who was a nice man and a very persuasive guy.

However, The Doc was at Preston and my old mate Stevie Doyle was there too, so that swung it. It was a new level for me, a lower level, but I looked at the PNE squad and thought they'd have no trouble coming straight back up; Alex Bruce was there, Mick Baxter, Francis Burns, some really good players.

Also, I'd played for Derby at Deepdale in the FA Cup a couple of years earlier and the atmosphere was unbelievable.

It was a really wet, muddy night and there was a good crowd on, about 20,000; really loud, great support. The pitch was horrendous *(we should have been used to that at coming from the Baseball Ground, eh?)* but we just couldn't get going and Preston hammered us 3-0.

After the game, The Doc was the angriest I've ever seen him.

Maybe because he'd been a North End player, he felt embarrassed that we'd been beaten so badly. In the dressing room, he turned on Gordon Hill (who was a top player and a great fella). Tommy Doc laid into him and at the end said: 'Don't bother putting your kit in the washing Gordon, it's like a mud bath out there and look at it - it's not even dirty.

'In fact, don't bother getting back on the coach. You're not coming back with us - you can flaming walk home!'

He was absolutely furious - he wouldn't let him back on the coach.

So that night stuck with me and, as I mentioned at the start, when I signed I thought I was coming to a club that would go places.

On the day The Doc was getting me to sign, he took me out on the pitch and when I saw Deepdale I just had this good feeling about it.

The big old Kop to one side, the Town End at the other, I could imagine it full and bouncing again and I thought: 'Yes, this is where I want to be.'

I'd not played in the Third Division before and I genuinely thought we'd be fighting for promotion. I thought the Doc would bring more players in and I didn't think for a minute that I would be the last new signing.

But almost straight away things started happening that were troubling.

People started talking about financial restrictions and all of a sudden, we were getting rid of good players. The lads I'd come to play alongside were heading out of the door. Mick Baxter went for big money, Franny Burns was gone, suddenly there was big change.

Whether it was purely financial, or whether The Doc didn't fancy them I don't know, but it started to look a different proposition to the one I'd signed up for.

It was very disappointing how quickly we lost some excellent players, not just that first season, but over the next couple too. The backbone of the team was lost.

And if you don't replace them properly, you're in trouble.

I think that was the start of things going badly wrong. I'm not blaming The Doc for what happened over the coming years, because I played under six managers during my time at North End - and every one of them was operating under serious financial constraints.

I know some of those managers had good ideas, identified good players, but they weren't able to bring them in - it was just a tough, tough time.

I don't think North End were alone in that respect, football was in a bad place in the 1980s and most clubs were just about keeping their heads above water.

There was barely any TV money, attendances were down, the grounds were falling into disrepair - it was a perfect storm really and it very nearly sank PNE.

Crowds were starting to drop to 3,500 at home and the club decided it was cheaper to buy a team coach for away games rather than keep hiring them every week. We heard about this and at first, we thought 'great'.

But then we saw the state of it . . . it looked like something from the 1950s - not exactly what you'd call luxury travel, more like an old banger.

If you were last on and ended up sitting by a dodgy window, you got soaked on the motorway because it was leaking water in.

I think the fans might have been getting on better buses than the team. On the pitch in that first season, we beat Portsmouth in the first home game, but struggled for wins after that for a long while. The Doc had been playing a 4-4-2 formation at Man United that turned rapidly into a 4-2-4 when they were attacking. When you're at that level, with top players like Steve Coppell and Gordon Hill, you can do that because of the quality at your disposal.

I think that was what he tried to bring in at Deepdale; 4-2-4 with the ball, dropping back to 4-4-2 without it.

But the problem was, we didn't have the players to do that. Stevie Coppell was more of a wide midfielder, who could get up and down all day, whereas at Preston we had more out-and-out wingers.

It became a problem for us on the pitch and results just didn't come. The Doc was sacked in December and that was a big blow for me, personally.

I'd signed a three-year contract, I'd just bought a house, I'd moved about a bit over the previous few years and I was hoping to be settled - to put down roots at a club and be successful. Now, the manager who'd brought me in was gone and everything was up in the air.

So it affected me in some ways, but in others it made no difference whatsoever, because I never forgot my Dad's words.

I still gave 100 per cent in every training session and every minute of every match - that never changed throughout my career, no matter who the manager was.

You want to be the best you can be. There are people PAYING to watch you, fans who would give anything to be out there in that shirt.

Please don't think footballers don't care about the supporters, because in my experience they do, for sure. OK, one or two might have a bit of an attitude, but when I was playing at Preston, people knew what it meant to pull on the shirt and to represent the club and the town. You owe it to the supporters, the club and yourself to give everything you've got.

That was always my outlook and I can look myself in the mirror and know that I was always true to myself - and my father.

You can't let your standards drop; 100 per cent effort every time.

Gordon Lee replaced Tommy Docherty and without even seeing four or five of us in action, he made a decision that we weren't going to play. There was me, Peter Sayer, Gary Buckley and one or two others; nobody came out and told us outright, we just weren't picked.

So that was that for the season for me - I went from playing every game up to December, to not kicking a ball again for the rest of the season.

I thought it was strange, but he's the manager, so what can you do?

Keep working and wait for your chance. People think Gordon was dour, but he had a funny, dry sense of humour. I've got to be honest, I'm not sure I always got it. I was walking down the corridor one morning, about to say 'hello' to him, but before I could speak he said: *'Do you love your wife?'*

No 'hello', 'good morning' or anything, just: *'Do you love your wife?'*

I said: 'Yes, of course I do.'

He said: 'If she fell out of an aeroplane, would you jump after her?'

I thought: 'What's he on about?'

I was flummoxed - so I said: 'Why do you ask?'

He said: 'Well, there may be a one per cent chance that if you jumped out after her, you could save her by cushioning her fall. So if you loved her, you'd jump out after her.' And that was that.

He walked off, leaving me there scratching my head.

Nearly 40 years later, I'm still wondering what that was all about!

Am I missing something? Was it a joke? Was he serious? Was it psychology? Just all very strange. Thankfully, my Mrs has never fallen out of a plane, so I've never had to find out!

So he had a few strange ways and ideas, but don't get me wrong, Gordon was a nice man and I got on with him as a person. In fact, I've no grudges against any of my managers, I had a glimpse of it later on at Preston and I know it's a tough job. They make decisions to try to win games; it's not personal *(well, OK, sometimes it is)* but as a player, you've just got to accept it.

Again, the following season, I only played three games in a short little burst, but then I was out again. Other teams came in for me, but moving clubs isn't as straightforward - or as desirable - as people might think.

On a personal level, my family was settled, and as a footballer, I didn't want to go. I wanted to stay and fight for a place in the team and be successful. I didn't want to be one of those players who has a new club every couple of years.

I believed I was good enough to get in the team and do well for North End so I saw it as a challenge to change the manager's mind.

And to be fair to Gordon, he brought in some good players, but he lost a lot as well. Again, you have to wonder whether it was his call, or whether it was down to the finances. Don O'Riordan went, Graham Bell went, Alex Bruce was released. Now, I know Brucie might have been in his thirties by then, but he was still a hell of a player.

When I was a kid, I'd trained with Denis Law at United and been lucky enough to be alongside Charlie George at Derby, but I'm telling you - Alex Bruce was as good as any I played with. He was just a natural born goalscorer. You couldn't teach what he had - it was instinctive.

Sometimes, you'd just stand back and watch him in training and it was an education in itself; a fantastic player, who absolutely loved Preston.

And then, at the end of the season, he was gone - just like that.

No great fanfare, no big send-off, nothing in the press thanking him for all those goals - just gone.

Again, whether that was financial or not, I don't know, but I do know I was sad to see him leave. I looked around and thought we'd been mid-table for two years and now the numbers were starting to look a bit thin.

By 1983/84, we had an 18-man squad really, with the odd loan and some youth players coming through. I came back into the team at the very end of Gordon's time, but it was only when Alan Kelly took over midway through that season, that things really picked up for me.

Kel had been in charge of the reserves when I'd been out of the First Team picture so I'd trained with him a lot. We got on really well and he was a proper football man; his record speaks for itself.

You don't have a stand named after you if you haven't achieved things at a club and he was brilliant for me. He was just a fantastic person; honest, straightforward and one of the nicest people I ever met in football.

He also knew the game inside out. Alan steadied the ship and suddenly we were scoring four or five goals.

He made me captain and, with a team effort, results improved. We finished mid -table again, having been in danger of relegation when he took over and I thought this might be the start of things heading in the right direction at last.

Finances were still tight though and pre-season was pretty basic; there was no tour away or anything, just a few local friendlies and then into the first round of the League Cup. We didn't have loads of new signings but Alan had instilled some belief in us and we actually started that fateful season really well.

Andy Murphy had come in and was doing great, Nigel Greenwood was just breaking through, so young players were starting to get a chance again too. It was all looking good.

The manager had got everything going behind the scenes, the spirit in the club was great and we all felt we were in for a successful year ahead.

We beat Tranmere in the League Cup and won four of our first five matches in Division Three - sitting near the top of the table.

One of those wins was away at Hull and maybe because there was a bit of interest in us doing well, the game had been picked for Match of the Day. This was back when they only showed three matches and hardly ever a Third Division fixture, so it was a big thing.

The Hull fans had these banners out saying *'We love Jimmy Hill'* and stuff, but to be honest, we ignored being on the telly - we just wanted to keep our run going.

Luckily, I scored the first goal from a corner routine we'd worked on in training. It was one of those where you can try it and try it and it rarely comes off, but that day the ball dropped to me on the edge of the box and it flew in on the half volley. I don't even remember hitting it to be honest, so I think it was more luck than judgement, but it's nice to look back on. My granddaughter is into football now and it's good for her to be able to see it on YouTube.

They sometimes show it on the big screen at Deepdale as the team comes out, so that's always a nice touch too. Of course, everyone remembers the second goal more than mine - and rightly so. Mark Jones came up from full-back and put an absolute screamer into the top corner to give us a 2-1 away win.

I don't know if it won Goal of the Month but it should have done - it was an unbelievable strike and, again, look it up on YouTube if you haven't seen it. We didn't really have 'assists' in those days, but I played the cross-field ball to him so I'm claiming one now, 30-odd years later Jonesy!

The funny thing was I can't remember being too bothered by it being on TV. We didn't have a video recorder and I was never one for looking back - as soon as the game was done, my mind was onto the next one.

Ironically, I look back now and wish I'd have kept more stuff; signed shirts, mementoes, etc. But at the time, I just focused on who's next.

Everything was going well, we were playing well, pushing at the top of the league and then . . . *well, football can be brutal, eh?*

We lost eight games in a row. Eight - unbelievable.

We had a game at Plymouth - all that way down there - where we were winning 4-3 and I got sent off towards the end.

We ended up losing 6-4 and that was a long journey back, I can tell you.

We were suddenly conceding a lot of goals and plummeting down the league. From being a season where we'd be fighting for promotion, we were quickly looking over our shoulders. In December, things hit rock bottom: FA Cup Second Round, Preston North End 1, Telford United 4.

(Can we leave a pause here - it might be time to take a sip of that drink!)

What can you say? Preston North End should not get beat by non-league teams. End of story. I know it's the FA Cup and it's been done before and since, but it just shouldn't happen. We knew that. Everyone knew it. I played in that game and I can't put it into words. Nearly 40 years later . . . ***no***.

The worst result and the worst feeling of my career.

There's no excuse and I feel sorry for the Preston fans who had to witness it. Look, Telford had some good players and back then, there was maybe more money in playing part time and having a good job than there was turning full-time professional. They were a good side, who gave Everton a decent game after us, but still . . . ***no.***

People might not want to hear this, but in a roundabout way, that day led to the biggest compliment any manager ever gave me.

On the Monday morning, we had a team meeting. Well, let's call it what it was: 'a crisis meeting' (although I didn't realise that at the time).

Everyone - the entire squad - had been told to assemble in the dressing room and we were sat there, waiting in silence. When Alan Kelly walked in, he pointed at me and said: *'You can leave the room.'*

So I went out and was hanging around outside on my own, wondering what was going on. The meeting went on for about an hour and all the time I was thinking about what I'd done to be excluded. Eventually when the players came out, it was clear the manager had torn them to shreds. The lads came out looking very stony-faced. They'd had both barrels and then a bit more.

Alan Kelly took me to one side and said: 'I didn't want you in the meeting, because I know you gave everything you could give in that game.'

Now, that's not to cast aspersions on any of my teammates, because I truly believe everyone was doing their very best.

But that's what the manager said to me and that's about the only thing I can take from that day. He was right, too. I had given everything, just like every other game - that's what I prided myself on.

So out of that terrible afternoon, there was an ember of small comfort in that the manager had recognised that I'd done what I could.

However, the harsh reality is that whatever we were doing as a team, it wasn't good enough. Unfortunately, things went from very bad to even worse and I don't think we won another game before Alan went and was replaced by Tommy Booth.

I don't want to talk out of school, but I think Alan was treated shabbily when he left as manager. He deserved better and it's good that years later, there's now a stand named after him - so there should be. He was a Preston legend.

Tommy had had a great career and was a really nice guy, everyone was right behind him and again, we thought this would be the change that would start to turn things around.

The thing was though, he faced the same problems as Alan.

Changing the manager was like rearranging the deckchairs on the Titanic at that point. There was no money. You can't change the personnel, you can't do what you want to do.

All those people who took over around then . . . they can't all be poor managers. Gordon Lee had managed Newcastle and Everton, The Doc had been in charge at Manchester United. They couldn't have been that bad, could they?

No, the problems ran deeper than who was in charge of picking the team - much deeper.

I think the lads were all doing everything they could, there was no lack of effort and no-one threw in the towel. But at the end of the day, if you're losing that many matches, then collectively, we weren't good enough.

For too long, the policy had been to get rid of the high wage earners.

But they were big earners for a reason - they were the best players.

Throughout my time at the club, that was a running theme; lose the higher wage earners and bring in lads who were cheaper.

Later on, Andy McAteer was another one who was pushed out. He was a great full-back and a Preston lad who loved the club. But he was one of the higher earners - and we're not talking a fortune here - so he had to go.

The way things were being done at the time, it's no wonder we ended up in serious trouble.

I think there were about 20 directors at one point and some of them would try to influence the manager.

One or two thought they were football experts because they'd chipped a few quid in. I can assure you they weren't.

I'm a bit loath to talk about this, but there was even one occasion when a director came to my house and physically threatened me.

I'd signed a new three-year contract and as part of the deal, there'd been an incentive that was paid in cash, which wasn't unusual at that time.

It was around the time we played Hull at Deepdale towards the end of the season. They were going up and they beat us 4-1.

As we came off the pitch at the end, their player manager Brian Horton put his arm around me and said: 'Well played son - I want you to sign for me.'

I said: 'Sorry, but I've just signed a new contract and I'm staying here thanks.'

That was it. End of conversation.

Anyway, the following day we had a team meeting and Tommy, for once, really laid into the players. He absolutely hammered us and then he said: 'You're a bunch of effing cheats.'

Well, sorry, but that was a step too far for me.

I stood up and said: 'I don't care what you say, but you don't call me a cheat.'

And I got up to walk out. He said: 'Hang on, you're the biggest cheat of the lot - I hear you're signing for Hull!'

I couldn't believe it. Whether someone had overheard the conversation with Brian Horton and got the wrong end of the stick, I don't know, but there was no way I was going anywhere and told Tommy so.

Despite me saying it wasn't true, this rumour took hold.

A couple of days later, I got a visit at my house from someone involved at board level at the club, who asked if he could have a quick word.

Straight away from his tone, I knew something wasn't right, so I suggested we go into the garden.

Basically, he said that if I left the club, unless I gave him back the signing-on fee in cash, he would have me knee-capped.

I couldn't believe what I was hearing and I sent him packing in no uncertain terms. Look, it was a long time ago and I don't know how serious it was. I had no intention of leaving anyway, so it all just went away, thank God.

But when people say it was a different world back then . . . it really, really was.

Back on the playing side, it was out of character for Tommy to have a go at the players like that, but we'd just been hammered 4-1 at home so a manager has to say something.

He was a good guy really and with the little money he was given, he brought in some great players for Preston.

Bob Atkins and Gary Brazil arrived for a pittance and went on to play hundreds of games.

So he could spot a player and was a decent coach, but really - and I think Tommy would say this himself - he was too nice to be a manager.

It's funny because he was such a tough player, a really hard centre half, but he just didn't like confrontation. He preferred to be one of the lads.

You often see that in football and I don't think he liked making those tough decisions about dropping people, or releasing them.

In a way that's a compliment to him, because he's such a nice man, but to be a manager, you've got to have that nasty edge and that's just not him.

As it was, I played nearly every game that 1984/85 season but no matter what we did, we just couldn't get a run of good results going.

We were among the lowest scorers up front and we had the worst defence in the entire league - conceding 100 goals.

(Now you know why I said to make that drink a large one!)

So, when you look at it like that, not scoring and conceding an horrendous amount . . . well, the writing's on the wall.

We were relegated to the Fourth Division for the first time in Preston's history.

Again, there's not much to take pride from in a season like that, but for me, there was at least the consolation of winning all four Player of the Year awards at the club; the Junior Whites, the Lancashire Evening Post, the Players' Player of the Year and the Official Supporters Club.

And I do look back with a lot of pride on that. It says that in the midst of all the turmoil, I was doing what I could. I've still got the awards as fond mementoes from my career, but as with most ex-footballers and their trophies - they're up in the loft!

So we were down in Division Four for the first time and it was a strange thing for Preston to be in there. We were all very confident about coming straight back up. Tommy had assembled a good squad when you look at it; John Thomas had come in and he was another natural finisher - a great guy who became a real hero to the fans.

Wayne Foster was there and, as well as Gary Brazil and Bob Atkins, young Alan Kelly was coming through - so the nucleus of the team that would go up a couple of years later was actually in place.

And yet the two seasons couldn't have been more different.

There was no complacency among the squad going into that season, but maybe teams raised their games a bit when they came to Deepdale.

Whatever it was, the standard was higher than we perhaps expected.

We started with a home defeat but were showing signs of life at times, winning 4-0 against Torquay and then beating Burnley at home. I didn't realise it at the time, but that game was really the end for me as a player.

I was stretchered off and at first the physio thought I'd torn my groin.

It turned out to be much more serious than that - I'd damaged my pelvis through wear and tear and suddenly things got very serious for me.

There was erosion of the pelvis and I was referred to various specialists. Three separate consultants told me that I'd never play again.

I was 26 - absolutely devastated.

Luckily, around that time, Brian Kidd had joined the coaching staff and he told me about this guy that Manchester United had used down in Harley Street, London.

The club fixed up for me to go and see him and I knew I was in the right place because there were three players in front of me in the waiting room; two from Real Madrid and one from Barcelona.

(Name please? 'Jonathan Clark, Preston North End.')

The chap's name was Jerry Gilmore - and he was an absolute genius. Later on he treated people like Jonny Wilkinson and Jeremy Guscott, as well as the wounded BBC war correspondent Martin Bell.

He told me more in an hour than the other three had told me in six months. He said he'd get me playing again, but I had to accept that I'd never be the same player I was. He was right on both counts.

I had an operation with him and did eventually get back, but really, that was it for me as a player. I was never the same again, even though I played on for a few years. Deep down, I knew. You just do.

But I had a family to support and people were always happy with what I was doing on the pitch, so I kept going.

And you get little unexpected things that tell you a lot about people. While I was out injured, I received a letter from someone I'd never met.

His name was Jimmy Armfield.

It was just amazing; he wrote saying he knew what I was going through, he'd had a very similar injury in his career and he was telling me how he got back to fitness, how to keep my spirits up, etc.

It was handwritten by an absolute great of the game from a real rival of Preston's and I thought '*wow - what a wonderful person'*. I had the privilege of meeting him later at an event and he was just a tremendous man. The Doc also got in touch to see how I was getting on.

A lot of people might not know this, but he was quite a religious person and he said he would pray for me. Again, he was a class act right to the end and it's sad that we've lost him recently.

Anyway, I was working on rehabilitation and getting fit behind the scenes as the season went on and results just seemed to get worse and worse.

Again, we weren't fighting for promotion, we were heading for re-election at the very bottom of the Football League.

For a team like Preston, that was unbelievable.

Tommy stepped down and Brian took over but even then, we couldn't get a win for love nor money. And we're talking about Brian Kidd here - a top player and someone who's gone on to have a career at the very highest levels.

You're not telling me he's not a good coach and that he doesn't know what he's doing. Of course he does, but the club was just in a mess.

Like I said, there were 20-odd directors at one point and, while most of them were fine and well-intentioned, some would try to get involved in team selection. It was crazy, listening to them talk when they didn't know the first thing about the game.

They had other responsibilities they should have been looking at, not least the finances and the state of the floodlights. When they got condemned and we had to play that game against Scunthorpe at 2pm on a Tuesday afternoon, well, we'd really hit rock bottom.

A lot of people know that was the game that Mel Tottoh played in and I think it was totally unfair on him. He was a good guy who would come in and train with us every now and then, but to expect him to work in the morning and play for Preston in the Football League in the afternoon?

No, it was out of order.

I was injured by then, but I was at the game and for me . . . that was the lowest ebb. I was a player, but I'd become a fan as well - I still am to this day. To look around and see the state of the ground, no floodlights, a non-contract lad up front, re-election looming, it all just really hurt.

And, of course, to really rub things in . . . we got beat.

I know they announced the crowd as just over 2,000, but I think it was lower than that in reality. The club was just too embarrassed to admit it.

Usually, clubs did it the other way round - they rounded it down to save some tax, but that day, I think it was embellished.

The only positive from that time was that sitting up in the stand, I was able to see the game from a new perspective and I noticed one or two things about how the team played. Tommy and Brian had always been at the top level but the Fourth Division was very different to that standard.

I remember one day we played Chester and our lads were told to back off their centre halves and let them have the ball. Well, they just came to the half way line, launched it into the box where there were a few knockdowns, bit of a scramble, the ball's in the back of the net and it's game over. This happened time and again. You could maybe afford to stand off in the First Division, but not where we were at where big balls into the box were food and drink to strikers at that level.

So again, results didn't improve and despite his coaching skills, Brian didn't last long.

People think it was a rushed decision when I replaced him, but it wasn't.

I've never told anyone this, but the chairman came to see me the week before and asked if I would take over if the manager went, because he thought there was going to be a change quite soon. It put me in a difficult position, not just because I was still a player, but because I liked Brian a lot - we got on well and went right back to my early days at Manchester United.

I think the board saw me as an honest guy and even though I was relatively young, I was well respected by everyone at the club.

On the day I took over, I'd been out to watch a young lad at Kirkham Juniors, but there were no mobile phones in those days.

So when I got home, my wife said: 'The Chairman's been on the phone for you - you need to get to the ground as soon as possible.'

Well, straight away I knew what it was about and I raced off to Deepdale.

There had been a discussion that morning and Brian had gone there and then. We were playing Southend at 3pm and by the time I got there, the team sheet had already been handed in.

Well, I wasn't having it - I wanted to make changes.

The first thing I did was take the captaincy off Micky Martin; I'd known him since I was a kid, but I said: 'Sorry Mick, I don't believe a loan player should be captain of a football club.'

To me, that just flies in the face of things. Mick took it well and I handed captaincy to Andy McAteer, who was Preston through and through. I also changed the line-up, but by that stage it was 2.15pm.

So I went to the referee's room and asked if I could change the team.

He said he couldn't allow that at that stage. He was adamant that it was against regulations. He said the only way we could change the team sheet was if the opposition manager agreed to it - and that was highly unlikely.

So someone went off to find the Southend boss and see if he'd let us do it. Luckily, he turned out to be one of the nicest guys you could meet.

He came in, cool as you like, and said: 'Yeah, no problem, you can change the team, that's fine.' It was a great gesture and I think everyone was gobsmacked, especially the ref.

But as the Southend boss left the room, he turned round and said to me: 'Oh, I hear it's your first game in charge son, good luck - all the best.'

And with that, he shook my hand and went back to his team talk.

It was Bobby Moore.

(What did I say about the best players being the nicest people? There's another one for the list.)

Back in the dressing room I said to the lads: 'I don't care about the second half. Go out from the first whistle and get the crowd behind you.

'Close people down, tackle, chase lost causes - do everything to get the crowd on your side.'

I just thought the fans were so despondent by that point that we had to do something to get them back with us.

I said: 'If we're dead on our feet in the second half, we'll live with it.

'Because, trust me, if we're in the game after an hour, you'll find a second wind and these supporters will carry you home.'

Gary Brazil scored and John Thomas got two as we won 3-2 and, yes, Bobby Moore was still just as gracious after the game as he had been beforehand.

After that, we went on a run of good results; we beat Tranmere - JT and Gary scoring again - and then went to Mansfield and won 3-2, where big Vernon Allatt got the winner. They hadn't lost at home for ages and afterwards, I got invited up to the boardroom there. Ian Greaves was their manager and he was another gentleman of the game who came up and said how well we'd played.

It was a real eye-opener seeing things like that and by the time we got revenge on Scunthorpe a couple of weeks later, we'd won five on the trot.

In our darkest hour, we'd put together our best run of results in the league since the 1960s.

I played Alan Kelly Junior in every game and from Day One I said to him: 'You come for everything in the air - and if you make any mistakes, I will take the rap for it in the press.' So Alan started taking a lot of responsibility for a young kid and fortunately for us, he was fantastic so I had nothing to worry about there.

I also took full-backs to one side and said: 'You're defenders first and foremost - so defend.' Previously, I'd noticed we had people attacking left, right and centre and as soon as we lost the ball, we were exposed at the back. So from then on, they could get forward if it's sensible, but their priority was to defend.

I also told the attackers to close down their defence whenever they had the ball, don't give them time to launch it at our box.

Up front, I said I never wanted to see their keeper getting the ball unchallenged. If it was a corner, I told Simon Gibson to make sure the keeper gets clattered - make him work for it.

So that's what we started doing and within 20 minutes of that first game, the crowd was right with us. They stayed with us right to the end of that season, too.

We were down to the real hard core on the terraces by that point, people who cared passionately about the club and we were now giving them something to shout about.

If we had to face re-election then we'd do it kicking and battling and fighting to the last - and that's what we did. I'm very proud about that.

Ultimately, we couldn't keep the run of wins going, but there were other things that maybe explained how we had got to that stage.

I don't want this to sound like an excuse, but we were due to play Colchester away - and the club wanted us to travel there and back on the same day.

Colchester? It's 270 miles away. And on that bus? Come on. No.

I wasn't having it and told the board I'd rather resign than do that.

I said to Keith Leeming: 'Chairman, this is Preston North End Football Club, I'm not taking the team all that way on the day of a game and then expecting them to get a result.'

By that stage it looked like we may well have to face re-election, but for me, that was irrelevant. We were still representing the club.

It got to the point where I offered to pay for an overnight stay out of my own pocket, because I just couldn't do it to the lads.

Eventually, common sense prevailed. Even though we ended up getting beat, we hadn't had the embarrassment of PNE turning up like a pub team.

We'd prepared properly, but they were a decent side and we just couldn't beat them on the day. We drew the next couple and by the time we went to Aldershot on the last day, our fate was sealed.

Luckily, there was no relegation from the league in those days, but we would still have to apply for re-election. I wanted some good to come out of it though, so I decided I was going to play the kids.

I wanted the young players to know what it felt like to play in a league game so that it stood them in good stead for the rest of their careers.

It would teach them a bit about the physicality, the levels required and they'd be better prepared for the following season.

So we went out there with Kel in goals, Nigel Greenwood up front, debuts for Andy Pilling and Nigel Jemson - and we gave it a go.

I was almost prepared for the defeat if it meant giving these lads a better chance further down the line. I knew they'd run all day for us and the fans would be great with them.

What I didn't expect was that so many Preston fans would turn up to support us that day. It was unbelievable.

Aldershot had this tiny little ground and in a crowd of about 2,000, there must have been six or seven hundred North Enders there.

When the team came out, there was ticker tape, cheers, singing - it was more like we'd won the league than finished second from bottom.

They were incredible and even though we lost 4-0, they did us proud.

The thing was, the Chairman had said to me before the game: 'Jonathan, whatever you do, don't let the players throw their shirts to the crowd at the end. We can't afford a new kit for next year and we need those shirts.'

Well, the supporters had been so brilliant that when the final whistle went I said to the lads: 'Get over there and give your shirts to those fans.'

I didn't care about a rollocking from the chairman, the fans deserved something back. So the players went over and they were throwing their stuff in - the fans got on the pitch and I think John Thomas had virtually everything stripped from him that day.

But we had a guy called Terry Gray playing for us and he was a smashing fella, even though the season hadn't gone well for him.

He threw his shirt in the crowd - and they threw it back at him!

Poor old Terry had to have two or three goes before anyone would take it. It was hilarious - the lads gave him merciless stick after the game.

For the club though, that day really was rock bottom and thankfully that proved to be the case. They've never been that low again and I hope they never will be.

Personally, I'd said from Day One that I had no intention of staying on as manager. I'd worked hard to get fit again and was going to focus on carrying on playing.

To be honest, some of the things that I'd seen over that spell stopped me going into coaching and managing later on. There were some wonderful people on the Preston board, so I don't want to tar everyone with the same brush. But as I mentioned, there were one or two who knew nothing about football and were just one step beyond for me.

I've got three children and I thought: 'Am I really going to put my family's future in the hands of people like that?' I'd seen the way Alan and Tommy were treated and just thought 'no'. Never in a million years.

Here's a perfect example. Wayne Foster had come in and was a shining light that season, he'd been an England youth international and was obviously going to have a good career.

At the end of the season, he came to see me and said his girlfriend was pregnant, so could he have a £20-a-week rise in his next contract.

I went to the Chairman and said: 'You need to keep this lad, he'll go far.' But they wouldn't do it.

For the sake of £20-a-week, he signed on a free transfer for Hearts in the Scottish Premier League where he did well for many years and played in the UEFA Cup. If they'd have given him the £20, they could have sold him for thousands later on.

At the end of the season, they also wanted me to draw up the retained list. For me, that was too much and I said I wouldn't do it.

I knew I had to go back into that dressing room as a player and it wasn't right for me to make those types of decisions. It just wasn't on.

What I did say was that they must get Alan Kelly Junior signed up to a three-year contract.

I said: 'If he'll sign for longer, get him for longer - as long a contract as you can get, because he is going to be one of the best keepers in the country.'

We made him a very well-paid goalkeeper for his age and it was a good investment, because he was a fantastic player and a big asset for the club.

Later on, I was told a deal was done for him to go to Liverpool but he got injured before it could go through.

I know Alan had a very good career, but I believe that if it wasn't for injuries, he'd have been a top flight goalkeeper throughout his entire playing days - he was absolutely outstanding.

The other big change that summer was the laying of the plastic pitch. I'd been advised not to play on it at all and it wasn't like the modern ones now that are really good. It was just a carpet laid on concrete really and anyone who played on it back then will know it wasn't the best surface to be on - especially if you're coming back from a long-term injury.

On the other hand, I'd played on six inches of mud every week at the Baseball Ground, so it was good in the sense that your passes would actually go where you meant them to (more or less!).

So, with my fitness returning I happily relinquished the manager's hot seat and got my head down to carry on as a player under the new boss, John McGrath.

When he came in, everyone had a meeting with him and I was looking forward to mine. I thought he might pick my brains about the squad, the previous season, etc. But instead, it was a real shocker.

The first words out of his mouth were: 'We're letting you go.'

I couldn't believe it.

He said: 'You're the highest earner and we can get two or three players in for what you're on, so you'll have to go.'

That was it. I think maybe he saw me as a threat to his position if he started off badly, but I wouldn't have been at all.

I'd made it absolutely clear that I didn't want the job.

But that's the way it was - a real kick in the guts.

What can you do?

Well, as ever, I didn't sulk. I gave 100 per cent in pre-season, every training session and fought my way into the team - even though the manager actively wanted me to leave. So, again, I take pride in that. I didn't let my standards drop and basically forced him to pick me.

My card had been marked though and when Bury came in for me in December, I was gone.

My last game was the 5-0 FA Cup win over Chorley and it was great to see 16,500 on Deepdale again - the place was absolutely bouncing that night.

I thought: 'Typical, isn't it? This is what I signed up for - and just as it starts happening, I'm going out the door.'

So I had real mixed feelings about leaving. I was glad that the club was re-emerging, a new team was coming together and you could see it was going to do well. But I was just so, so sad that I wasn't going to be a part of it. Having been through the darkest times, I was now missing out on the brighter days ahead and, yes, that hurt.

It still does, because I would have loved to have stayed.

That's the reality of football though and, looking back, I think it was still mainly a financial decision when I left. I knew I wasn't the first to have that happen - in fact, there's a long list - but I had deep feelings for the club and it was little consolation.

So with a heavy heart, my time at Preston was up and I left for Gigg Lane. It didn't really work out for me there and after a while I joined Harry Gregg at Carlisle.

Harry had been Swansea manager when I was a kid so I'd known him for years.

As a player though, if I'm honest, I was done when I left Deepdale.

I played on, but I was never the same and eventually I had to retire when I was only 29. When I stopped playing through injury in 1989, Harry offered me the chance to be his assistant up at Brunton Park.

My one big regret in football is that I didn't take him up on that offer.

I loved training and I should really have taken the job. Like I mentioned though, I'd seen what had happened to the managers at Preston.

I'd had a glimpse of it myself and that's what put me off. You can't dwell on these things though and I went on to have a good career in the hospitality and pub trade that I really enjoyed for 25 years or so.

Unfortunately, in 2014 I was diagnosed with Non-Hodgkin's Lymphoma and I've been battling that over recent years. The NHS has been absolutely brilliant for me and I can't thank the doctors and nurses enough - I know everyone says this, but they truly do an amazing job.

So I've had my ups and downs and these days I just try to take each day as it comes and enjoy life as much as I can.

That would be my advice to anyone.

I'm lucky that I've got a great wife, three great kids and even a granddaughter now, so family has always been very important to me and I'm very fortunate to have them.

I still watch football as often as I can - my lad Michael still plays locally so I tend to watch his games.

I was lucky enough to see him play in the FA Vase final at Wembley for Kirkham and Wesham a few years back and that was a very proud day.

But I get to Deepdale when I can and when my son stops playing, I'll be there regularly to support North End.

They were difficult times in the 1980s, but I love the club and the supporters were just a class above.

That day at Aldershot will live with me forever.

It's a great club, an historic club and it means a lot to me - it really does.

To be a Player of the Year and see my name alongside some absolute greats of the game is a very special feeling that I can't quite put into words.

Whether I'd have played one game or 100, just to have pulled on the Preston shirt makes me a very proud man.

Seeing where North End have come since my time is fantastic and I hope they can make that final step into the Premier League soon.

Whenever they do, wherever I am - I'll be raising a glass.

CHAPTER 6

DANNY DICHIO: ITALIAN STALLION

Music has always been a big love of mine. When I was younger, I used to host club nights under the name DJ Mellow D *(say it quick and you'll get it).*

You get the right vibe and everything just fits into place. It could be anything from deep house to Mumford & Sons, but you know when something's right. You can feel it.

That was what going to Preston North End felt like for me: Right Here, Right Now, right club, as Fatboy Slim might have said.

Because when I look back on my career, being at Deepdale was a brilliant encore to my time in England.

I played with and against some legends of the game in the Premier League, Championship, Serie A and European competition. Later on I made history by scoring the first-ever goal for Toronto FC in MLS.

So it was a hell of a journey and this might sound strange, but my time at Preston was the perfect swansong in the EFL.

It came at the stage of my career where often things start to wind down and I didn't want that. I wanted to still be part of something special and working with Billy Davies and the boys at Deepdale gave me not only a real challenge - but also one more shot at the Championship play-offs.

I loved the place. My daughter was born there and I'll never forget how friendly and welcoming everyone was. The fans stuck by me when I wasn't scoring and were brilliant with me throughout.

Trust me, it was a mutual appreciation - I loved those Northern fans.

To start at the beginning though, I was born to an English mum and Italian dad; the clue is in my full name I suppose - *Daniele Salvatore Ernest Dichio.*

As a young player, I was nicknamed the Hammersmith Horse - I'd like to think with a name like mine it was more about being an Italian Stallion than a bit of a donkey! You decide.

Anyway, I actually started off in midfield as a junior with QPR but one day when I was about 14, they said: 'We don't see that as your position, we want to see you up front.'

And that was it - I was a big lad and back in those days, there were a lot of 4-4-2 systems with a 'big man, little man' up top.

We had Kevin Gallen on the books and me and him had a formidable partnership all the way through the youth team, reserves and then the first team. So changing positions worked out for me in the end and maybe if I'd stayed in central midfield, I'd not have made it at the level I did.

I made my Premier League debut at Aston Villa where I was marked by Paul McGrath - so that was a hell of an introduction to the big league.

But I was lucky enough to score that day and also lucky enough to play for the England Under-21 team around that point.

I'd been involved in the England set-up from the age of about 15, playing in a tight group of lads with people like Nicky Butt, Sol Campbell and quite a few lads who went by the wayside, too. It was no guarantee that you were going to have a good career, even if you were a brilliant young player.

In the Under-21s Ray Wilkins was the assistant coach at the time and I worked with him at QPR, too.

He was a great mentor for me and pushed me forward a lot in my career, but at the time there were people like Robbie Fowler and Emile Heskey around so it was tough to get in the starting line-up.

I did play in a game away against Norway when we had people like David Unsworth, Lee Bowyer and Neil Shipperley playing.

Ole Gunnar Solskjaer scored for them in a 2-2 draw and it was just brilliant to be out there, playing for my country.

If I'm honest, my main focus though was getting into the QPR side, which wasn't easy as we had Les Ferdinand up front and no-one needs to be told how good he was. Sir Les was from my neck of the woods in West London and had come into the professional game slightly later than most, having played non-league at Hayes.

He was a superstar at QPR but he would always have time for us younger lads; little tips, technical things, positional advice - he was just brilliant to learn from and was always very generous with his advice.

It's not always the case that the top guys really speak to the youngsters in a way that gives them that extra little bit of knowledge, but he was great, both on and off the field. I played quite a bit for QPR, which was my dream, because they were my team. But my other big dream was to play in Italy, because I'm a bit of an AC Milan fan, too.

I'd scored a spectacular goal away at Wolves from about 30 yards out, which maybe brought me onto the radar out there as it got quite a bit of TV coverage, and not long after that, Sampdoria came in for me.

Serie A was the top league in the world at that time, QPR were in the Championship so I looked on it as the next step for me in my career development.

My contract was up and the Bosman ruling had just come into effect, so I think I was one of the first English players to move abroad using it.

I'm not sure how much they knew about me before I got there, but the Gazzetta dello Sport ran an article saying I was known as *'the best-looking footballer in the world'. (Don't laugh!)*

That must have been down to my long, flowing hair at the time, eh?

I dunno, maybe they were expecting someone else or maybe it was a misprint, but either way . . . grazie!

Sven-Goran Eriksson was the coach who signed me and the professionalism out there was completely different to anything I'd experienced in England at that time.

I'm not saying QPR wasn't professional, but the way the Italian players looked after themselves, the preparation, the training - it was all completely different.

The staff looked after players off the field in every way, too. They just wanted you to be able to focus on training and playing, so we had this beautiful house in a beautiful spot and we were looked after very well.

The Samp squad at the time was unbelievable; Christian Karambeu, Vincenzo Montella, Siniza Mihajlovic, Moreno Mannini, Gianluca Pagliuca, Sebastian Veron, Jurgen Klinsmann, so there was some really stiff competition to get minutes on the pitch. I played a couple of games and came on for Klinsmann up front in a UEFA Cup game against Athletic Bilbao.

Yep, Klinsmann off, Dichio on. Sounds about right (!).

Unfortunately for me, Sven left to go to Lazio and Cesar Menotti came in as coach. He'd won the World Cup with Argentina in 1978 and was a legend of the game, but I didn't have a very good relationship with him.

He was using the bigger, more established players and I got frustrated as I was a young player who just wanted to play matches.

I'd signed a three-year contract at Sampdoria, but I didn't think I would be an automatic starter, because I knew I still had a lot to learn. But despite training with these top guys, I wanted to be out there playing.

So I went on loan to Lecce, where I had a better chance of getting in the team. They were also in Serie A, so we were still coming up against the big teams and I was getting more game time.

I scored early on against Brescia (when they had a young Andrea Pirlo playing for them) and I had a good relationship with the coach there - Cesare Prendelli, who went on to be the national team manager and took Italy to the European Championship final in 2012.

He was brilliant and a bit of a maverick. Not just tactically either, he would sit smoking a cigar during the games - the epitome of a very cool, continental manager. He's only recently stepped down as coach of Fiorentina and it was fascinating to play for him. We got some great results and I remember we went to the San Siro and beat AC Milan 1-0 when they had the likes of Zvonimir Boban and George Weah playing.

What was funny that day was that a load of my Italian relatives were Milan fans and they came to watch the game. By the time it finished, half of them had gone home early and the other half wouldn't speak to me!

I'd have happily played the rest of my career in Italy, but when games started to dry up in Lecce a few English clubs became aware of my situation and I decided to go back.

My old QPR boss Gerry Francis was interested in taking me to Spurs, but eventually I joined Peter Reid at Sunderland and ended up playing in that crazy play-off final at Wembley against Charlton that ended 4-4.

That was the one where Micky Gray missed a sudden-death penalty and we had to 'go again' the following year, coming up as Champions with Niall Quinn and Kevin Phillips tearing up the division.

I then went to West Brom and had a brief spell at Derby on loan before joining Millwall back in London.

I was really happy there and that was the year we reached the FA Cup Final, but I didn't play after being sent off in a league match a few weeks earlier, which - as you can imagine - was a huge disappointment.

Hang on, no, that's too much of a cliche - it was absolutely flaming heartbreaking!

The sending off was for something or nothing off the ball and it was, well, terrible to miss that final - it's the kind of game you dream of playing in. I played in the Europa League thc following year against Ferencvaros when we drew 1-1 at home, but went out after losing the second leg. Dennis Wise and my old mentor Ray Wilkins were in charge by then, but when they left there was a really bad feeling around the place.

The club wanted to restructure the wages of the senior players and although the new boss Steve Claridge wanted to keep me, the club owners wanted me to move on. I was upset but at least Steve was honest with me.

Two days later, Billy Davies was on the phone from PNE. He said: 'Look Danny, we've just had a bad experience in the play-off final and the boys are devastated.

'We're looking for someone with experience who's been there and done it and can give us a bit of belief.'

I think Richard Cresswell was just leaving North End at the time and Billy said: 'Don't worry about that, we've got a young player called David Nugent who's going to be massive.

'He just needs a player to help him along with his development and I think you'd be perfect for him.'

Straight away, I really fancied it and Billy's passion for the club shone through - he made you feel like you were getting in on something special.

You wanted to be part of it, it was exciting and if you didn't sign, you'd feel like you were missing out. I felt at Millwall we were just a club that was fighting to keep its head above water, whereas Preston were really ambitious and on the cusp of something amazing.

The crowds were good, the manager was very well thought of, the squad was obviously good enough to get to the play-off final and the stadium was fantastic - everything was in place. I knew Chris Sedgwick a bit and also Carlo Nash and they both spoke really well about the club.

From a career perspective, I wanted to sign up, but I had to have a tough conversation with my wife before committing. We'd only just moved back to London from Durham after my Sunderland days and now I was asking her to uproot and go back up north - to the other side of the country.

And we didn't have much time to think about it, either. Billy was looking at another striker at the same time as me - James Scowcroft - but he could only afford to bring in one of us.

So I had to make my decision pretty quickly and a couple of days later I was heading up the M6 and checking into the famous Tickled Trout hotel.

I met the chairman Derek Shaw and he was a nice guy, very committed to the club and a bit of a classic northerner - very friendly and open about things.

Billy himself was a relative of the old Chelsea striker John Spencer who I'd been with at QPR so I think Johnny had put a good word in for me with him. I'd heard some stories about him, but he was brilliant with me; very full of life, a classic no-nonsense Glaswegian with the bit between his teeth to get the club into the Premier League.

It was his obsession almost - he was just so driven, when he said something you were convinced it was going to happen.

To be honest, he didn't have to sell the club to me that much, as Preston had a really good reputation in the game.

It was thought of as being well run, good transfer policy, good support, didn't sack managers every six months, big history, it was all there.

I'd played against North End over the years and always thought they were tough games; lots of Scottish and northern lads who would never make it easy for you. You knew it was going to be a battle when you played them, so I knew what they expected from me when I signed.

And they were brilliant with me and my family - they looked after us off the pitch and there was a real family spirit.

For me, the best clubs I've played at are very close to their communities and Preston was very similar to Sunderland in that sense. It had this real identity and you felt it just walking about; people would nod to you, say hello, stop and have a chat, but they were always very polite.

It was also a bit like Millwall, where there were other bigger clubs nearby, but the fans were choosing to support this team that, despite its massive history, had never been in the Premier League.

They weren't glory hunters, you know? They were proper football supporters and I loved that.

My old QPR teammate Trevor Sinclair gave me some house-hunting advice and we moved into Lytham St Annes, where a few of the Preston lads lived; Brian O'Neill, Youl Mawene too, really good lads.

BON was my roommate at North End and I still speak to him now. He's a fantastic person and exactly the type of character every team needs. He sets the standards on and off the pitch, but he also has a great personality and is a top guy to be around. We moved in near him in Lytham and it's a lovely place - there's kind of an acceptance that you might play for Preston or Blackpool, but people are very polite.

When I was living in Durham, I had Sunderland and Newcastle fans following me round the supermarket, looking in my trolley and saying: 'Why are you eating that?'

So that was a bit strange, but Lytham was great and it also had good access to the PNE training ground.

Springfields was an experience in itself, as it wasn't stuck in the 1980s - it was stuck in the 1940s I think!

You looked under the benches and expected to see Sir Tom Finney's name carved there. But it was also a big part of our success.

Everyone accepted it and, to be fair, the training pitches were lovely - in fantastic condition all the time.

Yes, the facilities weren't exactly state-of-the-art, but Billy was brilliant in turning what could have been a negative into a positive.

We used Springies as a bonding tool almost - being there brought everyone closer together and played a big part in our team spirit.

I know North End have moved only recently, but even back then, Billy was talking about getting a new, more modern facility.

He'd say to people at the club that if we were going to entice top level players we had to have Premier League facilities. It was one of his pet subjects, all the time.

In the meantime, we used Springfields like a toughening-up base; it became part of our identity as a team. We were tough, nothing fancy, but we had some real quality about us and if you were expecting a red carpet welcome and everything to be nicey-nice, you were in for a hell of a shock. The dressing room was absolutely brilliant, too.

Paul McKenna and Graham Alexander were there and they'd been at the club for a very long time. They had a huge amount of respect and were just so welcoming to me as a new player.

I looked around and saw BON, Callum Davidson, Youl Mawene and Matty Hill - guys that I'd played against many times - and I thought: 'Well, I know he's a decent player . . . and he is . . and he is . . . and this Nugent kid is as good as they've all said. We've got a real chance here.'

Up front with me, there was also Patrick Agyemang and I think he was even quicker than he realised. If he got on a chase with any defender in the league, you knew he would win it. He was a South London lad and a bit quiet off the pitch, but I wish he'd have had just a bit more bite to him, because he could have been absolutely top class.

But he was a fantastic guy to be alongside and credit to Billy for pairing the two of us up. I think he was looking at having different types of strikers to give him options in games. Obviously Nuge could do a bit of everything and was always sniffing around making darting little runs.

We had Pat whose pace would scare people to death, there was the experience of Brett Ormerod, with his know-how and scurrying little runs.

And then there was the big old target man like me who would take the challenges and the bruises and try to feed the players around me.

Speaking of feeding, I always had the same pre-match meal. You know how us Italian boys love our food? Well, I went for a traditional recipe - scrambled eggs and baked beans on toast.

When you find something that works, don't change it. (Same with superstitions. If I had a good game or scored, I'd always try to wear the same socks in the following match - although obviously I washed them first!)

It's funny though because Billy wasn't a big one for having lads eat before a game. He'd always say you needed a 'hunger in your belly' to go out and play well and I think he's right. I still say it to the lads I coach these days - in fact there's quite a bit I use from my time with Billy.

Training was short, sharp - and brilliant.

Everyone respected each other, so there was nothing silly going on, but I tell you what, we trained with the same intensity as you'd get in a match.

The tackles would fly in and you'd be expected to show what you can do. Training sessions mattered and you knew that you were always being watched, so standards had to be maintained. If someone was doing really well in training, they'd get their chance in the team. At some places, it's not like that, but Billy was always very fair - no favourites, just guys who could do the job.

And if you didn't, you were out, it was as simple as that. He'd set the standard in the pre-season training. I'd been at places where you'd just be doing run after run around a forest and you're all jogging along thinking: 'What are we doing this for?'

With Billy, everything made sense. You could see the exercises had been thought through and designed with a purpose - he was a brilliant coach and the boys all bought into it.

Everything was monitored, especially how many game minutes we had, either in pre-season or during the week between matches.

If some guys hadn't played sufficient 'match minutes' they had to top their levels up in training - proper games, to make sure they were ready.

In his team talks, he was passionate, but calm - and very well prepared.

He wouldn't go into every crazy, minute detail, because the onus was always on how WE played. He drilled it into you that if everyone did their jobs well, we could beat anyone. People might have this picture of him ranting and raving, but most of the time he wasn't like that. He was very intense, but calm - always thinking things through.

Occasionally, we'd be up against a 'big' team and he'd come out in the press and say something like 'we're just little Preston' but it was all mind games with the opposition in public.

In private, in our dressing room, he spun that on its head and would say how we were a match for whoever it was in every position: there's no such thing as a 'big' team, just eleven against eleven out there.

If the opposition were shouting and geeing themselves up in the tunnel, he'd give you a little knowing wink that said: 'Yeah, these boys are already done - and we haven't even kicked off yet.'

We'd be quiet, focused and then we'd get out there and slaughter them!

But you were certainly aware of the opposition and who you were coming up against. He was also keen on video technology and he'd put clips together himself. We'd always have a team video session on the Monday after a game.

If you won, there was always something to improve on - if you lost, well, it was a real 'Video Nasty'. You'd have to sit there while Billy would analyse what had gone on - the good, the bad and the ugly.

In the wrong hands, people would maybe have just switched off from things like that, but he was humorous about it and it was also very educational. You watched things back and learned from it - and this was a very experienced group we're talking about.

He was showing us things that we maybe hadn't picked up on, but he'd been away and maybe watched the game back two or three times. So I think we just got better and better and we had this inner belief about us.

If you were going to be left out of the team, he would always talk to you beforehand and explain the reasons why.

I got the impression he was very honest and when he looked you in the eye, you could see that he meant what he was saying - every time.

Don't get me wrong, it wasn't all plain sailing and there were times in that first season when I wasn't scoring. In fact, I wasn't really scoring at all, but I felt I was contributing in other ways.

I scored in the Carling Cup against Barnsley (on a night when we battered them at Deepdale, but went out on penalties) but I didn't score in the league throughout that first season. I'm sure some sets of fans would have turned on me. If that was at a couple of other clubs I'd played at, they would have been all over me and really shot my confidence.

But the Preston supporters were unbelievable; they could see what I was bringing to the team and they continued to believe in me.

They sang my name and stuck by me and I'll never forget that - I really won't.

Lots of players say they are oblivious to what's going on in the stands and if you are, if you can shut it out, then good luck to you.

But I think most players - especially forwards - know when the fans have lost faith and that then feeds into confidence, which becomes a vicious circle. You snatch at chances, you overthink things, it all eats away at your performance.

To know the fans are on your side and are willing you to do well makes a massive difference. I did get a couple in the FA Cup, including a last-minute winner, at Palace (which, as a former Millwall player, didn't go down too well with the home fans!) but I was just happy to be scoring again.

Paul McKenna put over two brilliant free kicks and I managed to get on the end of both of them. By that point, it was our 23rd game unbeaten and everyone had that feeling of momentum and confidence in the camp.

Brett was doing really well at that time and we just kept grinding out results. I once scored the winner in a Millwall v West Ham derby and I loved those big games, so it was fantastic to play in a Lancashire Derby against Burnley at Turf Moor and win 2-0.

The atmosphere - from both sets of fans, to be fair - was non-stop and those games were fantastic to play in. They had a guy called Wayne Thomas at the back and he was always a tough opponent, but he took it as well as he gave it out, so I never minded players like that.

I'm just sad that I never got to play in a PNE v Blackpool derby game because I've heard all the stories and whenever there was a cup draw, that was the one we were always hoping for (I hear those games get a bit lively!).

Either way, we were on a roll and I think we only lost twice after Christmas in the league and we won six out of our last seven games to finish fourth. People talk about momentum and confidence going into the play-offs and we had all that.

I'd been in there before and most of the lads had been to the final the year before so we went into it with nothing to fear. We were playing Leeds, who we'd beaten in the last game of the season and everything was looking good. We weren't over confident, but no-one was fazed by the challenge, let's put it that way. They were a good side, but we felt we could beat them.

I started up front with Nuge and Brett and when David scored to put us in front at Elland Road, it was a deserved lead, the way the game had gone. At that stage, we thought we'd got the job done.

Billy took BON and Nuge off for Simon Whaley and Patrick Agyemang and it was a real sickener when they equalised.

Eddie Lewis was an ex-North Ender and that just made it worse, but in reality, a 1-1 draw in the away leg wasn't a bad result. If we'd have been the ones coming from behind, we'd have seen it in a different light.

Either way, we'd been very strong at Deepdale all season and with our crowd behind us, I still fancied us to go through to the final.

People say Billy got paranoid about people watching us in training that week - but it was no more than usual. Even when we were on away trips, he would always be watching out for people taking an interest in us.

We ended up training before we travelled to games, rather than the other way round, which was unusual for clubs at the time.

Those few days before the second leg, he tried to keep everything very 'up' and positive, but something had definitely rattled him.

I don't know if it was something said in the press, whether he was worried about the game, I don't know.

But something affected his thinking and the game itself was just surreal.

There was a great atmosphere, a packed stadium, good preparation and everything was there for us. But when we saw the line-up . . . well, I think Billy was trying to surprise Leeds. If so, that probably worked, but it surprised us too.

We went with me, Brett, Nuge and Marcus Stewart, who had come in on loan towards the end of the season - four attackers in the starting line-up.

I think he wanted goalscorers in the team and with those three guys feeding off me, hopefully they would get chances and put them away.

It was an attacking approach and if it had paid off, people would have said it was genius. But, to be honest, I think the formation mucked us up a bit. We were getting overrun in midfield and we just couldn't get the service up to me, to knock down for the lads up top.

When it did come up, Leeds had Sean Gregan playing at the back and that was a tough, tough game against him. He was a very strong player and we just couldn't get going as a unit in the way we had in other games.

On top of that, Brett broke his leg after ten minutes and his running, buzzing about, was going to be the glue that helped link things up.

We definitely lost some cohesion when he went off.

Simon Whaley came on but he was a different type of player, so the whole strategy was under pressure from that point. Not only that, but Brett was a popular guy and we all knew it was a serious injury. There was a long delay for that, then there was another long delay when the floodlights failed, the plan wasn't working on the pitch and suddenly everything just got very deflated.

They got their goals within a few minutes of each other and then they were very clever at running the clock down. It was just a very sad night and frustrating too, because going into it, I really thought we were going to win.

If Brett hadn't been injured, if the lights had stayed on, if we'd have changed things around, if, if, if . . .

Afterwards the dressing room was just numb really; people were quiet, disappointed, down.

You're just empty - a long season's effort is gone in one night.

It still hurts to this day because that PNE team was so good and with the experience we'd had from the year before, I would have fancied us in the final against Watford - especially as Leeds got beat. I think our team was good enough to play in the Premier League and I think if we'd have got there we would have built on what we had and survived.

But it came down to one game, one bad night and the whole future of the club took a different direction.

Obviously, Billy left that summer to go to Derby and that was upsetting for me, because he was one of the main reasons I'd signed. I liked his way of management, his tactics and the way he treated his players, so I was sad to see him go - I think everyone was.

But I could understand his reasoning.

There had been a lot of talk about a big new investor coming in - Trevor Hemmings - but it didn't happen at that time and that was a major block on where Billy wanted to take the club.

He was frustrated because we were so close and if he'd had backing going into that following season, I think he would have taken us up. As it was, he went to Derby where the finances were different and got them up in his first year.

So it was a real blow to us as a group to lose Billy - and his assistant Ned Kelly, too. They were so integral in everything that we did and we'd lost a big part of the club. Whoever came in was going to have big shoes to fill and that was going to be very tough, without a doubt.

As it was, Paul Simpson arrived and he was a very astute coach with a couple of promotions to his name at Carlisle.

But in terms of man-management, he was totally different to Billy.

I didn't think he was as open and honest as Billy, but hey, different managers and coaches have different strengths and weaknesses.

I felt that Paul's mind was made up even before meeting me and a number of other players about the way he wanted to move forward.

His assistant, Dennis Booth, was already openly talking about players they wanted to bring in and I thought that was a bit strange before they'd even got to know or understand the players they'd got at PNE.

When you come into a club in a position like that, your first task should be to understand the players that are there and try to get them on board with a new way of working. OK, it might be different to what had gone before, but all the more reason to get players to buy into it.

That didn't really happen. Instead, it was a case of new names straight away, new players coming in and it was unsettling.

They brought Michael Ricketts in and that was a strange signing for us; nothing against the guy, but he wasn't really a typical Preston player like we'd had over the past few years. Things from Billy's time just seemed to be dismantled and I couldn't understand why. If we'd had a bad season, then yes, a lot might need to change. But we'd finished fourth, lost in the play-offs and still had the vast majority of the players who had done that.

It didn't need taking apart, it just needed a bit of refreshing, so it was a strange transition to say the least.

One of the biggest stumbling blocks for my relationship with the new manager was when Brighton came in for me that summer.

The first I knew about it was when the manager called me in and said they'd accepted an offer for me and I was free to go and talk to them.

Flat out, I said: 'Hang on, I don't want to go to Brighton.

'I'm enjoying playing for Preston, we got to the play-offs last year and I think we can push on this season and go one better.

'Not only that, but I've just moved my family up here, my daughter's just been born in Preston and we're very settled.'

None of that seemed to matter, because he said: 'Well, this is the club's decision - you should go and talk to Brighton.'

What was really poor was that he hadn't even seen me play a game at that point. Like I say, he came in and seemed to have decided on certain players without even giving them a chance.

I went to talk to Derek Shaw and he was very understanding, saying it was totally up to me, which was a big relief to be honest.

I just told him: 'Look, I'm loving it here. It's a great club, a great set of lads and I think we can be successful again this season.'

I knew I was coming into the last year of my contract at that stage and there was a fee on the table, but to be fair to Derek, he was very respectful and in the end, I didn't even go to talk to Brighton.

I didn't know what the future would hold beyond that season at Deepdale, but I told Derek I would give everything for the club and see where it took us.

I was around 31 at that time and in the back of my mind, I'd always known that I wanted to see out my career in MLS, but while I was there, my focus was 100 per cent PNE. To be fair to Paul, he brought in some great players like Liam Chilvers, Neil Mellor and Sean St Ledger.

And when the season came around, he put me in the team.

We started off really well and had some great results, beating Wolves at their place 3-1 and generally carrying on from the season before.

Then on October 14, 3.18pm it finally happened - I got my first league goal for North End. And of all the teams to come against, it was Sunderland, who were managed by Roy Keane at the time.

Grezza put in a great cross and I got in front of my marker at the back post to nod us in front. Did I celebrate against my old team?

Come on, it was my first league goal for about 12 months!

I even think I was ill at half-time that day, so I wasn't 100 per cent, but I battled on. When you're out there, all the other stuff that's going on behind the scenes has to be put to one side.

I don't think I was his first choice striker, but Patrick had been injured and whenever I was called on, I prided myself on always giving everything I had. We were 4-0 up against Sunderland that day and it could have been more. They got one back in the end, but really, we were by far the better team on the day.

A week later, I got another two league goals when we beat Hull and then we somehow lost to Burnley even though we'd been 2-1 up with less than 10 minutes to go. Everyone was determined to make up for that and the following game was against our old pals, Leeds at Deepdale. They had David Healy and Richard Cresswell up front that day, but we were fired up and we took them apart. I got one of my favourite Preston goals to open the scoring - a header at the Fulwood

End that I managed to get to, even though I was going away from the goal at the near post. In the end, we hammered them 4-1 so there were still some really good memories, particularly at the start of that season.

Despite the situation behind the scenes, I wasn't at loggerheads with the manager and the coaching staff on a day-to-day basis; I was always respectful and gave 100 per cent - people could see that every week.

Whether the coach likes you or not, my mindset was that I was playing for the club, for my teammates, for the fans, for the community, for the badge, for my family. I also thought I owed the PNE fans a lot, because of the belief and support they'd shown in me the previous year.

Those are the things that matter. The coach, in a way, is just part of the mechanics that put you out there.

But, irrespective of that, it's very strange to be playing for someone who's basically told you that you're not in his plans. You wouldn't be human if that didn't have some sort of psychological effect, but you push it to the back of your mind. I'd not had that situation before and if it was deliberately motivational, then you could say it worked.

Because every time I went out, I really wanted to prove him wrong.

When January came around, I had less than six months on my contract and there had started to be interest from a couple of MLS teams. I wasn't starting regularly by then and was just getting the last few minutes off the bench, if I played at all. I went to see Paul and asked if I could go on trial to Chicago Fire, who were interested in signing me in the summer.

There was a little bit of a pushback on that and he told me to go and talk to the chairman. Again, Derek was fantastic with me. He said: 'We don't want to stand in your way, you've been a model professional while you've been here and if you can get something sorted out, you've got our full blessing.'

So I went over and did well, but it fell through because there was a mix-up over my green card status.

I was gutted, to be honest, but not long after I got back, I got a call from former Scotland striker Mo Johnston who was at Toronto, where they had just started their first-ever season in MLS.

He said: 'The thing is Danny, we need you in the next two or three weeks. Is there any way Preston might let you leave early?'

I went to see the manager, who was reluctant to let me go, but I said to him: 'Look, I haven't caused you any problems, you're not playing me in games, I've shown you respect, all I'm asking is for some respect back so that I can sort this move out for my family now?'

He still wasn't convinced, so he directed me to Derek again.

Thankfully, he was brilliant. He understood the situation and basically ripped my contract up to let me leave.

I'll always be grateful for that and I hope the Preston fans understand my situation, because I think it was fairly clear I wasn't going to be offered a new deal by then.

My last game for North End was against Southend at home and it was a bit of a crazy one. I came on as a substitute just before Grezza put us in front with a penalty with about ten minutes to go.

Unbelievably, they got two goals in the last two minutes to beat us 3-2.

There were only four games left after that and the lads won two and lost two to just miss out on the play-offs. So that was a sad way to end my time at a club that meant so much to me and still does.

Out in Toronto, they had already started their first-ever MLS season and hadn't scored in their first four games. The stadium was still being built before then and my debut was actually our first home game.

Ironically, it was against Chicago, and it was a huge occasion; a beautiful sunny day, packed stadium and they'd put these special commemorative cushions on every seat.

It was a surreal moment when I scored in the 24th minute - it wasn't the best goal I've ever got, I just bundled it in at the near post, but it's one that's gone down in history as Toronto's first-ever MLS goal.

The place went wild and all these seat cushions went up in the air - it was mad, mad celebrations that the club had finally scored.

Unbelievable scenes and when I watch it back, the TV commentator shouts: *'Dannnnny Diiiiichiooooo! Bedlam in Canada!'*

People elsewhere might think that MLS lacks passion. Just watch that game - it was just incredible and to be part of it was crazy.

Even now, the Toronto fans sing about it in the 24th-minute of every game, which is a huge honour for me.

So I got the first goal and then later on in that same game - I got the first red card! They don't sing about that years later, funnily enough, but at the time, they did give me a standing ovation after getting sent off, which was nice - and also a bit of a first for me!

These days, I do a bit of media work and I'm on the coaching staff out here at Toronto and I love the place. I use all sorts of experiences from my own playing career to hopefully bring on a new generation of talent in Canada.

As I mentioned at the start, I had a great journey in my playing days and my time at Preston was one of the highlights. At that stage in my career, to have come into such a brilliant environment and to have seen what a real family spirit can mean at a club, it was a real lift.

It also meant that when I did leave England, I was going out on a high, with the honour of playing for one of the country's most historic and well-regarded clubs.

I'd like to thank everyone at North End for giving me the opportunity to pull on that famous shirt and especially the players and supporters for the reception and belief they always gave me.

I had no hair, but they didn't care - and I just hope they can make it to the Premier League soon.

That really would be music to my ears.

CHAPTER 7

ALAN IRVINE: PROS AND CONS

When I got the job as manager of Preston North End, I'd been around football for more than 30 years. I'd had a long career as a player, a youth team coach, I'd been in charge of two top-class academies and I'd been assistant manager at Everton in the Premier League.

I had done a very long apprenticeship and thought that at 49, I was prepared for the job as a manager in my own right.

But I wasn't.

I remember sitting back in my chair at the end of my first day at Preston and thinking: 'Well, I wasn't expecting it to be like that.'

It was a whirlwind - everyone wants a piece of you.

The chairman, the owner, the coaches, the players, the office staff, the media - the queue at the door never goes away.

That was a surprise to me, which it really shouldn't have been.

When I'd been assistant, I thought I'd known everything going on, but even after one day in the main job, I had a new perspective.

You're the only person who sees everything, from all directions.

You are The Manager, full stop.

You can have all the help in the world, but it's right what people say - when it's all on your shoulders, it can be a lonely job.

Not that I didn't revel in it and enjoy it, because I loved my time at Deepdale. It was genuinely one of the happiest spells I've ever had in football. A fantastic club, a great set of players, brilliant supporters - that's all true about Preston North End.

I'd been at Everton with David Moyes prior to joining and, when the position became available, Preston chairman Derek Shaw asked David to see if I was interested.

As well as confirming all the aforementioned things about the club, I remember something else that David said to me: 'They're good people.'

The fact that he was vouching for PNE made my decision easier, although it was still not straightforward.

One of the things I tend to do when making big decisions, is sit down and write a list of the pros and cons.

And when I looked at it, there were quite a few cons.

I'd be leaving a secure job in the Premier League to step down to the Championship, for a start. I'd be taking on a role that I'd never done before and one that came with a lot less security if things didn't go well.

It was also a big drop in wages, so I had to discuss it with my wife and basically say: 'I'm going to be taking on a lot more responsibility, getting a lot more flak, working God knows what hours, for a lot less money.'

So it wasn't the easiest idea to sell to her, either.

I also knew that there wouldn't be a lot of money to spend at Preston and that if a player did come good for a couple of years, they would probably be sold.

Oh, and on top of all that, North End were down at the bottom of the league, only out of the relegation places on goal difference.

So that list of cons was quite a hefty one.

But as for the pros, it all came down to one thing that outweighed everything else - opportunity.

The chance to turn things round, put ideas in place, learn things, acquire new experiences and be successful in my own right at a good club.

It was an exciting prospect and obviously, in the end, I said yes and stepped into 'the big chair' for the first time. To me, it was a natural step.

I have heard people say things like 'he's too nice to be a manager' but that's not the case. I treat people how I'd expect to be treated myself, but make no mistake, I have an edge to me and there's a line you do not cross.

My approach is that I show the players, staff and everyone I work with respect and when you do that, people respect you back.

I'm also a proud Glaswegian and people might have this image of me as 'dour' or 'grumpy' but that's not the case either - I enjoy a laugh and a joke as much as the next Glaswegian (!).

When I was a kid, I was playing at a decent standard for one of the well-known boys' clubs in the city, but at 15, they let two of us go. There was me and a guy called Jim Leighton.

They said we were both too small, which to be fair was maybe the case at the time. Obviously, I played in England for many years, while 'wee' Jim went on to play for Aberdeen, Manchester United and Scotland - so us 'little ones' didn't do too badly in the end.

At first, I joined Queens Park in the Scottish Second Division, where players were strictly amateur and it gave me time to work on an accountancy degree alongside playing football. A few years later when I finished that degree in summer 1981, there were 23 teams interested in signing me - from north and south of the border. I chose Everton because they'd have been trying to sign me since the previous October.

Gordon Lee, who went on to manage North End, was the manager who had been watching me and wanting me to sign at Goodison.

But on the very day I went in to sign, he lost his job - and was replaced by another ex-North Ender, Howard Kendall.

What was amazing was that just after Gordon had been given the bad news, he still took time to come in and see me.

He said: 'Look, I'm not going to be here any more. But I'm telling you - sign for this club, it's a fantastic place to play football and you'll do well.'

For him to do that was incredible; he must have been feeling devastated and a bit raw after losing his job, but he still made the effort to come and see this 22-year-old kid and urge him to sign for the club that had just sacked him. That says a lot about his integrity and what kind of a person Gordon is - and it was a brilliant piece of advice. I had a great career at Everton, really enjoyed it, then eventually moved to Crystal Palace.

Down there I struck up a great friendship with another guy who'd come to the professional game relatively late - Ian Wright. The two of us had been used to working for a living in the 'real' world and here we were getting paid for doing something we were used to doing for nothing.

We couldn't actually believe that when training finished, everybody went home in the early afternoon. We were used to much longer hours than that, so we'd go back out - I'd cross the balls over and he would keep lashing them home, hour after hour, day after day.

That was the way we were - it just seemed natural to us to do a full day's work and Ian's development when he was at Palace was incredible.

He had so much hunger for the game, as well as drive and ambition, but he worked so hard and he got his rewards. He is a model for any player to look up to. I enjoyed my time at Palace and then returned to Scotland with Dundee United for a while, before joining Blackburn Rovers.

When my playing days ended in 1992, I moved over to the coaching side, working with young players and heading up the Academy at Ewood under Kenny Dalglish. After that I also worked with Kenny at Newcastle United as coach, before looking after the Academy there, too.

In 2002, I first joined David Moyes at Everton as his assistant and we had some great success at Goodison.

But when Preston came calling, despite the list of pros and cons I mentioned earlier, I just felt that if I didn't take it, I would have always questioned myself. I would have doubted my ambition and my drive, things I always felt I had in abundance. I'd spent many years coaching and felt that if I wanted to carry on improving, I had to take this step.

And I don't regret it for a moment. David was of the same mind and when I asked him what he thought he was straight-up, as always: 'You should do it.' Looking back, maybe he just wanted rid of me!

I knew I was taking a big chance, sticking my head above the parapet as the boss, instead of quietly working away as a Number 2, but I felt it was something I had to do.

I'd had one or two inquiries from clubs before that, but not really at a good enough level for me to consider leaving Everton. There was nothing anywhere near as attractive as going to North End in November 2007.

Even though they were near the bottom of the Championship at that time, you could sense there was a potential there to really turn the club around and get it challenging at the top again.

David sold the club to me even before I spoke to the chairman, but when I met Derek, I liked him straight away. He talked very well about the ambitions for the club, but I went in with my eyes open.

I knew that we weren't going to have a lot of money to throw at things and that it was the type of club where you might have to sell people at times, but I was backing myself to be able to take it on and move it forward.

I can't remember if it was my very first day, but right at the start I do recall Paul McKenna coming in with his agent and saying he wanted to go to Crystal Palace. I think by that stage the deal was virtually done and here I was with a big decision to make in my first week.

I'd known about Paul from what David had told me about him and already seen how important he was so, in short, I said no to him leaving.

And that was a great call as it turned out, because he was brilliant for me. On the pitch, in the dressing room, training ground - just everything, he was fabulous and his attitude was always first-rate.

Some players might have sulked after having a move blocked, but he never wavered and was a model professional as well as a brilliant player.

Preston fans don't need me to tell them how good he was and how he caressed the ball, always looking for the right pass, not just the safe pass, always running, on the move, closing people down, offering himself, scoring goals - everything you want from a midfielder. He was just a phenomenally classy player on and off the pitch. And on top of that - he was the captain. So right at the start, I was a conscious that here was a great player and a big influence on the team and if I let him walk out the door, it was going to leave a big, big hole to fill.

Previously, of course, as an assistant, I'd only be advising or discussing it, but the final decision wouldn't have been mine.

Now it was and that was another big *'welcome to the job'* moment.

People ask about the long hours being a manager, but that's never been a problem for me - working with David, that's probably just as well!

It's football and for the people behind the scenes, the days are invariably long. Until recently, I was David's assistant again at West Ham and I was in before 7.45am most days and often didn't leave until 8pm.

It was the same at Preston, where I had the keys to the training ground - I would often open up and lock up.

By the time the players arrived, the whole preparation was done, the pitches were ready and straight away everyone knew what they were doing that session.

Yes it was meticulous, but I also hope it was enjoyable for the players and that they would learn things as we went forward. The more they learn, the better they get and the better they get, the better results we get.

I think the vast, vast majority of players want to constantly improve their game and if they see you trying to help them do that, they buy into it.

In winter, you start at Springfields in the dark and go home in the dark and, hey, I'm not complaining about it one iota - because I love football.

When I was at North End if there was a game that I wanted or needed to watch, I would always travel to it, no matter where it was, regardless of whether it was on TV. I wanted to be there, because you see so much more in person, and if that meant a few hours on the motorway and a late night getting back, then so be it.

I don't think I'm unusual in that - all good football people are the same and you see a lot of the same faces when you're out and about.

Everyone knows the score and no-one complains about the workload, because we all know how lucky we are to work in this industry.

It's a privilege as much as a career and there are millions - literally millions - of people who would swap places with us tomorrow.

Anyway, when things got started on the pitch, not only was my first game in charge at Preston against Charlton, who were flying, it was also live on TV - so a nice easy introduction, thanks for that!

It kind of summed things up that we played OK but got caught out right at the end of each half and lost 2-0. But even though we got beat, I knew we had the potential to be much higher in the league.

As well as Kenna, there was Youl Mawene, Callum Davidson, Sean St Ledger - some really good players.

Up front, we had two lads on loan - one of whom was a young kid from Blackburn called Paul Gallagher. What's interesting about Gally is that his position has changed over the years, because at that time he was more of a striker. He was always a hugely talented player, but back then as an out-and-out attacker, he was not a top striker.

He didn't really have the physical presence in that position that might enable him to play with his back to goal, and he didn't have the pace to get in behind and get away from people. But he was an extremely intelligent, gifted footballer. Dropping back into midfield was a fantastic move for him, because from that slightly deeper role, he's able to get on the ball and control games, with the play laid out in front of him.

He's so much better doing that than battling to try and make it stick up top, up against guys who are much stronger in the air.

He's done brilliantly since going back to Preston and, again, he's a model professional - someone who is proud to play for the club. He was a lot younger when I was there and it's been great to see his career progress so well and I'm sure he will be a success now he's moved into coaching, because he's such an intelligent guy.

The other loanee up front was Andy Carroll from Newcastle. In his time with Preston, he was just a bit too young to have a big influence on our situation and I let him go back to his club fairly quickly. I spoke to him about it and he was fine, he understood the decision and there was no problem with Andy behind the scenes.

In fact, apart from Gally, I let all the loan players go back to their parent clubs. I wanted people around who it really mattered to if we got relegated - people that would feel a cost if we went down.

I'm not saying loan players wouldn't be committed to the cause, but they're not as committed if they know that whatever happens, they can go back to their parent club.

The players that are under contract desperately need to get results to stay up for the sake of their livelihoods and with the situation we were in, I wanted hungry, desperate players who would fight like their lives depended on it.

With the club near the bottom the table, things obviously needed to change and the biggest issue when you take over on the back of a bad run is confidence. Losing leads to more losing and it's not as if I waved a magic wand on Day One and everything was suddenly fine.

In my first 10 games, we lost seven and only won three.

And one of those defeats was against Blackpool at Deepdale, so that probably counts double for some Preston fans!

As we came into the New Year, I sat down and reckoned that we needed to win nine out of our last 21 games to stay up. That was a tough task but there was no point keeping it to myself.

So we had a meeting with the players, putting up all the stats on a board and making the situation absolutely clear. I'd worked out how many points had been needed to stay in the league over the past five seasons, how many points per game we had been getting and how many we needed from that point onwards.

I said to them: 'Listen, we are in serious, serious trouble here. We need a run that is automatic promotion form. That's the size of the task.'

We'd picked up a bit before that meeting, but the last thing I wanted was for anyone to think that a few good results had pulled us out of things, or we'd maybe scrape enough results just to get above the dotted line.

They had to know and accept the gravity of the situation, starting from NOW - not the last five games when everyone is in panic stations.

And to be fair to the lads, they were brilliant - attitude-wise, they were spot on. There were a number of factors that helped turn things round and I'd be very conceited if I said it was all down to team talks or working with me on the training ground. It was a team effort right across the board.

It does take time to get new ideas and ways of working across to a squad and that was part of it, for sure. But I think the players were growing in confidence and, just like losses breed losses, wins breed wins and they were starting to believe that they could get results.

Once we got on a run, you could see the belief come backing the group.

We beat Burnley in a local derby at their place, where Neil Mellor and Gally were superb up front. Then we beat West Brom and Stoke, who both went up automatically that year. You get a couple of good wins like that and performances really start to lift.

Sometimes, things just go your way though. I remember we'd played Southampton at St Mary's that winter and it was probably THE worst preparation for a game I'd ever been involved in.

We were flying down there and actually got all the way to Southampton when the pilot announced he was going to have to turn round because there was some problem and he couldn't land there.

We flew all the way back to Manchester, then had to wait for a coach to come and pick us up to drive down. The lads were having pizzas and burgers in the airport before we frantically set off for the south coast again, this time by road, a journey of about five or six hours.

We ended up getting to the hotel at about midnight, where we had soup and sandwiches and packed the lads off to bed. The next day, we skipped the normal routine and just had a pre-match meal before setting off for the stadium. And after all that, when we got there . . . the pitch was frozen!

There was a big to-do with the ref about whether the game was going to be on or not. Well, given that our lads had had all this drama and hardly any sleep, I was desperate for it to be off.

I was going through the full poker-face routine of trying to influence the ref: 'We can't play on this, look at the state of it, it's dangerous, etc.'

But he wasn't having it and, much to my dismay the game went ahead.

Andy Lonergan made a great save towards the end, but we were well organised and it looked like a dull 0-0 draw until right at the end . . . Lewis Neal popped up in the last minute and grabbed a winner - incredible! I joked with Derek afterwards that maybe that's the way we should prepare for every game - if only we could afford the jet fuel.

As it was, that gave us three wins out of four and again, it all added to the confidence in the camp.

I knew January was going to be important in getting some new faces to keep the momentum going and we were fortunate to bring in Richard Chaplow and Chris Brown, who was just sensational for us.

Chappy gave us energy and legs in the middle of the park to complement Kenna's passing and Browny was just the perfect target up front, his workrate was phenomenal and he never let defenders rest.

Those two made a huge impact for us and we knew we had to get those signings right. We didn't have a huge network of scouts - in fact I think we only had one guy.

Beyond that, it was myself and the coaching staff and talking to Derek.

The good thing is that football is like a village; everyone knows someone who knows someone. So we were able to check up not only on those guys' ability, but also their character - that's a huge, huge thing.

A lot of what you do is common sense and it's not rocket science to see that if you take a guy who's got all the talent in the world, but he's the wrong type of character, you're taking an almighty risk bringing him in.

All managers will say the same; if someone is known as a bit of a prat, or a bit of a lad, you'll either have to be brave or desperate to bring them in. It amazes me sometimes how some players are unaware of the reputations they've got.

In our situation, we couldn't take any risks and, thankfully, Richard and Chris were superb. One of the good things about working in youth development is you come across players at a young age and you remember them down the line. I'd been aware of those two from years earlier and you don't forget them, even if they're playing against you.

On the downside, we lost Patrick Agyemang, who was a guy I loved working with. If you paired him up with someone like Gally who could always pick a pass, he just kept getting in behind people and was doing really well for us. Unfortunately, he did so well that QPR came in for him and it was a deal we couldn't refuse.

I remember Patrick coming to see me, almost apologetically, saying that he was loving it at North End, but it was a massive opportunity for him, it was back in London and I recognised that. But I was sorry to see him go.

As it was, Browny came in and scored two great goals when we beat Charlton at the Valley - one where he flicked it up and volleyed it in was a real Goal of the Season contender.

But then, I remember Darren Carter scoring from long-range at Leicester around that time and that was an unbelievable goal, too. You look at that goal, which was almost the last kick of the game down there, and then they got relegated by one point, while we finished in mid-table.

So it's fine margins in every single game in that league.

Sometimes you might be disappointed with just a point, but in the final standings everything is vital.

Given where we'd come from in the league, we understood the situation from the start, whereas some teams that only get dragged into it late on, only realise the danger too late.

That's why our January meeting was so important - and I knew we had the characters who would respond.

I've mentioned Paul McKenna, but Callum Davidson was brilliant too, a proper leader and someone you always knew would give everything out there. Again, it's no surprise to see him doing well in management.

Youl Mawene was another great guy, not quite as vocal as one or two others, but someone who led by example and was universally loved.

Sean St Ledger was someone you could just see was a natural footballer. He wasn't the biggest for a centre-back but he was quick and he was good on the ball. Sean says, kindly, that I changed things for him in his career, because he did have a bit of a tarnished reputation in the game.

He'd been part of that daft TV documentary at Peterborough, which could have killed him, but the move to Preston and the way he developed there put him back on the right track.

Everyone will tell you, he's a fantastic guy and I still speak to him to this day - he always makes me smile, he's just one of those people.

One of the things we did with Ledge was use Kenna to screen just in front of the centre forward. Instead of Sean having to compete against the biggest lads, I let Paul do it in front of him. Kenna had a great spring and for someone his size, he was unbelievable in the air - one of the best I've worked with. You'd see attackers thinking they were going to get an easy life when he picked them up, but then he'd be beating them in the air every time.

It must have been a nightmare for them - this little guy always there and frustrating the hell out of them.

That allowed Sean to drop off a bit, pick up the pieces and get us playing from there. It was a simple move, but it was effective and caught so many strikers out because they weren't expecting someone of Paul's size to be so strong in the air.

Little things like that helped turn results around. We won five games out of six and by the end we were well clear of the drop. We finished 15th and I thought that would give us a platform for the coming year.

The biggest thing I'd learned from that first taste of management was that recruitment is massively important.

Years ago, someone said to me: 'If you want to be a good coach, get good players. And if you want to be a great coach . . . get great players.'

Now, that's a bit simplistic, as you can have great players and not put the puzzle together very well. So it's not guaranteed, but it certainly helps.

I think those January signings made a big difference to us; they gave us a lift on and off the pitch and they contributed massively.

At the end of the season, one of the players we tried to sign permanently was Gally, but Blackburn wanted an awful lot of money for him and we just didn't have it.

We did get Barry Nicholson in from Aberdeen on a free and that was a great piece of business, as he was a lovely player, who gave us that spark of creativity and could play in a number of positions, too.

I also knew that this was my first chance in pre-season to get some proper work done with the lads. It's very difficult during the season to get anything done other than a few tweaks, especially in the Championship.

It's *game/recover/game/recover* and it's relentless.

So I knew pre-season was going to be massive for us and we worked the players very, very hard. But it wasn't just physical; it was about bedding down the principles that we felt were important.

My preferred formation was always a 4-3-3, but you have to have the right players to make it work. When I was coaching at Blackburn, I had James Beattie down the middle, Damien Duff on one side and Damien Johnson on the other, so you can see how that worked very well - especially with David Dunn behind them.

But what I also learned was that because your squad inevitably changed, you couldn't just have one system, you had to have contingencies and crucially, you have to fit the system to the players.

I know some managers would try to get the players to fit the system, but I don't agree with that. The players you've got dictate the system you play - that's the way I see it. You pick your best team and that then determines what your formation is.

The alternative is trying to squeeze round pegs into square holes. You might get away with that as a one-off, but it won't deliver results on a consistent basis.

I knew I wanted fast, tricky, wide players and we were able to bring in Ross Wallace that summer on loan from Sunderland, who was a fantastic player for us. I knew about Ross from Glasgow and it was quite a challenging one to get over the line, because I had to really convince him that it was a good move for him, bearing in mind he was at Sunderland at the time and they are a massive club.

It was going to be a step down for him and he wasn't sure about it, but I actually went up to his house in Glasgow and persuaded him to come.

I was happy overall with the recruitment and look, no manager ever gets every player he wants. You're always going to have to compromise somewhere along the way. But when you've got a winger like Ross, who could whip crosses in if you gave him just a few inches of leeway, you need someone on the end of them.

We needed a focal point and I think we really, really got that when we signed Jon Parkin from Stoke. A lot of people would look at Jon and think he was just a big lump, a battering ram and that's about it.

But for me, he was an extremely talented footballer - technically he was very good and his touch was excellent.

His positional play was also spot-on, which is a good job, because he wasn't anywhere near fit enough when he arrived.

He'd missed the pre-season we'd had and I don't think he enjoyed that physical side of the training *(that's hardly a trade secret!)*, but he was a really, really good footballer.

Obviously the big question mark was his lifestyle and I spoke to Tony Pulis about him beforehand. Tony actually gave him a glowing reference. He said:

'He's a big daft lad at times and you've got to keep on top of him. 'But he's got a heart of gold and he's a good player. He'll get chances and he'll create for other people too.'

And to be fair, that assessment was spot-on.

He was away with Stoke preparing for their game at Middlesbrough on a Friday night, but we got hold of him and pushed through an emergency loan so he could play for us the next day against Charlton at Deepdale.

He only met the rest of the lads a couple of hours before kick-off but he came in and put on a fantastic performance, especially as he'd not played much football for Stoke. That's the nature of the guy - he just wanted to play football, score goals and do it with a smile on his face.

With him, Browny, Stephen Elliott and Neil Mellor, I thought we had a good blend and a lot of goals in us.

And so it proved, because in that 2008/9 season, we started like a house on fire. In the first six games, we won four and drew two and were obviously pushing at the top of the table at that point.

But I knew it wasn't going to be as easy as that and we hit a bad run, starting with a loss at Deepdale to Wolves on a day when a couple of decisions went against us and Chris Iwelumo got a hat-trick for them.

We then lost six out of the next seven (!) so that just illustrates that the Championship is a 'streaks' league; you can win four games in a row and then very easily lose four games. And if you sit down and try to differentiate between the results, it's very hard.

What you do find is that there are a lot of teams in there that are of similar potential and results come down to who plays best on the day.

That sounds obvious, but in the Premier League for example, you can largely see which teams are going to be there or thereabouts most seasons.

The Championship is normally a lot more unpredictable. There would have been people who looked at us the previous season and not thought we'd make the play-offs that following year, but, of course, we did.

The margins are so fine and all it takes is a couple of decisions, or individual errors and your results can look very different.

When you're winning, these things go for you and inevitably, when you're losing, that's when they've gone against you.

Fans sometimes don't want to hear that, because some will judge things purely on results, but it's frustrating for a manager when he's been happy with a performance and then been undone by one bad moment in a game.

It's a cliche, but you've got to try to separate the two when you analyse things - don't get too high when you've won, or too low when you've lost.

I understand that it's different for the supporters; your team's won; that's it, go crazy, celebrate like mad.

But for a manager, you've got to keep a limit on emotions at times - that's not being a dour Scot, that's being professional.

Obviously, it's worrying when you go on the kind of run we did that autumn, but it was also a reality check. We were going way beyond expectations at the start of that season and when we dropped from second to about tenth, that probably put us somewhere more realistic. It was a case of looking at things and seeing if there was something we'd started doing differently. We examined it and decided that we weren't; the players and staff hadn't become complacent.

So we kept on the same track, kept working hard, went back to basics and hoped that things would turn for us, which thankfully, they did. At the time, I wasn't panicking - but I was probably as miserable as sin about it!

But if you need cheering up at Preston, the best way to do it is to beat Blackpool and in November, we went to Bloomfield Road for one of those derby games I'd heard so much about. For me, derbies are derbies.

I'd played in them elsewhere and I don't get why people think that a Merseyside derby is bigger than Preston against Blackpool.

To the supporters, it means exactly the same - they are the games that everyone looks forward to and people thrive on.

It was a great occasion and I remember our fans were in a temporary stand down one side of the ground. I don't know how, but somehow that really helped generate a whole load of noise and the atmosphere was incredible that day. Mells got a goal and just dived into the supporters and it was great to see that togetherness, there was a connection between the players and the fans and that was another positive step.

I think we had one or two injuries at that time and we were just getting people back, but on the bench we had people like Youl, Baz Nic and Parky who didn't even get on, so it was a strong squad, for sure. The other thing that lifts people is a big cup game and that year we were fortunate - or maybe unfortunate - to be drawn against Liverpool at Deepdale.

What was great about it was that it created a real buzz in the town, the ground was absolutely full and I think we gave a good account of ourselves.

If you play well against a top side and come out with credit, you take that forward into the league and I think we took a lot of belief out of that game.

I'm not saying anyone thought we could compete with them on a regular basis but in a one-off, we gave them a good game. Ledge actually had the ball in the net at one point, only for the linesman to flag for a foul by Jon Parkin in the build-up. But the atmosphere was brilliant, it was live on TV and again, it got people talking about the club. It was only 1-0 until the very last minute when we were pushing up and really going for it.

Obviously, that left us a bit exposed at the back and Andy Lonergan, who'd played brilliantly, was left all alone against Steven Gerrard and Fernando Torres in the last minute for them to make it two.

So, yes, we lost, but those nights are great for the club and the town if you've shown a bit of fight and quality, which we had.

I think maybe people had written off our chances of being in the play-offs that year, but it shows what you can do when you keep going right to the end. And it also shows again that it's a 'streaky' old league.

Going into the last four fixtures, we not only had to win them all, but also turn round a massive deficit in the goal difference on Cardiff.

They only had to win one of the last four games, which on paper, they should have done quite easily.

But of course, the game's played on grass and that day when they came to Deepdale, well, what can you say about that? They were probably thinking there was no way we could catch them, not just on points, but on that goal difference. Our view was: 'Well, we've done OK, we'll just do the best we can to the end of the season.'

We didn't have any real hope of getting into the play-offs going into that game and we played like the pressure was off.

The guys went out and expressed themselves and, yes, it was one of those days when things went well for us, with one or two deflections and little nicks helping us get the first two goals early on.

But on the other hand, we deserved the result.

We got the LMA 'Performance of the week' award and it's a nice memento that I keep at home, along with one or two others from my time at North End and it's a day that I always look back on with pride.

More importantly, it was a 12-goal swing in the goal difference and, obviously, that made all the difference in the end.

After that, we suddenly looked at the fixtures with new eyes; they were tough, but we now had an outside chance. Next up was Birmingham away, where I think they only needed a point to be sure of promotion that year.

It was a big day for them, live on the TV and I don't think they expected us to turn up and spoil the party - but, of course, we did.

They were 1-0 up and maybe they were cruising with 20 minutes to go, but I tell you what, you don't let Paul McKenna have a clear shot from 20 yards out, because he'll punish you - a lesson they learned the hard way.

So that was 1-1 and then you could feel a bit of tension in the stadium.

I still don't think they expected us to go on and completely ruin things, but in the very last minute Ross Wallace hit one of the best free kicks you'll ever see - absolutely perfect, bending right into the top corner.

So 2-1 in the last minute and the North End fans were going crazy, quite rightly too. Brilliant scenes, just brilliant.

Obviously, we weren't the most popular people in Birmingham that day, but I have to say, neither was the referee, Phil Dowd. He gave Ross a second yellow for taking his shirt off in celebration and sent him off, which was ridiculous.

Let me just pause here because I mentioned earlier on that I loved football growing up. Well, I loved it more back then than I do now, with some of the rule changes that have been introduced over the years.

That madness about getting a card for taking your shirt off is one of those. He'd just scored a really, really important goal for us and I don't see how a young fit guy taking his shirt off - when he's got another one underneath - is offending anyone. But no, the new rules say he couldn't do it and he was off. It was crazy. Come on. It's emotion - and it's one of the things we love football for.

It's the same thing as VAR - when are you supposed to celebrate? The moment the ball hits the net? Or when some guy sitting 60 miles away presses a button on a computer screen three minutes later?

Look, referees make mistakes. It's part of the game, always has been - sometimes it goes for you, sometimes against. If you now take that and add an extra layer of technology on it, you lose something.

Even worse that day, earlier on, he had sent Lee Williamson off after a tangle with Lee Bowyer and it was another ridiculous decision - just terrible. There was no way he did anything wrong in that situation, he was the aggrieved party and to get the red card was ludicrous.

It didn't cost us that day, but I do think it cost us when we went into the play-offs. We appealed it, which was unusual for me, because I'm not normally someone who bothers with that process.

As I've said, referees make mistakes and you just move on, but that sending off was one step beyond and with the play-offs on the horizon we really wanted Lee involved.

He was looking at a three-match ban for violent conduct, which was just ridiculous, but sadly the appeal failed and the ban stood.

It was a real kick in the guts, because Lee had given us a real presence in midfield alongside Kenna and I think we missed him when we eventually came up against a really physical Sheffield United side.

Either way, we still had work to do to reach the play-offs.

Going into the last game at home against QPR, you'd have said Cardiff were the clear favourites at kick-off.

All they had to do was draw at Sheffield Wednesday. They could even afford to get beat, as long as they scored more goals than us - that's how tight it was. We just went into it knowing that we had to do our job and hope that would be enough.

We got off to a great start and I think Jon Parkin's goal sums things up; he scored from an incredible angle at the Town End, a brilliant strike. You don't take those types of shots on maybe if you're feeling pressure, but instead, it was an instinctive, confident finish and that set us on our way.

You could almost guarantee that if someone was going to score against us, it would be Patrick Agyemang but we kept going after he equalised and we got our rewards.

Personally, I didn't keep up with what was going on with Cardiff's game, but obviously people in the stadium were aware and it filtered through. When Sean got the winner, it was a just reward for our efforts and even if we hadn't made the play-offs, we'd have been finishing the season on a real high.

As it was, there was one more twist to come when Darren Carter cleared off the line with the last kick of the game - that would have been hard to take if it had gone in, but again it comes back to fine, fine margins.

I know the fans piled on the pitch at the end, but one of the things I'm big on is always being respectful to the people in the opposition dug out.

There's nothing worse than managers running up and down touchlines or running on the pitch and things. I would never do something like that, so my first response is always to shake hands with the opposition manager and staff and then enjoy the moment from there.

Don't think for a minute I wasn't jumping around inside though - it was incredible and a brilliant, brilliant day. And coming with the late run, we had momentum going into the two games against Sheffield United.

We carried that on into the first half of the first leg at Deepdale, where Sean got another really well taken goal and Jon Parkin hit the post. If that had gone in, I think it would have been very difficult for them to get back into it. I thought we were by far the better side at that point, but I knew that 1-0 wasn't enough to take to their place.

We didn't actually want half-time to come in that first leg because I felt that the longer it went on, the more chance we had of getting the second goal. In the break, the talk was about how we could keep getting at them and extend our lead, there was no talk about keeping what we'd got or settling for a draw - absolutely not.

Unfortunately, they equalised right from the start of the second half and I think that knocked us off our stride a bit. That's where we missed Lee Williamson, with his aggression and physicality to get us back on the ball and on the front foot.

Our intention was to go for a winner and get back in front, but there's two teams out there, they were a good side and sometimes you can't do what you want to do.

Going into the second leg, we changed things round a bit tactically, with Ross drifting in behind the strikers. One of the reasons for that was that they had two excellent full-backs in Kyle Naughton and Kyle Walker.

At the time, they were both very young and very quick and I felt that Ross's strength was not pace. He was brilliant in so many ways, but the one thing he lacked was that burst of speed to get away from a quick full-back, which was possibly the main reason why he didn't make it at the very top level.

He was great at dribbling and could dig a cross out from anywhere with that beautiful left foot, but he didn't have that zip to get away from fast markers like Sheffield had. I didn't think he would get any change out of those full-backs if he was up against them in a conventional role.

Throughout the season, he could play on either flank and I would always look to play him on the side where I thought he would do best.

We were able to do that because the other wide midfielder was Chris Sedgwick, who could also cover both wings. Now, Sedgy wasn't the creator that Ross was; he did all the dirty jobs, all the tracking back, all the covering, all the tucking in, doubling up, all the leg work - he was Mr Reliable. Wherever you played him, he was always seven out of ten.

You knew what you were getting from him, but you knew what you weren't getting as well. And as a manager, that was fine - you need those type of players to knit things together.

They're never going to get loads of headlines or plaudits but for his teammates and for me as manager, we knew his value to the side, even if sometimes the supporters didn't always see it straight away.

It's something I speak to players about to this day - doing all the horrible jobs well; the tracking, the filling in - all those things that nobody says 'well done' to you for. That was Sedg. He epitomised a team player, even though he rarely got the credit he deserved for it. But I tell you what, the lads loved him and he was vital to what we did.

Either way, when the game at Bramall Lane got started, we didn't play well and it was a disappointing night. It was our poorest performance for some time and it was just one of those nights where we didn't get going.

It was a horrible game, with not a lot of football played by either side, and in the end they edged us out 1-0, so that was very, very frustrating.

Looking back, we needed to be going into it with a goal lead or ideally two - that would have changed the approach and the dynamics of both sides. But as it was, we came up just short and it was a painful one because we'd had a lot of confidence going into it.

I suppose when the dust settled, even though we were disappointed we could look back and say we'd had a season that had maybe exceeded expectations and there was plenty to look forward to next time out.

I was looking forward to a summer of strengthening the side and a tough pre-season. However, I knew we would have a big hole to fill, because Nottingham Forest had made an approach for Paul McKenna.

I'd promised Paul right at the start that if he gave me a year or so, I wouldn't stand in his way if another big opportunity came around.

I think he was around 30 by then and it was the right thing to do. The club would make some money, he wanted to try somewhere else and I'd really appreciated what he had done for us during my time at the club.

I couldn't in all conscience stand in his way at that point. So very reluctantly, we lost him to Forest and that left us with a big gap to fill.

He was more than just a major player in the team, he was a presence right throughout the club and losing him was a massive blow. We'd been lucky to have him for so long because at his peak, I think he could have played in the Premier League. Probably the only thing that went against him was his size and maybe a lack of pace, but I believe he'd have been good enough to compensate for that if he'd gone up a level. He was such an intelligent player, he'd have made it happen.

Now we needed a big replacement and the guy we thought would fill Paul's shoes was Charlie Adam. He was at Rangers but had been on loan at Blackpool where he was represented by David's brother, Kenny.

I'd had long conversations with Kenny about the deal and he reckoned we would get him for about £300,000 - at the time, I don't think the club could pay any more than that.

So we put the bid in and we were hanging on thinking we were the only people in for him. Rangers were haggling a bit on the price but we thought they would eventually give in on it and we'd get him for that amount.

I thought that was the case. Derek thought it and, crucially, Kenny - the boy's agent - thought the same, too. It was just a matter of time in our eyes and the deal would get done.

It was summer, some time passed and, all of a sudden . . . well, you know the rest. Blackpool came in with a £500,000 bid.

Painful as it was, we just didn't have the money to match that bid - it was as simple as that. He wasn't 'in the building' or on pre-season tour with us, it never got that far. We were just outbid

Missing out on him was a real blow, because Charlie was a talented player and he was keen to come to Preston.

Looking back, it was a big lesson for me and if I had my time over, I'd have pushed harder to get the deal done as soon as possible. I would have pushed Rangers harder for an answer and tried to put some 'time pressure' on them.

But at the time, everyone involved thought it was going to happen eventually so there wasn't the need to get on Rangers' case about it.

Once I became more experienced, I realised that you need to tie these things up as soon as possible.

You learn from situations - and I learned from that one.

Also, I knew from the day I arrived that we were never going to have loads of money and, to be fair, I'd been backed to bring one or two people in during that first season.

We'd received a fee for Paul McKenna, but it was never a case of getting £750,000 there and having that to spend on replacing him.

That's just not the way it worked. The club was going to need some of it towards running costs and I would get a certain amount to spend.

I think it's the same at North End now - they have to sell their best players to help balance the books, we've seen that again recently.

And they're not alone in that - let's be honest, it's a financial reality at many, many clubs. Inevitably, that has repercussions on the team.

In my time, it was losing Paul and Sean St Ledger that summer - they were two absolutely key players for us.

Sean went to Middlesbrough and that was another purely financial move, because there was no way I wanted him to go, especially as it happened as a loan deal right at the end of the window.

I used to joke with Derek that on transfer deadline day, the two of us would sit in my office, both looking at the phone . . . he was hoping it would ring and I was hoping that it wouldn't!

Certainly in that window, we weren't going to be signing many players. One that we did get in was the Macedonian Veliče Šumulikoski, who was put to the club by an agent.

I didn't know a lot about him and neither did anyone else really, but we saw enough in him to think that he would be a decent player for us.

Would he be able to replace Paul McKenna? Highly unlikely.

Was it the case that we chose him over Charlie Adam? Absolutely not.

If we'd been able to do the Charlie deal, we would have done it and that would have been that. But it was gone by that stage, he'd signed for Blackpool and we needed a midfielder.

It wasn't a hugely expensive deal - it was within our budget, let's put it that way - and unfortunately, it didn't work out as well as anyone wanted, but that happens sometimes at every club.

Not every transfer is a success, but it doesn't mean that they're all bad players, sometimes it's just the wrong fit.

I think what made that one stand out more is that we had been linked with Charlie, who went on to do very well with Blackpool.

And of course, the boy was trying to replace Paul McKenna, which would have been beyond most players coming into the club.

We also sold Simon Whaley to Norwich that summer and I'm sad the way things turned out for him, because he was a lovely lad who had everything in his locker; pace, skill and a shot like a cannon.

But sometimes you get lads who perhaps think they've made it and they lose that hunger. They stop developing, they stop learning and if you do that, you start to go backwards.

The good ones know that there's something to learn every day, every week, every game - they never stop taking things on board and that's what gives them good careers.

Out of the blue, plans for the 2009/10 season were disrupted even more when there was an approach to the club for my services from West Bromwich Albion.

On paper, it was a very good opportunity for me; I could have hugely increased my wages with a team that was probably going to get promoted, where there was money to spend and the Premier League on the horizon.

But I chose to stay because I felt I owed it to North End.

They had given me my first opportunity and I was really grateful for that - they'd taken a chance on me.

Also, it was just before the season was due to start and I knew that leaving at that stage would have caused a massive disruption for the club.

Obviously, Derek didn't want me to go and said to me quite clearly that if I left, they would be in a bit of a pickle trying to get someone in at that late stage. I didn't want to do that. It would have been wrong to the club, the players and the supporters to just walk out right on the eve of the new season - I'd have been leaving them in the lurch.

Loyalty is a big thing for me and I felt a loyalty to Preston.

I'd loved my time there and I thought that we could kick on in the season ahead and be successful.

We were missing some key components from the previous year but we made a good start and only lost one of the first eight games in the league.

We came up against Spurs in the early rounds of the League Cup and that was a memorable night as it was the start of Gareth Bale coming to the fore. He hadn't really been playing regularly for Tottenham and when he had got in the side, it was at left back.

But that night Harry Redknapp played him as an attacking player and he was absolutely sensational against Billy Jones.

After that, he moved forward permanently and the rest, as they say, is history.

Peter Crouch got a hat-trick, Jermaine Defoe scored, they had people like Robbie Keane playing - it was a 5-1 defeat but sometimes you come up against opponents that are just too good, so credit to our boys for sticking at it with Chris Brown getting a goal towards the end.

We went out in the next league game and beat Leicester away, but results weren't coming as consistently as we'd like.

However, I had no inclination at all that pressure was building on my position. So when the end came it was a complete surprise. In the previous 10 games, we'd won two, drawn four and lost four, which is nothing to write home about, but I wouldn't say it's sacking form.

Sometimes, you can feel these things coming, but there was nothing whatsoever. The supporters hadn't turned, I had no problem with the players and we were still in the top half of the table. I genuinely thought once the season settled down and if we made some clever additions in January, we would be challenging for the play-offs again.

As I said, it's a streaky league and I think the players thought we'd be challenging at the end of the season - and probably the supporters too.

We had a game in hand and if we won that we'd have been five points off the play-offs with more than half the season to go - we hadn't become a bad side in the space of a few months.

It was following almost the same pattern as the previous season; great start, bit of a dip and then a charge at the end.

The way that David and I work is that we work extremely hard in pre-season so that our teams tend to start well, maybe have a dip around November/December, then regroup and finish strongly at the end.

I have absolutely no doubt that if I'd been able to stay, we'd have bounced back in that manner. The players were on board, the fans were on board, everyone was feeling optimistic and calm.

Well, everyone apart from the people in the boardroom apparently.

We had played Sheffield United the night before and lost to a goal with about three minutes to go from an in-swinging free kick that went all the way in. It was a freak, but it meant we lost when we didn't really deserve to lose, at a tough place. If I remember rightly, we were only three points behind where we'd been the previous season. So we'd have been well-placed, especially as Sean St Ledger had just returned from his loan early.

The day after the game, the players were off but I was in my office watching videos of our next opponents. Derek appeared at the door and I thought we were just going to have a normal chat. When he told me I was being sacked, I was absolutely shocked . . . virtually speechless.

I couldn't get my head around it and just said to him: *'Why?'*

He looked quite crestfallen and obviously it was a grim task to deliver the news. But he just answered: 'I don't know.'

I thought: *'You're the chairman, how can you not know?'*

So I'm not quite sure about that and, in all honesty, I don't think that is the case - a chairman knows why a manager is being fired. But that's what he told me on the day.

Let me say here though that I have absolutely no problem with Derek - I worked subsequently with him at Blackburn and he's a good man. If I saw him out tonight, I'd go over and have a pleasant chat with him - there's no animosity between us, no hard feelings.

It was done properly from a contractual viewpoint, but to this day, it's the biggest disappointment of my career.

Being at Deepdale was one of the happiest times I've had in football and leaving it was definitely the lowest.

I just couldn't get my head around it, especially with what had gone on just a few months before when the club said they didn't want me to go to West Brom. I'd shown loyalty to North End and yet within six months I'd lost my job, which was just . . . well, it's hard to comprehend.

I didn't understand it at the time and if I'm honest, I still don't now.

I felt my loyalty deserved the club's loyalty - and I didn't get it.

But despite what happened, I don't regret staying that summer. It was the right thing to do and when I've been back at Deepdale over the years the welcome I've received has made it worthwhile; the people outside the ground, the staff, the applause from the Town End. That means something to me that you can't measure in pounds, shillings and pence.

I get stopped in the street by Preston fans to this day and they all say the same nice things. I'd much rather have that than them thinking I'd walked out on the eve of the season.

Don't get me wrong, to get sacked from a job I was loving still hurts - it hurts like hell - but I'm still pleased I made the decision to stay.

I don't regret it and it was the right one. I can look myself in the mirror and know I was loyal to the club, the players and the supporters.

If I'd have gone to West Brom, I would have hated the idea that the fans or the players felt I'd let them down.

Some people can do that, just walk away, but I'm not one of them.

I know the players reacted badly to the decision to sack me and I felt sad to be leaving such a good group of guys. Obviously, that wasn't my decision and I think one of the factors was that the club had probably already got Darren Ferguson lined up to come in and replace me.

To be fair, most of the time when clubs sack someone, they know who's coming in next. I suppose that's the way they have to operate and in football, everyone understands that when someone loses their job, someone else is going to get it. Alex Neil, for example, lost his job at Preston and Frankie McAvoy stepped in. Alex, meanwhile, will wait around for another manager to lose his job and it starts all over again.

Everyone knows how it works, but sometimes you get a better crack of the whip than others and I don't feel I got that. But you live and learn.

There's probably a lot of things I would have done differently if I look back. As I mentioned, I'd probably have been a bit more pushy with the Charlie Adam signing, but going right back to my list of pros and cons at the start, I was aware that the club wouldn't be spending big money - and I was aware that the club would sell when good offers came in for the best players.

I knew what I was getting into on that side of things.

So you can't take the job on that basis and then start whinging when the club can't spend the money that you would like. You have to accept things that are out of your control and that includes the decision to sack you.

I had to go away, reassess things, look at what I'd learned and move on.

It was such a good experience that it didn't dim my enthusiasm for wanting to be a manager in my own right and I went on to take charge of Sheffield Wednesday and, ironically, West Bromwich Albion in the Premier League.

I'm probably better known as a coach and I've been an assistant to three managers now - David, Paul Lambert at Blackburn and Alex Neil at Norwich - even though I didn't know any of them before I went in.

I shared an office at Norwich with Frankie McAvoy and he's a smashing guy, really nice and very knowledgeable about the game.

When Alex left, I took over the team there for a while, but when he went to Preston, there wasn't the opportunity for me to go back to Deepdale with him and I don't think I would have come anyway. To have been the manager then to go back as an assistant would have been difficult.

If I'm honest, I'd love another crack at management but I think it's unlikely to happen. I've never applied for a job in football and I'm now 62 - so I don't think this is the time to start.

I've turned down more jobs than I've accepted and even though I've left West Ham recently, I'm very, very happy.

I keep a close eye on all things at North End and I've seen similarities between the difficulties Alex Neil had during his time and the challenges I faced at the club.

You lose good players and you're not going to spend the same amount of money you've received to replace them. That's it in a nutshell.

It's extremely difficult and that cycle becomes harder and harder as the years go by - the recruitment has to be absolutely spot on, otherwise you're in trouble.

Parachute payments for the teams coming down again make that task tougher financially, but I would love someone to be able to bring success to North End.

The club gave the both David and I our first opportunity to manage and it holds a special place for us.

For me, I'll always look back on North End fondly, because despite the way things ended, the happy times far outweighed the sad.

I love the club and if I sat down now to draw up a list about my time there, there would be a lot more pros than there are cons.

I certainly became a better assistant from having been a manager, because I understood more what the role entails. You can't gain that knowledge in a classroom, from the outside, or even as an assistant - you have to do it for yourself, otherwise you'll never really know.

When you're in charge, there's a lot of people - including myself beforehand - who have an opinion and question things: 'Why has he done that? What is he thinking there?'

Until you've sat in that big chair yourself, you never fully understand.

It's a privileged position at any club, but to have had that opportunity at one as special as Preston North End is something I will always be grateful for. It's a great club - a proud club - and I wish everyone there every success in the future.

As someone once told me, they're good people.

The kit, the sponsor, the pitch, the Town End and Tepi - a perfect picture

Alan Irvine - 'I thought I was prepared for being a manager. I wasn't.'

Phil Brown - 'Injuries killed us'

Graham Westley - 'I signed too many good players'

Darren Ferguson is greeted by the crowd before the FA Cup tie against Chelsea in 2010

Jonathan Clark - player, then manager, then fan

Tommy Booth (right) alongside Brian Kidd (centre) on the way to relegation against York City in 1985

Feed The Beast - Jon Parkin celebrates a last-minute winner against Birmingham

No hair, but we don't care - Danny Dichio putting his body on the line for North End

Chairman wow - Bryan Gray led the BAXI revolution at Deepdale

Fresh-faced Declan Rudd shows his colours (left) Older and wiser (right)

'You always knew what you were going to get at Deepdale' - Phil Brown

Jermaine Beckford in FA Cup action against Norwich City in 2015

Ouch - Mick 'Baz' Rathbone working his magic on Iain Anderson at Coventry in 2000

Mick Rathbone putting David Eyres through his paces at Springfields

'It was a magical time' - Ricky Heppolette in action at Deepdale

CHAPTER 8

DARREN FERGUSON: IN HINDSIGHT

You might not believe this, but the year I had at Preston North End was one of the best I've ever had in management. I was young, I was brash and I got a lot of things wrong - but you learn from your mistakes and in terms of a learning curve, it was fantastic.

I appreciate that might surprise some Preston fans because in essence it's a failure on my CV, but there were a lot of extenuating circumstances and a lot of unexpected changes at the club during my time. It was a hell of a challenge and, despite it not going well, I'm glad I took it on, following in the footsteps of some very successful Scottish managers up there.

Strangely though, I didn't apply for the job at Deepdale. North End had parted ways with Alan Irvine a couple of weeks previously and they got in touch with me to see if I was interested. I went up to meet Derek Shaw at his house and, to be honest, it wasn't the greatest meeting I've ever had.

Derek was a nice fellow and obviously Preston through-and-through, but he didn't seem overly ambitious for the club.

Maybe I'm being harsh there because he wasn't unambitious, but obviously I wanted to push on as much as I could and get into the Premier League and I didn't detect that same drive on the day I met him.

Funnily enough, I left Derek's and went straight over to meet the people at Sheffield Wednesday, who had also been in touch about the manager's job at Hillsborough.

To be honest, I came away from both meetings not really enthusiastic. Neither of them blew me away and my gut instinct was saying don't take either of them.

I said I'd go away and think about things and really I was on the verge of walking away from them both.

I then got a call to say Trevor Hemmings was flying down to Peterborough in his helicopter with Derek to meet me and talk about things in a bit more detail.

We met at the Haycock Manor Hotel near Peterborough and after talking to Trevor, things were more positive in my mind. I came away thinking: 'This could be an exciting project.'

He explained certain things in more detail and he did say there was going to be a big, big investment into the club.

Obviously, that never materialised, but I didn't know that at the time and I had a decision to make between North End and Wednesday.

In all honesty, I still wasn't fully convinced and spent the full day 'umming and ahhing' before finally making the decision to go up to Preston.

The next day I was heading up the M6 and getting ready to meet the players.

That first meeting with the players is always very important, very pivotal. They may have heard things on the football grapevine, but now they're meeting you in the flesh for the first time.

You've got to be confident in how you come across, your messages have got to be clear, you've got to instil that first impression on the group about who you are and the direction you want to take.

However, of all the first meetings I've had as a manager, that one at Preston is the one where I came away thinking: 'I don't think that went very well.'

The setting wasn't right for a start; everyone was in this tiny little Portakabin and it was very dark, dingy, everyone crammed in, not the best setting for such an important introduction.

On top of that, for some reason I wasn't very confident on the day and I just didn't come across to the group as well as I would have liked.

It was only my second managerial job - I'd only been doing it for two and a half years at Peterborough beforehand, so I was still very much a young pup in management terms.

I'd had two fantastic seasons at London Road, but this was a completely different dimension to what I'd been used to, a different dressing room and a different approach.

I wasn't going into a club that was rock bottom of the league and I was replacing a manager who had been popular with the players.

Alan Irvine was a very good coach, very organised, the players enjoyed working with him and PNE had been in the play-offs the previous season.

I think they'd gone through an horrendous run of results just before I arrived, but were still around 10th in the table, so it was not a disastrous scenario by any stretch.

That was one of the reasons that I took the job on - I looked at it and thought: 'If we get on a run, we could be in the play-offs again this season.'

It wasn't that long ago that they'd been in the play-off final, so there was some good experience in there, lots of solid Championship players.

But there was also no doubt that it was an ageing team. It needed some freshness and that's not something you can do overnight.

So there was a lot for me to take in and adjust to right at the start.

I don't think we had a game for about three weeks when I took over because the weather was so bad, so we were training mostly at Manchester United's Carrington complex at the start, indoor and outdoor.

When we went back to Preston, the first day we trained over there was at an indoor place about 15 minutes from Springfields and I'll always remember the goalkeeping coach Andy Rhodes telling us he knew the way.

Lo and behold, he got us lost and we ended up getting there 15 minutes late, which again wasn't a great start.

Maybe that was a sign of how things were going to go.

When I arrived, one of the key things was that I wanted to play a different way to Alan - every manager has their own way of doing things.

But coming in mid-season, it was difficult in those first few months to get my messages across effectively, especially when the games are coming thick and fast in the Championship.

Also, one of the biggest challenges was motivating the players, because there were a lot of people there on a lot of money - money that was completely different to what I'd been working with previously.

Quite a few seemed very happy on their contracts and it was hard to motivate them to do things differently, let's put it that way.

I brought Kevin Russell in as my assistant and on the day I took the job I phoned David Unsworth, who was in charge of the youth set-up at the time.

I asked him to come with me on the first team, because he was a fresh pair of eyes for me and also he knew the club and the players.

When I told him I was bringing a fitness coach in, he thought that was a very good idea because I don't think there had been one before that.

Having said that, I don't like it when managers come in and say 'I don't think the players are fit enough'.

I think it's a bit of a 'get-out', if I'm honest - it's one of those easy things to say.

For me, having a specialised fitness coach wasn't a criticism of anything that had gone before, it's just that I see fitness coaching and sports science as a pivotal part of football now.

You bring people in because they see things differently to you and they are experts in their fields in terms of fitness, conditioning and preparation.

All that work is vital to having players perform at their peak. So there was Kevin, fitness coach Scott Taylor and myself, along with Unsy, who was fantastic. That was the backroom team and we got on with it.

The first game (eventually) was Bristol City away where we were 1-0 down after two minutes and eventually lost 4-2, so not a great start.

But OK, you study the game, you learn things on the day and then you watch it back and you learn things afterwards. Then we had Chelsea at Deepdale in the FA Cup, which was great to see the ground full, brilliant atmosphere, loads of interest in the club and the town, even though we lost 2-0.

We weren't disastrous - I remember Darren Carter missing a good chance - and we weren't embarrassed at all. Again, you look at those early games and all the time, you're learning about players and how they react in certain situations.

One of the things I took from it was that if we could get up into the Premier League, the crowds were there and the stadium was fantastic.

There's no doubt it's one of the best places to play football; very well designed, very traditional and very fitting for the surroundings and the club. You only need to see a glimpse of it on TV and you know that's Deepdale - it's unique.

We were able to bring in Danny Welbeck on loan from United quite early on and he gave us an injection of youth and quality and also Matty James came in on loan to give us fresh legs in midfield.

And I like players who get fans off their seats, who can entertain but also be effective as part of a team.

One such lad was Keith Treacy at Blackburn, who was an enigma. He had all the talent in the world, if he could just sort his head out.

Some people maybe thought signing him was a gamble, but he had so much ability, it was worth the risk and, to be fair, he did some great things at Preston.

It's just a shame his career didn't match the natural ability he had, because he was a lovely lad.

So we were able to bring in some new faces at the start, but in reality, it was already quite a big squad and overall it was a case of 'go with what we've got' for the rest of that season.

For whatever reason, I soon realised that my hope of pushing for the play-offs that year just wasn't going to happen.

We had some good results; we beat Billy Davies' Forest 3-2 and also beat quite an expensive Cardiff side 3-0, so there were glimpses of what we were capable of. But we weren't consistent enough to make any real challenge for the play-offs and it was a case of assessing things for the following year where I thought we could have a real go at it.

As I mentioned at the start though, I made mistakes at Preston and there is so much I would do differently now I'm more experienced. In that first half-season, I went in all guns blazing when what I really should have done is take a step back and just analyse things a bit more clearly.

Instead, I went in two-footed: 'This is what I want, this is what's going to happen, etc.'

I learned from that, big time.

You've got established players that are looking at you thinking: 'OK, you've done well at Peterborough, but this is the Championship.'

It works both ways; I had to earn their respect as much as they had to earn mine and although it took a bit of time, I think we got there eventually.

I didn't set out to take anyone on in the dressing room and there was never anything personal - in fact I got on with the players very well.

Yes, there were some big characters, but people like Jon Parkin were fantastic for me. I loved the guy and he was a very, very good player at that level.

He used to come in for training with a Twix in his pocket, so I banned them and there were other things I tried to change about him. But he was doing the business on the pitch and so loveable off it, what can you do?

I remember one time I called him into the office and said: 'Parky . . .'

But before I could finish the sentence he said: 'Gaffer, let me stop you there - if you're asking me to move nearer to Preston, I'm not doing it.

'Everyone's tried to get me over here and it's not going to happen - I'm a Barnsley lad.'

The pair of us just burst out laughing and that was that.

But he was brilliant and unplayable at times, teams just couldn't handle him. He had his own way of doing things, that's for sure, but sometimes you've just got to accept that you're not going to change the boy. You just do what you can to get the best out of him and I got on fine with him, no problem at all.

I don't remember having big fall-outs with anyone really, it wasn't a fractious atmosphere or anything. In the end, we kind of drifted along and finished 17th which was nowhere near good enough, I know that.

But it had been a case of finding out about things in that first period and getting used to the club.

The issue was that, as time went on, I realised it wasn't exactly what I'd been promised when I signed up.

For a start, I hadn't expected there would be so many changes off the pitch.

One of the biggest was getting rid of Derek and bringing in Maurice Lindsay as chairman. Instantly, it went from being a situation where I was expecting big investment, to being a huge cost-cutting exercise instead.

It was a total '180' from what we'd talked about before I took the job.

For example, that summer Burnley came in for Ross Wallace and the club agreed a fee of about £1 million. I didn't want him to go and when I spoke to Ross he didn't want to go either, which was great news. I thought that would be the end of it, so I phoned Maurice and told him Ross was staying. He just said: 'Look, you have to sell him, otherwise we can't pay the wages.'

It was as simple and as stark as that. That's the way things had become, very quickly.

To be fair, £1 million was probably good money for Ross - I think he was coming into the last year of his contract and it was a good financial deal for the club.

Another big surprise was a winding up order from the HMRC that landed in May, so clearly certain things needed to change.

I understood the financial situation, I knew how things worked, even if I didn't necessarily like it.

The template now was to cut costs, with no sign of the promised 'big investment' coming in - just the opposite in fact.

To an extent, I didn't mind some cost-cutting in principle, because as I've mentioned, some of the wages flying around were just staggering to me. I was absolutely stunned by the salaries when I arrived - they were huge for a club like Preston.

So the board and I were on the same page; we wanted to refresh the squad and if we reduced the wage bill by doing so, everyone would be happy.

I had no problem with that because one of the things I try to do with all my squads is have young, hungry players in, average age around 23/24.

The squad we had at Preston at that time had done very well, but the average age was much older and I knew I'd have to move a lot of people on. In hindsight, I could maybe have accepted things the way they were and done things more gradually maybe.

But at the time that wasn't me - I had my own approach and, like any manager, you have to believe in what you are doing.

If I'd backed off or watered it down, I wouldn't have believed that was the right way to go about it. And if you start doubting yourself, then you're in trouble.

Really, I thought the squad needed to be broken up and for us to forge a new identity. To do that, I needed to free up some very big wages to be able to rejuvenate the squad.

When you're bringing younger players in, you know the money isn't going to be anywhere near as high, which it wasn't.

You'd get people who were still making their way in the game, still hungry in a way that maybe some of the older lads weren't.

For example, I'd brought in Paul Coutts from Cove Rangers at Peterborough for five grand - and the boy could do everything; tackle, cross, pass, score goals.

He was outstanding and we were able to bring him into Deepdale for a decent fee, but not outrageous, and I knew 100 per cent that he would be a success.

When you've worked with someone like that, you don't have any doubt about them stepping up. If I could have done more deals like that, I would have.

But the problem I had was trying to do too much, too soon in terms of reshaping the squad.

Obviously, you make decisions that people aren't always happy with, but it's never personal, it's always what you think is best for the club.

Towards the end of that first season, we beat Scunthorpe at Deepdale with about four games to go and that was us mathematically safe.

After that, I could do what I wanted and I thought: 'OK, I'll make some decisions now so that everyone knows where they stand and if that gives people time to get fixed up elsewhere then it's all to the good.'

So I sat down with people like Neil Mellor, Chris Sedgwick, Neill Collins, Richard Chaplow and one or two others in a respectful manner.

I told them they weren't part of my plans and they were free to arrange something somewhere else. Collectively, the wages of those players were considerable and I was hoping that it would free up a decent chunk of the budget to let me bring new people in.

The problem I had was that during the two months we had off, no-one took them. So I was left coming into pre-season with an issue straight away. I've told them they can go, but no-one wants them and I've now got to decide whether I want them back with the squad or not.

In the end, I made the decision to have a separate dressing room for those players and concentrate on the ones I was going to use.

Now, I know that's a dangerous thing to do as a manager, for two reasons.

One, if you change your mind, you've shown weakness.

And two, you're taking them on a little bit, you're saying: 'You're not going to be part of my plans, regardless of what happens.'

But that was the decision that I made. Looking back, would I do it again?

Probably not.

The problem was that by the time we got back for pre-season, I expected they'd have been sold. Whether it was wages or something else, I don't know, but no-one took them, so it was an issue.

Consequently, because they were still there and the wages were still being paid, it stopped me getting the players in that I wanted. So it was a bit of a mess and again something that I learned from. Things don't always go the way you expect them to and you don't always get the scenario you imagine.

In terms of players we missed out on, we were trying to sign Matt Phillips, who was at Wycombe at the time.

Instead, he ended up at Blackpool and has had a great career - he's played for Scotland and is still in the Premier League now with West Brom. There were one or two others, but as a manager, you have to learn to cope with not always getting everyone or everything that you want.

It comes back to that learning curve again.

I'm not criticising anyone here, but circumstantially things changed at the club and in hindsight I think that's one of the reasons they brought me in. As I mentioned, some of the salaries were staggering when I arrived and the club had obviously had a right go for the past couple of years, unfortunately without it paying off.

Now things were getting tighter money-wise, they had taken on a young manager who wanted to work with younger players and develop players without that big ongoing cost, week-in, week-out. They were looking for players who, if necessary, the club could sell to offset things financially.

It was a departure from what had gone before because as we discovered, some of the lads who were the biggest earners were hard to shift and had little resale value.

So that was the new plan and it was a challenge that I enjoyed, even if it didn't work out in the end.

We were able to bring some players in that summer; David Gray came in, Matty James came back and Paul Hayes also came in, so we were able to get some new players over the line without spending any money at all on those three.

Paul had had a fantastic season with Scunthorpe and been their Player of the Year, so it looked a good signing, especially on a free transfer.

But it didn't work out for the boy at Deepdale sadly; he struggled to settle in the area with his family and sometimes things like that happen, no matter how good the player is.

We gave money for Craig Morgan and it's a strange one because he had a good career and ended up with four or five promotions under his belt, but he was another one where it didn't work out at Preston. He'd been used to being part of successful teams and it's a different challenge when you're struggling a bit and fighting for every point at the bottom of the league.

You have to be mentally very strong and that's why we signed people like Wayne Brown and Leon Cort, guys who would give us experience at the back to help the younger players coming through.

In September, we were able to bring Iain Hume in and he was fantastic for us - a really good player, first-rate attitude - just a top guy.

So having tried our best to freshen things up . . . we lost six of the first seven games in the league.

Now that's undeniably bad, but four of those were by the odd goal and one of them stands out for me all these years later - the 4-3 defeat away at Burnley. Obviously, that's always a big derby game anyway, but we went there and played ever so well.

We were 3-1 up with about 10 minutes to go, Keith Treacy had scored a cracker, Adam Barton got the second and Parky got a fantastic breakaway goal for the third, so we were comfortable and playing well.

The fans were right behind that goal when the third went in and I was thinking it could be a real turning point for us.

In the end, it was - just not in the way I'd hoped for.

The key moment was when Billy Jones went to take a throw-in on the far side; he picked the ball up, had a look down the line, and the ref Kevin Friend blew up.

I was thinking: 'What's he seen here? There must have been something we haven't noticed.'

Then next thing, he's pulled out a second yellow, a red card and he's off.

It was a ludicrous decision, absolutely awful, but even then, we should have seen it through. The problem was, they scored almost straight away to make it 3-2 and suddenly we were all over the place.

We collapsed and within minutes it was 3-3, by which point their crowd was up, maybe we were still fuming about the injustice and, of course, to rub salt in the wound, they won it 4-3 right at the end.

I was absolutely fuming and got into trouble for what I said to the referee - I admit I went over the top. I won't repeat what I said, you can imagine it.

But in the heat of that situation, it was very hard not to be incensed.

It would have been different if it was a clear red card, but it was a joke and from being a result that could have turned us around a bit, it put us deeper in trouble. I went away and looked at it and sometimes you start to get the feeling that 'maybe it's not meant to be'.

But then you just have to pick yourself up the next morning and go again.

Not long after that, we played Forest at home and again, from being in a winning position, we lost 2-1 to another late goal.

After the game the lads were all down and I was down - it was a real low point. I said to the boys: 'Look lads, I'm going to have to have a serious think about what we're doing here.'

And I got up and went to my office.

A few minutes later, Unsy knocked on the door and said: 'Gaffer, the lads want to see you.'

I went back into the dressing room, not really knowing what to expect, but they said: 'Don't even think about quitting, we're all behind you. We probably need to change one or two things, but we've got to stick together.'

So that meant a lot to me and, as I say, they were a good group of players.

We then went and beat Coventry at their place and after that was a midweek trip to Leeds, which, well . . . what can you say about a night like that?

It was certainly the most incredible turnaround I've ever been involved in and an amazing match for the supporters - although not the managers involved.

Simon Grayson was in charge of Leeds that night and the pair of us went through the mill and back again.

I sat up in the stand for the first part of the game, to get a better view and perspective from there and at the start, we went 1-0 up when their keeper fumbled one for Parky to tap in. So far, so good, here we go.

We then had another really good chance when Humey went close and everything was going well. Then before you know it, we were 4-1 down and I thought: 'Oh my God, we've collapsed here, we need to sort this out.'

I went downstairs and just on half-time as I got into the tunnel, Parky scored to make it 4-2 - a really good goal, too.

Straight after that, we had another half-chance and as we went off to the dressing room, I noticed their crowd were having a right go at their players.

So at half-time, my message was quite a simple one: 'Lads, even if it takes until the 80th minute . . . if you get the next goal, you'll win this.

'Their punters are going mad at them - they'll go under if we make it 4-3.'

And in that second half, we just blew them away. We were absolutely outstanding.

It was an incredible performance, we won 4-0 in the second half effectively and Parky and Humey absolutely destroyed them.

Regardless of how things went over the 12 months I was there, I'm proud that we were able to give them something they can still talk about years later.

We were the first team ever to go to Elland Road and score six which I was delighted about (so you can imagine how gutted I was when Bournemouth went there the following year and scored seven - unbelievable!).

On the night we beat them, I came away thinking 'that's a hell of a win' and also: 'You know what, we've got the makings here. If we can just improve on a few more things, we've got a chance, we can turn this around completely.'

We may have been at the bottom of the league, but I didn't think we were dead in the water, that's for sure.

We then drew at home to Reading in the next game and despite beating Crystal Palace at Deepdale, we lost a couple more and I knew things were getting frosty with the supporters.

No complaints, it's understandable when you look at the results overall. What was frustrating is that we lost a lot of games by the odd goal and I don't think we were getting outplayed on a weekly basis.

You try to change things, obviously, but you've got to stick to your beliefs and make sure the players don't think you're changing things too much.

They'll see right through that and think panic has set in.

We got Michael Tonge and Danny Pugh in from Stoke on loan and it was a case of bringing in experienced players who I knew I could trust to perform. Those two were great pros and were people who I knew would be really up for the fight.

We were in a relegation battle, there was nobody hiding from that, but we starting to get one or two decent results.

I always felt that we were one win away from getting out of it, but you also start to sense you're only one defeat away from the sack.

They are the two extremes and you can see it coming, you really can. You're just hoping that things turn around in time and unfortunately for me, they didn't.

It was a shame because I'd got my head around the challenge towards the end and I was enjoying it, even though it was one I wasn't used to.

I rolled my sleeves up and was getting really stuck into it and if we'd pulled away a bit, I think we could have gone on to be successful.

But the early part of my time there, which is pivotal for a manager, I know I made mistakes that I would never make now. That was down to inexperience; me being young and trying to do things too quickly. That upset quite a few of the players, because it was different to what they'd been used to.

There had been quite a low-key atmosphere in the sense that Alan wasn't a bawler or a shouter. I'm not saying I am either, but the lads had been going in a certain direction when I arrived and obviously, I wanted to change course a bit.

So it was a different type of thing from what they'd been used to when I went in. Sometimes players can resent that and maybe one of two noses had been put out of joint - I think that's inevitable in any line of work sometimes.

But I was always going to do it my way. Whether it was successful or not, you live and die by your own decisions - there's no point doing it any other way.

And the bottom line is that as a collective, we weren't good enough at that moment in time; me, the players, the backroom staff, all of us.

We just couldn't go on a run to string three or four results together that would have carried us up a few places and really lifted things in the camp.

I tried everything I could in terms of personnel and formations, but we couldn't find that consistency that would have kick-started us.

It's right that you are where you are in any league because that's where you deserve to be. Yes, you can point to one or two big decisions going against you and not getting the rub of the green, but it is what it is and as manager you take responsibility for it.

There's no doubt that there were moments where I found it quite difficult, dealing with the situation and some of the things that went on.

But you only get better by going through things, understanding them and then learning for the next time.

So I was disappointed when the end came, because I still thought we could pull away - I was settling to the task and I'd seen enough in the lads to think we would get better as the season went on.

Instead, Maurice came to my house with another director and as soon as you get the knock on the door, you know what's happening.

We sat in the lounge and when he told me I just said: 'I don't think I've had a fair crack of the whip, but I respect your decision, so I wish you all the best.'

That was it - over within two minutes.

I don't know if the club had already lined Phil Brown up, but we'd played Hull City on Sky a few weeks earlier and he was the TV summariser that night.

A couple of weeks later, he had taken over my job as manager, so make of that what you will.

There was also a bit of controversy about the loan players from Manchester United, but really that was a smokescreen.

Once I had gone, the United players asked to go back. As I understand it, they didn't get pulled back by my father. They asked to go back and my dad said: 'OK.' It was a simple as that, as far as I can remember.

It obviously became a big issue because it looked like he'd taken them back because I'd been sacked, but that wasn't the case at all.

Maybe it suited some people for it to be a bigger thing and it's something that's been used a lot down the years, which is disappointing.

There's a lot said about it, but in reality Josh King had only played about half a dozen games that season and Ritchie De Laet had played five.

Both their loans were due to end the following week anyway and Matty James had also only started 10 games in the league. So things need to be kept in perspective.

Look, if they want to sack you, then absolutely fine, they've sacked a lot of managers. They make a decision and they're entitled to do that.

But the loan thing all became a bit of a nonsense and, yes, that's disappointing.

It certainly didn't help me in terms of me going back to Deepdale since then, when there's tended to be an atmosphere that isn't needed, because I gave my all for the club and only ever want it to do well, even to this day.

Sadly though, if people hear things often enough, they start to believe them when it's not always the case.

But I'm not bitter towards the club or the supporters at all - I've got nothing but admiration for them.

And I don't let the odd bad reaction colour things too much because hand on heart, I enjoyed it - I really did and I think it's a great club.

Don't underestimate how proud I was to have been manager at Preston North End, because it was that lure of being somewhere with such a great history that was a big part of me taking the job in the first place.

It will always be a disappointment to me that I couldn't bring the success that the people there deserve and I really wish it could have turned out differently.

Make no mistake, if and when Preston get to the Premier League it will be a great day for football in this country.

For me, I took a lot from my time there and if I could turn back the clock and have that time again, maybe things would have worked out differently.

Unfortunately you can't do that, so for me it will always be a case of 'right club, wrong time'.

CHAPTER 9

PHIL BROWN: INJURY TIME

When I was a player, you always knew what you were walking into at Deepdale. It was feisty, it was frenetic and it was full-on. You had to fight for every inch of that terrible plastic pitch and one of the things we were always told when we went to North End was that you had to match them in the battle before you could win the game.

Mind you, I was playing for Bolton and, dare I say it here, Blackpool on those occasions so you know you're not going to get a friendly welcome!

I remember playing against John McGrath's team where he had Sam Allardyce in a back three, which was an unusual formation in Division Four of the English Football League in the 1980s, that's for sure.

Most teams were playing 4-4-2, but John had a set-up where he could get extra men in midfield or defence when needed, because the wing-backs were so good.

Atmosphere-wise, Deepdale was always intimidating with how close the fans were to the touchline, especially that wooden stand on the far side.

You took your life in your hands just going to take a throw-in over there.

When they knocked that down in Moyesie's era, it lost a little bit of something while it was being developed, but they did a fantastic job on it and the stadium now is as good as any at that level.

Some grounds have lost a bit of atmosphere, but with Deepdale still being at Deepdale, the original site - and being a traditional stadium design, I think it's a wonderful place to play football.

And also to be a manager, which I was lucky enough to be.

Funnily enough, my time as a player at Bolton coincided with one of the darkest days for North End in the early 1990s. I was playing in that horrible, scrappy game at Burnden Park when we won 1-0 and went up - and Preston got relegated. In a 700-game career, it's one that stands out for me because there was so much on it.

But I remember the football was awful. There was so much pressure on both sides that neither team could trap a sandbag. Those were the days when the referee would speak to you during the game. I was having a shocker and I remember the ref saying to me: 'Browny, calm yourself down lad!'

That was in the era of people like Gareth Ainsworth and Ryan Kidd playing for PNE, while big John McGinlay eventually got the penalty for us and we saw it out - just about. When the final whistle went, the Bolton fans piled on the pitch in celebration, but I remember the Preston fans were unbelievable that day too.

They were getting relegated, but they were there in big numbers and sang their hearts out right to the end.

Obviously, the clubs moved in opposite directions for a while but I think everyone in football was delighted to see the resurgence in the mid-90s under Gary Peters and then Moyesie.

I went on to see out my playing days before a successful coaching career at Bolton and then managing Hull, before joining North End as manager in 2011.

How it all came about is blurred lines, really.

Obviously, I replaced Darren Ferguson at Deepdale and one of the sad things about it is that Sir Alex fell out with me over it.

I think he thought I'd been touting for the job when Darren was still in place, but I have never - *and would never* - try and jump in a man's shoes when he's still in a job. It's just not on and I'd never advocate that. It's something the League Managers Association are very big on and quite rightly, too.

It's an unfortunate thing in the world of football that when someone is struggling, the vultures start circling.

But I can categorically state, hand on heart, that I wasn't one of those vultures.

Unfortunately though, Sir Alex heard through the horse-racing community that I'd had a meeting with Trevor Hemmings at Haydock Park, when there was no such thing in reality. We met purely by chance and there was no talk of the Preston job at all.

I had a table that day in the Owners and Trainers room and so did Trevor, who was on the table next to us with his secretary and a couple of people from North End. Sir Alex got wind of this and said that I had purposefully set up a meeting to get his son out of work.

I want to put the record straight, because that just wasn't the case at all.

What had happened was that a group of us had a runner that day - a horse we'd bought as a syndicate from our Bolton days, called European Dream.

Sir Alex knows the people I was with - Sam Allardyce, Peter Reid, Bobby Saxton, Brian Horton, Neil McDonald, all sorts of people in the football world who he could check with.

I remember Trevor coming over to our table and jokingly saying something like: *'Oh God, a table full of football managers - the bane of my life!'*

We had a laugh about it, but there was absolutely no talk about the job, or Darren, it was all just the usual pleasantries. I never thought for a second that I'd be working for him a few weeks later.

If anything, the way he was talking that day, I think he'd have been happier taking over the team himself, because he was so fed up with the way things had been going.

So I didn't make any approach at all. Instead, I got a phone call from Trevor after Darren had gone, we then had a meeting and things went from there.

But unfortunately Sir Alex accused me of setting a meeting up beforehand, which was just wrong and I'm disappointed if he still thinks that's the case.

The reality is, Preston were bottom of the league and, if anything, I'd say one of the reasons Darren probably stayed in the job so long was because he was Sir Alex's son. I'm not sure other people would have been given so much leeway.

I certainly wasn't a year later, but we'll come onto that.

When I took the job on, it was a hell of a challenge - I think everyone could see that.

Up to that point, I'd been used to managing teams at the top end of the tables or in the Premier League. So it was a real task to come in with a team that was rock bottom of the league. What sold me on it though was the ambition.

It was a case of staying up that season, then having a real go the following year with a 'treasure chest' from the owner. Part of my job was to make him fall in love with the game again and that was going to be a difficult task.

I think he'd sunk £27 million into the club at that point and not had a lot in return. He was spending more than he had anticipated and I was under no illusions that budgets were going to be cut if we went down.

So he was a bit disillusioned with it all. He loved the club but he was fed up with how much it was costing him, I think.

The guy who really had all the energy and enthusiasm at that time was the chairman, Maurice Lindsay. He had a Rugby League background, but he was a hell of a businessman and a great innovator.

This is a guy who was driving a Maserati around Wigan when he was still a teenager - that's how good an entrepreneur he was. When he spoke, you listened and I built up a good working relationship with him.

Obviously, being in the Championship and pushing for the Premier League is a different world away from being in League 1 and trying to get back where you started.

We were 10 points adrift from safety when I joined but I was convinced that if we managed to stay up, we could relight Trevor's fire and have the resources to do a proper rebuilding job.

Stay up and then take the club forward from that base, that was the plan.

Could I see Preston North End in the Premier League? Definitely. It had the stadium, the supporters and it reminded me of Bolton and Hull.

Not the most glamorous destination, but in football terms, a hugely credible club that would not look out of place in the top flight.

Did I think we could do it? Yes, again. If we had a charge in the second half of the season and re-ignited the owner's passion, we would have every chance.

The first job staring us in the face though, was to stay in the division. As it was, we didn't manage that but the task was made harder right from the very start.

North End had three Manchester United players on loan - Matty James, Ritchie De Laet and Josh King and also two Stoke City players, Michael Tonge and Danny Pugh. On my very first day, they were all taken away from us, which was a hell of a shock.

I think everyone could see why it happened, but the way it was done - particularly the Stoke City element - was just wrong, in my opinion.

So the rug was pulled right from under our feet and that wasn't a good first day at the office, by any stretch. Those guys had been playing regularly for Preston and I think they could have made a difference for us - Matty James and Josh King have gone on to have very good Premier League careers.

But on Day One, they were gone.

People think it was done because the club had sacked Darren, but I think maybe there was a bit more to it than that and that Sir Alex was thinking I'd set up that meeting behind his back.

As I say, that's not right and more than being disappointing for me personally, it left us right in the lurch.

So it was an interesting start, made all the more bizarre by meeting Keith Treacy's luggage even before I met Keith Treacy himself.

I pulled into the training ground and found his stuff all strewn about the hedges. I thought: 'What the hell's going on here?'

Apparently, the lad had fallen out with his girlfriend and been sleeping at the training ground. She had found out where he was and 'delivered' his belongings to him the night before.

So as an opening day, when I was planning to come in and galvanise the team to survive in the Championship, I'm suddenly five players down and playing Agony Aunt to a tricky winger, who's sleeping on the couch.

Welcome to Deepdale!

The one thing I'll say about Darren, and this isn't meant as a criticism because different managers do things in different ways, is that he was all about getting the ball out in training and playing. He was 'pure football' and I think the strength and conditioning work that was required maybe came second to that.

I don't know how much sports science he had behind it all, but no-one had more sports science than I'd been used to with Sam at Bolton and I'd always carried that into my own managerial career.

I always thought that proper strength and conditioning work was a big, big part of keeping your key players out there and without it, you were susceptible to a string of injuries, which is what the club had that season.

That was a major, major part of doing things differently.

But I tell you what, despite the loans situation, the 10-point gap, the budget . . . I honestly thought we could do it. And I believed we would do it.

I never wavered and when I looked around, we obviously needed bodies, but there was some real quality there too, if I could just get them out on the pitch. The first task was obviously to lift people, because confidence was on the floor. You're losing, you're bottom of the league and you need to get out of that rut.

When a new manager comes in, you've got to get to know each other and everyone has to deal with new ways of working.

It doesn't mean there was anything drastically wrong with what the previous guy had been doing, but it's just that the results weren't coming. You've got to recognise that, establish why and then go about building from there.

We didn't have bags of time, so it was a case of a lot of team meetings early on, for people to get to know me a bit and understand what we were going to be doing. When the five lads were taken away on the first day, I used that situation as a positive with the players that we had.

Psychology plays a massive part in the modern game and I tried to instil a siege mentality with the group: 'Everyone's turning their backs on us, they think we're already down, but we're going to show them.'

And you can do that at Preston North End.

They've had their time in the doldrums and not had their day in the Premier League sun - yet.

So it was a case of 'we are what we are' and 'we know what we are'.

You look at the city and it's a traditional, hard-working community with a lot of working class supporters who are grafting their nuts off Monday to Friday and want you to do the same for an hour and a half on a Saturday afternoon.

That's the bare minimum and without it, you're not going to get anywhere. The supporters had been very patient and we had to get them onside with the new situation. I think they understood that when I came in, I wasn't walking into a team that was firing on all cylinders, it was just the opposite.

But they knew - *well, I hope they knew* - how much hard work and effort and thought and planning and commitment was going into every single game.

And that was from me, the players, the coaching staff, the chairman, the tea lady, everyone involved. I felt we had to give the supporters hope and that's why it was important that I went in the lounges before and after games to meet the people in there, answer any questions and just be open about things.

Even if we lost, I didn't shy away from that and it's interesting to see the reaction in people when you're open and explain what you were trying to do in a game, why you set up the way you did, why you changed things, why you made the substitutions.

All that transparency is vital because we're talking about people who are on our side here. Everyone wants the team to win and everyone has an opinion - especially after the game!

But if you can explain why you did things and back it up, then I think people understand it a lot more and you build a better relationship with them. I'll be honest, when I got in, I wasn't trying to be a tactical genius - it wasn't about that.

It was about putting sweat on shirts, rolling sleeves up and putting a damn good shift in.

Obviously, we didn't just send them out without any game plan, but it was that spirit, that enthusiasm, that commitment to leave everything out there that had served me so well in the past. We had it at Bolton, we had it at Hull and I'd seen what could be done if you're a team that is fired up and in people's faces from the first minute to last - it's hard to play against.

I wanted the players to feel the same passion for Preston North End as the supporters did. They want to be entertained first and foremost, but they also want to see blood, sweat and tears. They want to see a return for their money.

And if you don't give them that, they have every right - *absolutely every right* - to have a go from the terraces and stands.

I've seen teams get applauded off after losing, because the supporters know that every man on that team has given his all during the game. You can't win every game, but you can sure as hell give everything in every game.

If you're going to lose, go down fighting to the very last whistle and then you can walk off with your head held high.

The other thing that I was very big on at Deepdale was bringing through younger players from the Academy. Sometimes it was out of necessity, but I had no problem putting young players in. Before a ball is kicked, it gives you that link between the youth set-up and the first team.

Players see that pathway is there for them and respond to that. The first team is not some far-off, distant place that you're not going to see for years and years.

If you've got the talent, you can get the opportunity and that was a big part of what we were doing at Deepdale while I was there. The guys running the Academy were first class and I was very keen on promoting from within.

The one thing you absolutely know you're going to get is those lads will wear the shirt with pride. We had Adam Barton, Jamie Proctor and Danny Mayor - guys who, by and large, have gone on to have decent careers in the game.

In my first game, we lost 2-1 at home in the FA Cup to Nottingham Forest and that kind of summed up where things were at the time.

We'd been winning 1-0, had some good chances to extend the lead, then went down to a last-minute winner. We then went 11 games without a win, but six of those were draws and I think the only time we got a real chasing was when we lost 4-0 at home to Bristol City, who were a very good side that year.

That was the game where we lost young Conor McLaughlin to a broken leg and that was a tragedy, because he was showing he could be a real prospect. (And I'm so pleased he's got over that injury in subsequent years, because he's a cracking lad.)

We were showing signs of life, I thought; we were 2-0 up at Watford but got pegged back to 2-2 in the end and we were beating Forest 2-1 at their place before they grabbed an injury-time equaliser. So we weren't being outclassed.

You looked at the team sheet and you thought: 'Yes, these lads will do a good job today.'

Iain Hume was up front and he was a real pest for any defence, Billy Jones was solid at full-back, Sean St Ledger was there - players who had proved themselves at that level. We got Eddie Johnson in on loan and he was a USA international, as well as Nathan Ellington, who had a very solid record at that level.

Unfortunately, we'd lost Jon Parkin just before I arrived and Richard Chaplow went soon afterwards, too. I know the club had paid decent money for Chaplow but I'm not sure if that affected the owner's thinking with regards to transfer fees - you'd have to ask him.

What I do know is that not long after I arrived, we had a deal set up for Jamie Vardy to come in from Halifax.

I'd seen him, all my staff had seen him and everyone was of the same opinion - we *had* to get this lad.

Luckily, I had contacts at Halifax and was able to set up a deal that was all just waiting to be signed off. I put it to the chairman, because he'd been quite clear that I was to go through him for decisions like that.

Trevor didn't have time for dealing with every single thing so with Maurice it was a case of: 'You deal with me and if needs be, I'll pass it up the chain.'

That was the way it worked - end of story.

I couldn't change that and, if I'm honest, I didn't want to change that. Dealing with one person was better than dealing with two.

So I put the Vardy deal to Maurice; there's been a lot of talk about it over the years but it was £80,000 down, rising to £125,000.

Ultimately, agonisingly, as everyone now knows . . . it wasn't sanctioned.

All I can say is when I spoke to Trevor later on, it was clear that the proposal hadn't been conveyed in the way that I would have conveyed it.

The system clearly wasn't working in the way it should have.

That's not saying that Maurice did anything wrong. I think he was getting it in one ear from the owner and getting it in the other ear from me - and somewhere along the line, communication broke down.

The chairman is the buffer for the owner and there's always a danger of these things happening. When I've worked with an owner who's also the chairman, and had a chief executive in the mix, I've found that works better.

As it was, Vardy went to Fleetwood and the rest is history.

Some time later, when they sold him for big money to Leicester, Trevor came in and threw the newspaper with the headlines on it across my desk.

I gave him a rueful nod and a sort of knowing look. Then I went over to my filing cabinet, took out the reports and showed him the work we'd done on Vardy when we were looking to sign him. They were all 'A*'.

We had top-rated Vardy in every sense; me, the staff, the scouts - it was unequivocal that we should sign the guy and he was going to be a huge success.

Trevor looked at them and it was clear this was the first he'd heard about these reports, let alone seen them.

(It wasn't long after that that Maurice hung his boots up where football was concerned and in walked Peter Ridsdale. But, again, we'll get to that later.)

Back in 2011, there were one or two others we missed out on.

We wanted to bring James Vaughan in, but we couldn't make that deal happen either and it was a challenging time transfer wise, as we were effectively looking at frees and loans and that was about it.

Brian Horton was my assistant - he did a lot of scouting and had a huge network of contacts in the game and there were a lot of Under-23s we were looking at bringing in. But with the situation we were in, you could almost detect that they didn't have the experience, attitude, stomach for the battle, call it what you will, to help with our situation.

We needed the right mentality for our situation.

I'd rather give the lads in our own Academy a chance than bring in someone on loan who can just walk away if we get relegated, no consequences.

It's stating the obvious that it's a lot easier to come into a club that's doing well and everything is hunky dory. It's harder when the chips are down every week and the pressure is on right from the start.

So we were looking for the right type of characters to come in, who had the mental strength to handle that situation on and off the pitch.

That's why my first permanent signing was Ian Ashbee from Hull. Ash had all the characteristics that we wanted; he was an absolute diamond and was someone that had done brilliantly for me elsewhere, but unfortunately his time at the club was hampered by injuries so Preston fans never saw the best of him.

The other challenge in recruiting people was there was no guarantee what was going to happen at the end of the season. If we went down, we might well not be able to offer them a contract for the next year, so again, that hampered things.

So there was only a certain market to look at, where there were experienced players who weren't playing and wanted to get first team football and maybe earn a contract either at Preston, or back at their parent clubs.

We got Bongani Khumalo in from Spurs and he was a player with a great pedigree, having played and scored in the World Cup.

But again, you find out about players' characters. I remember we played Millwall in a TV game and the weather that day was terrible. Then just before kick-off there was thunder and lightning and he looked up at the sky, a bit fearful.

I thought: 'Blimey, my big, tough centre half is worried about the weather here - that's not a good sign.'

I took him off in the first half and put Bailey Wright on, but we didn't turn up as a team that day and got thumped 4-0. I remember that day because it was rare for us to go down so easily - we were battling at that stage.

We'd only lost one of the previous seven and a win against Millwall would have lifted us out of the relegation zone.

They had a decent side to be fair, but they were still doing all the usual mind games; the tea was cold, the changing rooms were sweltering, all that nonsense.

But whatever it was, I thought it was rare for us not to give them a real fight, especially as we were so close to pulling out of the bottom three.

The other thing that hit us hard that season was the number of injuries to key players. Paul Coutts was injured for long spells, Chris Brown was out, Callum Davidson was out, Sean St Ledger was missing, the list just went on and on.

Browny was a focal point for the team and had an unbelievable workrate, while Couttsy was just a very, very good, intelligent footballer - he still is.

He could pin down that right-hand side or dominate things in the middle and if we had him on the pitch, we had a good chance of winning the game. The challenge was obviously getting these lads out there and keeping them out there.

One of the key turning points was when a friend of mine - *well, I thought he was a friend of mine* - Owen Coyle, pulled Ricardo Gardner back from us.

We'd got him in on loan from Bolton where Coylely was the manager. With Ricardo and Keith Treacy, we'd boxed off that left hand side of the pitch completely. They were absolutely terrorising teams and I thought if we could keep that combination going, we would have a real chance of staying up.

But then Owen took him back and there was nothing we could do. He said he wanted to give the lad a chance to earn a new contract at Bolton, but I just didn't understand that. The lad had played at Bolton for 12 years - they knew exactly what he could do. *Earn a contract? What the hell's all that about?*

I haven't really seen eye-to-eye with Coyley since then to be honest.

If you're going to tell me a story, tell me the truth. I can handle the truth, I'm a big boy, y'know?

I honestly don't want to make excuses, though. In the final analysis, over the course of the season, we weren't good enough. I never gave up on us and I don't think the players did either. But I think inheriting a club, not just a team, that had been staring down the barrel for too long was what did for us in the end.

You can only lift people so much and we just weren't able to do it in time.

If the season had gone on for another three or four games, I think we'd have nicked our way out of it, because there were teams that weren't as good as us in that second half of the season and we would have caught them up.

However, football doesn't work like that and when it happens, you have to take your medicine, as bitter as that may be.

I remember the game at Deepdale against Cardiff when relegation was confirmed like it was yesterday. It sounds daft talking about it 10 years later, but their goal was offside and we had a penalty shout on Keith Treacy in the second half that was an absolute no-brainer. I can see it now, unbelievable.

You look at their team sheet that day and they had Craig Bellamy and Peter Whittingham up front, Jay Bothroyd, Tom Heaton, all top quality players - and we matched them.

Browny hit the post, Nathan Ellington had one cleared off the line - we were so unlucky and it just summed up our season.

Afterwards, I was completely drained because I was convinced, utterly convinced, that if we'd won that game and then taken it to the last day, we would have stayed up. We'd scrabbled a team together over half a season that was finally clicking into gear and also, we had bottle.

Again, I remember going into the lounges after that game to talk directly to the supporters that were there, so they could hear from the horse's mouth.

I wanted to look people in the eye and let them see that I felt what they felt and also let them know that we would do everything we possibly could to get back the following season.

It was the first time I'd ever been relegated as a player or manager and it hurt like hell.

You could say maybe I didn't have long enough to turn things around that season and undoubtedly one or two key things went against us, as I've outlined here. But at the end of the day, my name was on the door when the club went down and I had to take responsibility for that.

It hurt at the time - and it still does now, but you can't dwell on it.

Straight away, I was looking to the future and next week we went to Ipswich with a team that had Danny Devine and Scott Leather at the back, Danny Mayor out wide and Adam Barton and Jamie Proctor in attack.

We lost 2-1 but we were in no way disgraced that day and it was about getting those young lads some experience and minutes under their belts so they would be better prepared next time out.

The following week, I think we ended up with five teenagers on the pitch as we beat Watford 3-1 at Deepdale - and that was against a side that had Troy Deeney, Danny Graham, Andreas Weimann, all with bags of experience.

It meant we finished second off the bottom, which psychologically was something good, and it meant we'd shown fight right to the very end. I was so proud of the lads that day and thought we'd seen a glimpse of the future.

(We also saw a glimpse of the noisy neighbours, flying that stupid banner over Deepdale. I don't like things like that. It's distasteful to say the least and after the game I said if I had a gun I'd have shot the flaming thing down. Blackpool have had their issues since that day and I hope whoever organised that little flypast now knows that what goes around comes around. Why tempt fate, you know?)

Anyway, at the end, something came over me and I got on the microphone to say a few words and, yes, I got quite emotional.

I wanted the supporters to know that I felt what they felt. I was hurt just like they were. I looked into the faces in the crowd and I was genuinely fighting back the tears.

It wasn't for show, there was nothing false about it and if people think there was, they clearly don't know me. It wasn't something I'd planned, but I felt a lot of good could come from speaking directly to the supporters.

It would help get rid of this terrible feeling inside me, but it would also let people know that planning for next season started THAT very minute.

The club had just been relegated for the first time in donkey's years and as manager, part of my job was to lift them for the close season and let them know that we'd be doing *everything humanly possible* to get the club back up the following year - starting from now. I wanted to galvanise the support, for them to understand that, yes, we've taken a hell of a blow here, but we'll come back fighting.

First though, there were some tough conversations with the owner and Maurice about the budget. Basically, it was a 50 per cent cut in the wages budget and obviously there was going to be quite a lot of turnover in players when you're in a situation like that, with a lot of the high earners leaving.

Now, supporters aren't daft. They can see what's happening as the weeks go by and people head out the door. But as manager you can't always go public with things when they are taking place. You've still got a responsibility to the club and you can't start talking things down.

If you come out and say the budget's been slashed, I've got to get rid of these players, fans pick up on those things and I didn't want the season to be seen negatively before a ball had been kicked.

My plan was to get a couple of exciting signings in, have a good pre-season and get some optimism back around the place.

There was always a solid bedrock of the Preston faithful who would get their season tickets no matter what, but if we could tap into people who maybe hadn't been near the ground for a few years, by having a new era coming in, I thought we'd really start to see forward momentum that we could carry with us back into the Championship.

In the previous season, we'd been firefighting from when I arrived, but now, it was a clean slate, a chance to show the type of football I wanted us to play and to get everyone to buy into that.

Neil Mellor had been on loan at Sheffield Wednesday the season before, but I spoke to him and he was genuinely excited to be coming back, even though the club was now in a lower division. I thought Mells and Humey would absolutely tear up that division and with the likes of Proctor, we'd have goals in us.

The other thing I wanted was a really strong team spirit, so I took the squad up to Scotland to do some SAS-style training and it was brilliant for bonding the lads. Fair play to the club for allowing us to go, because it was going to be hard and I was running the risk of injury, illness, all sorts.

(Maybe the fact it wasn't going to cost much played a part in their thinking!)

It wasn't just physical either; the players underwent psychological profiling of themselves and I think everyone learned a lot from that.

Me included - because the first thing I said to the Regimental Sergeant Major (RSM) was there was no 'staff' and 'players' we are one group: Preston North End Football Club.

While we were there, I wasn't 'boss' I was just Phil. The only one who sat it out was Brian Horton, who was a bit too old for the course and became almost our own Sergeant Major, bawling instructions and laughing his head off at what we had to do.

We were put into FOBs - Forward Operating Bases - behind 'enemy' lines and given situations that the military really faced.

So we had a 10-mile march, then we had to make sure all our kit was ready and dry for the next day - especially your socks, to make sure your feet were OK.

You'd be absolutely knackered, collapse onto your camp bed at God knows what time, thinking you'd be back at it at 6am.

But then the alarm would sound at 2am and there's the shout: 'Man down in the field! Get out and help him!' You'd pile out of bed and be grabbing a stretcher to go and rescue whoever it was.

Of course, in our little group who was the man down? David Unsworth - all seventeen and a half stone of him.

So it took five of us to get out in the dark, find Unsy and carry the bugger back without being captured - or breaking our backs!

If you did get captured, you were interrogated - and they weren't messing about. Again, it was all very psychological but one of the guys had a sack put on his head and was given the smell of petrol and the sound of sloshing around his feet. In that moment, he thought they were actually going to set him on fire.

Of course, it was only water, but when you're exhausted, pushed to the limit mentally and physically like that, it doesn't half prepare you for the challenges ahead. Suddenly, playing Colchester away on a freezing February night doesn't seem so tough, y'know?

We were put in a sweat box and then had to climb up these sand dunes on the beach, which were practically vertical - especially when we'd been up them about 20 times. Then we were walked into the sea; freezing cold, arms interlinked, until we were told to stop as it got deeper and deeper.

Well, of course, the lads were all different heights and I remember poor old Humey being lifted up by the guys either side just to keep his head above water.

But we were all in it together.

The fitness levels were off the scale too and the RSM was asking me at night: 'Are your lads OK? Are we pushing them too hard?'

And I just kept saying: 'Nope, these boys can take it.'

So I think we surprised the instructors a bit, too. These 'namby-pamby' footballers were taking everything without complaint, doing the tasks and working as a team with smiles on their faces. It was brilliant.

The main thing though was the spirit and togetherness that an experience like that fostered. It was just incredible - you couldn't put a price on it.

I still bump into some of the Preston guys now and they always say: 'Hey, you remember that trip to Scotland?' I'll always remember on the way back, we had to change our train from Arbroath in Glasgow to catch the train to Preston.

We had one-and-a-half minutes to get off our train and get on the next one - 90 seconds. You've never seen teamwork like it; we had three or four groups of lads, one doing luggage, one finding the platform, one with the tickets, even lads with the food for the journey. Talk about military precision.

Everyone made the train and the way it worked was just a thing to behold. It might sound daft, but when you've got that teamwork and that togetherness, even on a non-football task, it counts for a hell of a lot and I thought: 'Yes, we're ready for the season here.'

At that time, when we got back to Preston, we still had Keith Treacy with us and for all his flaws, I thought he would absolutely tear up League 1 - he was streets ahead of that level.

If we could keep him in good order, he would be pivotal for us that season. It's well documented that Keith was making wrong decisions off the field and the main reason was probably that he was homesick for Ireland.

I kept telling him about players I'd had previously at Hull, Bolton and Derby, where I'd actually gone over to Ireland and physically dragged them back. I loved the Irish lads, they always seemed to have that flair along with grit and determination.

But, they also loved going back to the Emerald Isle and as a manager, you never knew when - or if - they were coming back. We had to create an environment where Keith wanted to stay in England and that didn't just mean playing him on a Saturday afternoon, he needed babysitting off the pitch.

So when we got a decent financial offer from Burnley late that summer, we had to weigh everything up.

In all honesty, I thought that as long as the money was coming my way to re-invest in the team I thought it was probably best to get rid of the problems and try to replace them with something else that could work for the team.

The key phrase there, of course, is *'as long as the money was coming my way'*.

Unfortunately, it didn't.

I suppose it made the club breathe a little easier and if you're the manager and the owner sees you give a little bit of ground at times like that, you're hoping that he'll remember it further down the line if you go knocking on his door.

You hope that there'll be a time in the future where you'll get a bit of leeway or a nice surprise with the funds. That's the theory, anyway!

We'd been able to keep hold of one or two big hitters and going into the season, I thought if we kept everyone fit, we'd have a good chance.

Right on the eve of the big kick-off, I managed to get Graham Alexander back to the club and again that gave everyone a lift. The fans were important to me and I know that fans can keep you in work - or get you out of work. But that wasn't paramount in my thinking with Graham.

One of the things I'd honed from my time with Sam was getting the most out of players who were coming to the end of their careers and extending the time they had left. At Bolton, we'd had Gary Speed, God rest his soul, Youri Djorkaeff, Fernando Hierro and lots of other guys who we had playing until their late thirties. We also had Jay-Jay Okocha - no-one even knew how old he was, but who cares when you were as good as that?

So with Graham, it wasn't just a sop to the fans to put bums on seats, I knew he'd looked after himself in the right way and he could still do a job for us.

At times I'd bumped into him in restaurants around Preston and he was always eating the right things, refuelling properly. He was basically the epitome of a model professional. So he would also be a good influence in the dressing room and, on top of all that, he loved the fans and he loved the club - absolutely loved it. People might have looked at it and thought that maybe I was bringing in a guy who could be my successor if things didn't work out, but I was never bothered by any of that talk.

I always knew he was going to go into coaching and there might be times when supporters would be looking at him to take over, but I never, ever minded that pressure - I thrived on it.

That's life, that's football, and if you do it to the best of your ability and you win games, you keep your job no matter who's in the background. So I loved having Graham around for many reasons and there were no negatives for me at all on or off the pitch.

At the other end of the age scale, we had a good set of young lads coming through who I had a lot of faith in. As I mentioned, I always like to give youth a chance and around that time, we had Barton, Mayor, Proctor and one or two other lads who I thought had a good chance of making careers in the game. To an extent, that's been proved right.

Adam, in particular, was a great young player and there was a bit of interest in him. He was a very elegant passer, who had a touch of the Glenn Hoddles about him, very graceful and always had his head up. What I was looking for from him was a bit more grit, a bit more naughtiness in his game, getting your head in where it hurts sometimes for the team and if you get a cut or a bruise then so be it.

He didn't really have that devilment side to his game and he had a knack of dropping too deep because he wanted to collect the ball, whereas he'd have been more effective further up the pitch. He's had a half-decent career up in Scotland, but I think he could and should have played at a higher level.

Danny Mayor could always handle a ball and was a brilliant dribbler. When Keith Treacy went, I looked at what we had coming through and thought he could step up. He's another one who's done really well at a certain level and maybe if Preston had subsequently persevered with him, maybe he'd have had a chance higher up too.

I always loved watching the Academy lads training and playing on a Saturday morning before a game at Deepdale and I think it's important for them too to see the manager there, keeping an eye on them and letting them know that if they're doing well, it's not going unnoticed. The worst thing would be for them not to see a path to the first team.

As for the first team itself, I was happy to play an attack-minded side and let the opposition worry about us.

I looked at the defence, with Grezza, Clarke Carlisle and Craig Morgan and I thought we'd have enough in our locker at the back and I think in the first game of the season we started with Barry Nicholson, Paul Parry, Paul Coutts in midfield and a front three of Jamie Proctor, Iain Hume and Neil Mellor.

I think that showed our attacking intent . . . but lo and behold we got beat 4-2 at home to Colchester.

We then stuck with virtually the same side and won seven on the trot in the league and won a couple of Carling Cup games too.

I thought - and I still do - that our forward line would have taken the league apart, and so it proved while they were all fit.

We had Mayor coming off the bench to torment defences late on, we had Mells, who was just a natural goalscorer, and Humey just never stopped running.

Iain could play anywhere across the frontline; he could go as a Number 10, go as the lead attacker, he was vital to our game plan of never letting the opposition rest and play the ball out from the back.

Jamie had the lungs to keep going for 90 minutes, the physicality and enthusiasm of youth and he also had that special feeling for the club. Being a local lad, it was ingrained in him.

We could play 4-3-3, we could play a diamond, we could do all sorts with the formation during games because the players we had were so flexible.

We had ball players in midfield with the likes of Coutts and out wide Paul Parry and Baz Nic, who could all pick a pass.

One of my passions is *'play the right ball at the right time'* and that doesn't matter if it's through the midfield, long from the defence or straight from the goalkeeper.

We had three guys up front who were lively and were covering the entire top third of the pitch - their movement was magnificent. The fans were loving it and we were playing some fantastic attacking, flowing football.

They could all finish and we were flying, absolutely flying.

I never counted our chickens, seven games doesn't make a season. But when I saw the team click in that first part of the season I thought: 'Oh aye, here we go.'

I could just see goals in us and then it was a case of getting a defence to build from and I thought we had that too so I was very optimistic with the way things were going.

And then . . . we lost all three of them in two games.

We went from having three lads who we'd worked with and got playing like a unit, to not having any of them, really.

That game at Walsall where Mells got injured was the end of the world.

We ended up with a young kid from the German second division, Juvhel Tsoumou, who wasn't ready for what he was being asked to do. He didn't have the physical side of the game to lead the line up top and at the back, Iain Turner got injured, so we called in another young kid, Andreas Aristidou, and we were asking too much of them.

They were products of the finances at the club, because they were really players who were there to be developed and maybe come in at some point in the future.

We'd used a fair chunk of the budget on keeping some of the big hitters from the year before, so the back-up lads weren't really in the same bracket.

We were asking too much, too soon and it showed.

We lost the first-choice keeper and the three first-choice strikers, so suddenly we went from one extreme to another results-wise and won only one of the next 10. We were bringing in young lads like Danny Devine at centre half and it was a difficult time.

But look, you can't go crazy in the changing room because a) that's not my style and b) the lads were giving everything they had.

You're just desperate for that treatment room to empty and you can get your team back out there - the team you'd prepared in pre-season, the one you'd worked on in training, the one that had shown it would get results.

We got Mellor back and straight away we won away at Hartlepool and I was hoping there was some light at the end of the tunnel.

It was just whether the owner would have the patience to understand the situation and play a bit of a longer game.

I had a good relationship with Maurice Lindsay and the owner, so I thought I'd maybe have a bit more time to get people back and turn the corner.

Instead, what happened was Maurice went and Peter Ridsdale walked in.

I'd met him a couple of times when he was at Plymouth and bumped into him in a restaurant, so he seemed like a nice guy in a social setting. When it came to running a football club however, his history with what had happened at Leeds goes before him.

The very first meeting I had with him was when he came into my office at the ground. One of the first things he said was that he liked the office - and then asked if he could have it. Well, come on, I couldn't really argue with that and straight away I thought: *'Oh hello . . . here we go.'*

He gave me some spin and said he just wanted to be able to see the workplace better, but I think the writing was on the wall from the first minute.

Funnily enough, I took a call from Peter Reid later that day, who had worked with him at Plymouth. I told him about the office move and Reidy laughed out loud - he said he'd done exactly the same thing to him down there . . . then the following week, he'd got the sack.

As for me, I survived a couple more games including a Johnstone's Paint Trophy game where Graham Alexander missed a penalty. (When that happens, you really know your luck is out!) We then drew with Stevenage at Deepdale, so we'd gone three games unbeaten, we were starting to get people back and as soon as we got them up to speed, I thought we'd be back at it.

Instead, that was it - just as there was light at the end of the tunnel, the curtain fell on me.

And I've got to say it was a surprise.

You think when a new chairman comes in he's going to take a look at things and obviously, there's a reason a new man has been brought in.

Was it the fact that I'd left the former chairman exposed a little bit with the Vardy situation? I don't know.

Maurice wasn't in the best of health at that point and he was always having to deal with that label of being a Rugby League man running a football club, even though he knew what he was doing and was a good business operator.

I had a good relationship with him and I think when it came to my job, he would have fought my corner with the owner a bit more, let's put it that way.

Instead, when the new guy comes in, you're looking at the calendar thinking: 'Is it going to be today?'

Maurice was always someone who called a spade a spade and was very straight-talking, to the point of being abrupt at times.

I didn't get that with Peter and, in the short time we were together, I found myself second guessing him on things - it was just a very different relationship.

I was hoping that over time, he'd get to know how I worked and vice versa, but obviously that never happened.

When the change in chairmanship had come through, I thought that this new guy's going to be a lot more active on the football front, a lot more proactive possibly even with team selection, I don't know. It never came to that.

Anyway, he knew how strong I was and he knew what I wanted.

How much of that affected him and the decision by Trevor in the end . . . I can't answer. Only they can answer that.

As it was, I was called into my old office - *Peter's new office* - and given the news. It's never a good day when it happens, but it's happened to the best in the world and you've just got to take it on the chin.

A lot of the factors I've outlined here could - *and I believe would* - have made a difference if things had played out differently and I'd have had the players available, but that's the game, unfortunately.

Going back to the very first day when I lost five Premier League players, to the very last when we were still scratching around to get guys back fit and up to speed.

You look at teams who get promoted and very often they're the ones that manage to keep their first choices out there for most of the season.

If we'd been able to do that in either season, I think we'd be telling a very different story now, but I accept that it's ifs, buts and maybes and a big part of the job is making the best of what you've got.

We just didn't have enough to fall back on for long enough when the time came. I'm convinced though that if the front three had stayed fit, we'd have been promoted that year. So, yes, I think it was harsh, but I imagine all managers who lose their jobs say the same thing.

But do I think I got a fair crack of the whip?

Not really, no.

I did think I'd be given time to create a new working relationship and environment with the new chairman.

Sometimes performances catch up with you, sometimes the fans can influence decisions in the boardroom.

But it's results that get you in the end, not chairmen.

The fans hadn't really turned and I give great credit to the Preston supporters for that. You always get one or two voices in the crowd, but I think a lot of people could see what had happened with the injuries and were prepared to give us a bit of leeway to get things back on track, especially given how good we were at the start of the season.

I have no doubt whatsoever that if and when we'd got Mellor, Hume and Proctor back together we'd have gone up that season. Without a shadow of a doubt, losing them is what cost me my job at Preston and that hurts, because it's a great club and one I thought we could take all the way.

Instead Graham Westley came in and if I'm honest, I've never really seen eye-to-eye with Graham.

We've locked horns many times, none more so than a few years back when I was at Southend and we played Stevenage in the play-offs.

He was 'crash, bang, wallop' in your face all the time - I'm sure you know what he's like. So we decided to go toe-to-toe with him and beat him at his own game, which was a source of pride for me - and a lot of pleasure too, I can tell you.

Everyone in the game knows what Graham brings to the party. For him to follow me in at a club like Preston North End . . . I didn't think it was the right move then and I still don't now.

Each to their own, I suppose.

Would I have been comfortable doing what he did in terms of breaking the squad up? No - and I don't think it needed doing, either.

But they employed him for a reason and, unfortunately, that reason didn't work.

I take no pleasure in that, because at the end of the day, I want to see Preston North End in the Premier League.

I hoped I'd be the man to take them there and I'm proud - very proud - to have managed the club.

It's one of the great names in English football and one of the most historic clubs in the game worldwide.

I've managed in India in recent years and when people see the name Preston North End I'm always quick to tell them that they were the first champions in the first league in the world.

And once upon a time . . . I was their manager.

CHAPTER 10

GRAHAM WESTLEY: AIMITA

It's September 8, 2012. Gigg Lane, Bury, around 4.30pm. The sun is shining, the fans are singing - and my Preston North End side are 2-0 up. We are on the verge of going five games unbeaten, scoring 12 goals in the process. Life is good. Really good.

I don't normally do this during games, but that day I stopped - just for a moment - and took it all in.

I looked onto the pitch and saw a team that was working as one unit; not quite perfect *(it never is for any manager),* but heading in the right direction for sure.

Scotty Laird had put in two great crosses, Akpo Sodje got his head to one and Shane Cansdell-Sherriff got the other. We were comfortably holding a decent Bury side at bay. So I paused and looked around the ground, where there were more Preston fans than home supporters; a sea of white and blue, bouncing around and belting out: *'PNE! PNE! PNE!'*

They were awesome. They just brought the house down with the noise they were making. And I just thought . . . *wow.*

It was a taste of what we could expect if we could get this club going in the right direction again; the passion, the pride, the energy.

It was exactly what I wanted and what I'd signed up for. I never needed any extra incentive to succeed, but if anyone else ever did, it was there that day.

You could feel it from those Preston fans, transmitting it to everyone involved on the playing side: 'Give us success and this is what we will give back to you.'

It was loud (very loud) and clear.

And loud and clear back I can look them in the eye and say: 'I tried.'

I gave it everything. Mistakes may have been made along the way, as they always are, but any lack of success wasn't down to effort or endeavour or hard work or commitment on my part.

We didn't lack any of those things, as I'm sure even the harshest critic would agree.

That day at Bury wasn't the first time Preston North End had taken my breath away. I agreed to join the club on Friday the 13th (yes, I know!) of January 2012 and the following day the team played Wycombe Wanderers at home.

I'd been to Deepdale a couple of times before; once on a scouting mission with Stevenage and then when we came for the subsequent fixture.

When I first laid eyes on the place it was another '*wow*' moment; the stadium, the Sir Tom Finney statue, those iconic floodlights - the whole set-up was a world away from Stevenage.

And why wouldn't it be? We're talking about a club that is aiming to play in the Premier League, compared to one that had only recently come from non-league football.

No disrespect to Stevenage; it's a fantastic club, but obviously with a ceiling to what it could realistically achieve. With Preston, I thought there was no ceiling.

We could go all the way.

On that first scouting mission I thought: 'Now . . . this is a football club.'

The history, the size, the expectation - all of it was just fantastic.

For me, it was love at first sight.

I'll be honest, I didn't really know enough about Preston before that first visit. It was against Yeovil on a Friday night under Phil Brown and there was just something about the place.

This book is called North End Souls and it's a fitting title; there's this 'soul' to the football club that you can feel the minute you set eyes on it.

There was a genuine passion and care from the fans about the club. It meant something out of the ordinary to the people and it just felt like a football club should; a living, breathing thing.

It didn't hurt that the game itself was a 4-3 thriller, with PNE seeing off a Yeovil side including Paul Huntington, Nathan Jones and Luke Ayling, among some other very good pros. The cheer that greeted the final whistle was spine-tingling and, again, it stuck with me.

On the way out, I spotted Peter Ridsdale in the foyer of the Sir Tom Finney Stand and as I caught his eye I nodded and said: 'Hello Chairman.'

I don't think he had any idea who I was, because he looked at me as if to say: 'Who the hell are you?!'

Later on we'd laugh about that first meeting and let me say here and now that throughout my time at Preston, Peter was a great support to me.

He's a fantastic football man, a top administrator and, in the final analysis, he backed me for as long as he could. So there will be no negativity heading his way from me - or anyone else for that matter.

I'm not one to bear grudges, nor am I one to wash dirty linen in public, so if you're expecting to hear me say this or that about individual players, you're going to be disappointed.

That's not my style, despite what you might have read or heard elsewhere. There are lots of Chinese whispers and far-fetched anecdotes bandied about that can quickly become 'fact' when they are far from the actual truth. Football can be a great gossip factory, but my advice would be don't believe everything you hear.

On the plus side, it's also that gossip grapevine where you first hear about potential transfers, loan deals - and managerial moves.

I think the link with me and Preston started in early December when Stevenage went to Colchester and won 6-1. That made people sit up and take notice about the team and start casting eyes in my direction. At first it was probably just one or two things on fan forums, but then questions started to get asked by the local press about the link. I'll be honest, it excited me.

Those two trips to the North had left a great impression on me and the minute I got a sense of the interest, it was very much somewhere I wanted to go to.

Sure enough, when Phil left, contact was made and I had the opportunity to talk to Preston about how we might take things forward.

The appointment process was very thorough and diligent - I had a meeting with the board and I'm sure they were appraising their options throughout that period.

At no point in the process did I think the job was mine until I had confirmation, but when that came, my feeling was just one of sheer excitement at the opportunity I'd been given. It was my big break and I couldn't wait to get started.

I wasn't naive - I knew it was going to be tough.

The club had been on a downward spiral over the past few years and in that time, two very good managers had failed before me.

Darren Ferguson had achieved great success with Peterborough, so he was clearly a talented manager, as he's gone on to prove again. Similarly, Phil Brown had taken a team into the Premier League and managed at the highest level. Darren had lost 51 per cent of his matches in charge.

Phil had lost 41 per cent of his games.

Clubs that lose that level of football matches are not losing for no reason.

Darren and Phil were people with proven records of success who had not been able to repeat that at Preston.

You have to ask: 'Why?'

On a personal level, I hadn't ever managed away from the London area really. My home was in West London, where I'd joined QPR as an apprentice at 16, straight from school.

My career had been interrupted by injury and eventually early retirement from playing at the age of 28, when I began to focus on business interests.

Having been successful in that, I had a solid base in the city, kids in school and a settled family life. I didn't want to upset that aspect of my life, so when I joined Preston I spent a lot of my time travelling to and fro.

I'd get up in the early hours to be at Euston for the first train north, working all the way. I'd be up at Springfields for training then get a late train back, often arriving back at 10pm, then be up again at 5am to do the same thing again the next day. None of this was a problem for me. It was my work ethic and I just ploughed on. I'd probably stay up North for half the week then do that travelling routine for the rest, depending on games, training schedules, scouting, etc.

Looking back, if I'm honest, my one big regret is that I didn't recognise the toll that all the travelling took on me. At the time, when you're doing it, you just crack on. It's the job and you're just giving it everything. It's really only later you see the toll that takes on body and mind.

When I did stay up North, I moved around various hotels; some near the ground, some further away in Preston, some in Manchester, the Lakes even.

It was a good way of getting to know people and I bumped into a lot of fans out and about, who always wanted to talk about football, the team, tactics, etc.

There were times when I literally couldn't get a moment away from football and PNE if I stepped outside, but I loved it and the people were really friendly, so I never minded a chat - even if we didn't always agree.

Overall however, if I was to have my time again I'd probably find a semi-permanent base up there and do a bit less travelling. For me at the time though, I had a young family and I felt it was the right thing to do. The train journeys gave me time to think about the many challenges at the club and why it had not been successful for several years.

When you looked at it from the outside, the whole place was geared up for success. In League 1 it was one of the biggest teams in there, great supporters, big attendances for that level, huge away followings.

People might ask about the training facilities at Springfields, but I came from Stevenage, where we'd do weights in the open air and train on a car park sometimes.

And at the time I left Stevenage to join Preston, we were up around sixth in the table, pushing for the play-offs with a fraction of the resources, while North End were down in the bottom half.

In fact, we'd been to Preston earlier that season and got a 0-0 draw in a fairly grotty game, but it was a big result for us. We were little Stevenage, coming from non-league just a couple of years earlier, getting a result against a team spending millions on their squad with a former Champions League winner in it.

That sort of thing isn't supposed to happen. So when I took over I started to really look at the Preston playing squad.

When I did, I saw a group of players that had become 'satisfied' - comfortable in their surroundings and used to doing things a certain way just to get by.

In some cases - not all, but enough to have a serious impact - there was a lack of hunger; no desire to do better and improve. There were people who had been in the game for a long time and were on that treadmill. For them, just 'getting by' was fine.

Well, for me, it wasn't.

I know the difference between a hungry player giving 110 per cent every game, really pushing himself to the limits and straining every last sinew to win that tackle, that header and ultimately that match.

And then compare that with a 'satisfied' individual who's maybe gone stale, is on a good contract and is happy to give 90 per cent because he's a talented player and thinks 90 per cent is 'good enough' to get by.

I can't accept that; not at Stevenage, not at Preston, not anywhere.

I couldn't tolerate it.

It was unacceptable and I don't think that's unreasonable. I don't think the supporters would have found it acceptable either.

So if you come into that situation, the reasons why the club has lost two good managers in two years and is half way down League 1 start to become clearer.

I don't think it came as any great surprise to Peter or others at the club that there was this attitude kicking around. They'd clearly brought me in to shake things up, draw a line in the sand, make the necessary changes and then build from there. I was inheriting problems that had built up over quite a long period in football terms.

The extent of those footballing problems would only become clear when I walked through the door. And on top of that I was also inheriting the problem of taking the best part of £5 million out of the wage bill.

That was not going to be easy, especially when what you're inheriting on the playing side has already been losing a large proportion of matches.

I wasn't the first manager to be asked to go into a club and do that, but it was always going to be messy and painful in that first phase. As manager, you need a strength of character to see that task through. It would mean moving a lot of players on and bringing in people with a completely different mindset.

Of course the players who are going to be affected will react to that.

I didn't know much about the North West or the media up there and I felt the effect of that early on. And not in a good way.

Now for me, what goes on in the dressing room is sacrosanct. It's widely understood in football that what gets said in the dressing room stays there. That didn't seem to be the case with some players whose worlds were about to be turned upside down.

Some reacted negatively. One or two used their contacts in the media to push stories out to maybe undermine what I was trying to do. There were a lot of things said about me in my early weeks that just weren't right.

The club was brilliant about it and actually appointed lawyers to deal with some of the press and got compensation paid for some of what was printed.

There were a lot of lies told and when you're new to the region and you haven't got the media contacts, your ability to fight back is restricted.

So there are maybe one or two myths I can dispel here, starting with the *'Medal Winner'* nickname.

When I first met the Preston squad, I gave a brief introduction about what to expect from me and what I expected from them. Every single new manager does the same thing.

Now, I'm quite a light-hearted kind of person, albeit in the serious business of winning. In that session, I jokingly - *jokingly!* - said that my kids referred to me as 'Medal Winner'.

It was 100 per cent in good spirit, banter, call it what you like. It was clearly humorous, said with a huge wry smile on my face - same as I have now looking back on it. I was laughing when I said it. There's no way anyone can genuinely have taken it seriously in that session.

My kids had never called me 'Medal Winner'.

Until of course the players announced it to the press, at which point my kids took great delight in bantering me about it!

It's all about context and if you go away with the impression of some self-serving lunatic who goes around saying things like that in a serious manner then you couldn't be further from the truth.

I'm a much more humble person than that; I've worked very hard at everything I've done in life and I take hard work very seriously.

But like I say, I'm a light-hearted guy in many ways and sometimes people can use that against you, when things get written down in black and white, taken out of the context and away from the meaning that's intended.

I certainly would never be so brash as to go out there to a room of colleagues and talk about myself in such glowing terms.

Anyone who knows me knows that's not me.

We all have a laugh about it and that's the way it was intended in that meeting. I think, deep down, everyone who was there knows that.

Similarly, there was a lot of talk about me sending out text messages in the early hours the night before a game.

Let me tell you, on the night before a game, I'm tucked up in bed and I'd expect the players to be exactly the same. There's no way I'd ever seek to disturb that.

We're going back quite a few years now when technology wasn't quite as sharp as it is now, so maybe the odd one or two messages sent earlier in the day got stuck in the system and ended up arriving later than planned.

If so it wasn't deliberate and I can't recall anyone ever raising it directly with me. If they had, we'd have looked into it and made sure it didn't happen again.

Instead though, these things got leaked to the media who made a big thing out of it: 'Oh, he must be crazy, look what this guy is doing at Preston!'

Give me a break.

File it under the category of 'don't believe everything you read in the press'.

Let's be honest, there were a lot of people who wanted to give me a bad name. We were asking players to leave a club that they didn't want to leave. So things get twisted and used by people for their own agendas, to make me look daft, call it what you like.

As for texting, messaging, emails or whatever, I use all of those to communicate with people; who doesn't? It would be weird if I didn't.

The reality is, the players knew that I was there with a remit to shake things up and make big changes.

It was not going to be pretty for a while, but once we'd gone through that process, I firmly believed we would come out of it with a younger, hungrier squad that would more reflect my values - and also represent Preston North End and the people of the city better.

There is ALWAYS going to be a lot of hassle when you're a manager going in to do that job. You're not going to be popular with those players. You're shaking up their world. They are going to resist changes and go into protection mode - let's not kid ourselves about how these things work.

I could have shied away from it. One or two people - some very experienced football people - warned me against going to Preston because of what had happened to Darren and Phil, but I never shy away.

Everything was geared up for success, we just had to go through the process first. I saw it as a hell of an opportunity, but also a hell of a challenge.

As I mentioned, I was moving to a completely new territory; I didn't know the North West area, I didn't know the recruitment, the media, I had no natural support network around me. I was upping sticks to a new part of the country and starting from scratch.

On top of that, I was going to have to take a lot of players out of the squad, a lot of well-paid players and - in some cases - a lot of well-liked players. So it was going to be a tough, tough task. I was going to have a lot of explaining to do, fans were going to question what I was doing and it was all going to take time.

Most of all, I knew - 100 per cent - that to succeed I would need a huge amount of luck. Because it was a tough place to go to and bring winning standards in.

The one thing I know for certain is that no manager could have worked harder for the club than I did.

I'm sure every manager that walks in the door works really hard, but none of them could have worked harder than I did.

I just couldn't quite crack the code quickly enough.

I turned the squad round at super fast speed that one summer I was there, but I just couldn't get the results going in the right direction fast enough for the club.

I knew I would get there, given time. In fact, my loss record was 37 per cent, so a bit better than my immediate predecessors. It's not a seismic change, but given the circumstances, I fully believe we would have got there in the end.

The backdrop to everything we were doing was the finances at the club. It speaks for itself that a Championship football club will have a very different budget to that of a League 1 club.

The payroll will be entirely different and that adjustment needs to be made pretty quickly or you can be in big trouble. You only need to look at the financial aspects of the television money to know that you can't afford to carry the same level of expenditure you had previously. It just doesn't add up.

So we had to take a knife to the payroll and at the same time try to raise money through the transfer market. We sold some really brilliant talent; the likes of Danny Mayor, Paul Coutts, Jamie Proctor, Adam Barton all went.

We had some exceptional talent at the club that there were suitors for and those lads went out the door.

Beyond that, it was just a very expensive payroll with lads that were above the pay grade for a League 1 club, so part of my remit was to tackle that.

It was about a new approach and a new culture, so partly we turned a necessity into an opportunity by bringing in players who had a different outlook to being at a club like Preston.

It was clear from the outset that there was a problem with the squad - you just had to look at the results. Darren Ferguson was a winning manager who had struggled with the squad, Phil Brown was a winning manager who had struggled with the squad and I like to think of myself as a winning manager who struggled initially with that squad.

It needed to change.

You can pussyfoot around, but I wasn't there to pussyfoot around. This was my big break. This was a job that I intended to succeed at.

If you were being critical of me, you could say I didn't show enough appreciation of the consequences of taking a knife to the thing. Critics may say I did the job, but I didn't do it with enough sensitivity.

But there were so many players with such a losing habit that I just had to act. I'd come from an environment where all we'd done was win. That's what we had to create.

It wasn't about 'me or them' or 'me versus them'. Not in my mind anyway.

It was about Preston North End FC and the direction the club was going in as opposed to the direction it wanted to go in.

At some point in a downward spiral, you have to hit the brakes and take action to turn the thing around.

The club can't keep being dragged down and down. It was my job to stop that and looking at what's happened since, I think I achieved that.

One of the phrases I've used many times is *'attitude is more important than ability'* and I think that can sometimes be misunderstood.

Ability is what you need to succeed. It's a major part of winning.

But I think attitude makes an exponential difference to whatever ability you've got. Let me give you an example. In 1959, Formula 1 driver Jack Brabham was leading on the last lap of the last race of the season, the Sebring Grand Prix. Four hundred yards from the finish, his engine packed in and the car rolled to stop.

Now, he didn't jump out of the car and throw his helmet to the ground in a strop. He jumped out and started pushing it up the hill.

Other cars went past him, but he managed to push that car up the hill and over the line and finished in fourth place.

And that fourth place was enough to make him World Champion.

Now, Jack Brabham was a top class driver. His ability took him to the brink of being World Champion. But he actually became World Champion because of his attitude. He didn't sit around and moan about bad luck. He did what he could do and he did what he needed to do to create victory.

So when I emphasise about attitude being more important than ability, that's what I'm talking about.

Making the decisions to go the extra mile; to do more than the next man. So whatever ability you've got, you get the very best out of yourself.

A big part of the attitude I look for in players is the ability to self-appraise - and to do it honestly. To work out where they are strong and where they need to improve. I'm looking for players who will work to create that environment for improvement and players who have got the capacity to identify and act on the changes that need to be made.

On top of that, they've got to have the ambition to push themselves to be the best that they can be. Working with people who have those qualities inspires me.

That's what I look for in players and I think when I look at the players I brought in to Preston, the majority of them had those attributes.

They weren't satisfied; they were hungry, ambitious and a lot of them - not all, but a lot - have gone on to be great acquisitions for Preston, or at least have success at other clubs.

At Stevenage, we had a lot of players like that and we were a real unit. Everyone bought into it and there was a clarity of purpose.

What I found when I came to Preston was that the nature of the team I put out had to be different from what we'd had at Stevenage. And I only really realised the reason for that after I'd done my initial recruitment.

Because what made the big difference was . . . the pitch.

The playing surface at Deepdale was among the biggest in England. So it becomes even more important on a big playing area like that to control possession.

If I made a mistake, it was probably around the fact that I recruited players with great attitudes and physical qualities, but I didn't quite recruit enough players who could help us dominate possession. I didn't quite bring in enough ability to allow us to control the game, especially at home.

If I'd have gone on longer in the job, I'd have looked to add that extra tier of ball-playing ability alongside the athleticism you need on a pitch of that size.

That way we could have pressed and used our defensive attributes without the ball, but then also controlled the game when we had possession.

Some people have asked why we didn't look at changing the dimensions of the pitch, but I don't think that's what the club is all about. The club is bigger than that. Our pitch is our pitch, we are what we are. It's a very traditional club and I don't think messing with the size of the pitch is something that would go down well. My take on it was: 'Let's crack on and be the best we can be.'

And a big part of that was working hard on the training pitch.

Now, I make no apologies for my approach to training; if you want to be successful in any walk of life you have to work hard. It's as simple as that.

I break my training programme down into several core parts; firstly, there are technical, tactical and teamship skills. Firstly, footballers need to work on *technical* aspects of the game if they are going to become better players.

If you're a full-back, you're going to throw the ball maybe 20 times in a game - so learn to throw the ball properly. You'd be amazed how many players from one game to the next don't throw the football in properly.

They just throw it back into the game. Well, I'm not a believer in that. I'm a believer in doing everything you can better, learning that skill properly and acting to disciplines every time you play. That's not unreasonable - that's common sense.

Tactical is learning the way we want to play for the game that's coming up. Some of that is in a classroom, on a whiteboard, watching videos; some of it is out on the grass.

Teamship is seeing how people work together; maybe giving them a task completely away from football and seeing how they share ideas and communicate. Then there are *personal*, *professional* and *physical* elements.

You want players who are happy in their lives; you want to know where they live, how home life is, what they do in their spare time, etc and that's very much about one-to-one conversations in informal settings.

Professionalism comes down to detail, preparing properly for the games ahead. If you're a corner taker, have you studied the dimensions of the pitch and factored that into how you'll strike the ball? Have you checked what stud the pitch is going to take? Have you got the right studs in the bag?

These sound like the sort of basics you'd assume every player gets their heads round - but often they don't.

And then on a physical level; it's about having players that know how to fuel right, whose muscle mass is right. A gym to me isn't there to be stared at, it's there to be used. I believe in putting the hard yards in to make sure players are in the best physical shape to succeed.

At Stevenage, we had one training pitch, a few little astroturf pitches we had access to, a changing room and a little dance studio. That's not unusual for the level Stevenage had been at.

We used to pull weights out of a cupboard and do them in the rain if needs be.

And yet we were in sixth place when I left and Preston were well down the table having lost 11 out of their last 13 games when I arrived.

Springfields felt luxurious by comparison. So, I was quite happy with the facilities. They were what they were. There were pitches, there were balls, gyms, an indoor five-a-side court, it was great.

The only thing I didn't like was the row after row of beds we had in the massage room. It's a football club, not a health club.

Never mind getting your legs pampered, how about getting out there in the rain and training with the rest of the lads?

I think the most uncomfortable place in a football club should be the treatment room. I don't believe that players should have any incentive to be away from training. Obviously, no player wants to be injured, but I believe they should be given every encouragement to get back out on the grass. I'm just not one for a comfortable treatment room. That's always been my stance.

There's also been talk of asking players to lift 'imaginary weights' and I'm genuinely not sure where that comes from.

Maybe there were stretching exercises that resembled those movements, but clearly you can't lift an imaginary weight, so it's a new one on me.

Sounds like another case of *'don't believe everything you hear'*.

Having said that, every manager at every level has their own psychological approach. There's nothing complicated about my psychological approach (and, no, it doesn't involve imaginary weights).

I did a piece of work when I was younger with Daley Thompson, a World and Olympic Decathlon champion. I actually wrote a book with him that was on world class performance.

I was absolutely staggered when I met Daley and learned things about him and his mentality. His dedication to achieving success took my breath away. The amount of hours he spent on the training ground was absolutely astonishing.

He would camp in the hillside in Germany to try and get a glimpse of his opponents in training; to learn their best practices and integrate them into his own regime. When you're in the company of a genuine World Champion like that, it shapes your mindset of what you are prepared to do to be successful.

When I arrived at Preston, I'd come from a club that had won at Wembley, won a championship, gone to Old Trafford and won a play-off final.

We'd smashed Sheffield Wednesday 5-1 at home, beaten Sheffield United, knocked Premier League Newcastle out of the FA Cup - we were winning football matches by doing whatever it took. It was a combined effort; everyone in the camp had the same mentality; how can we learn, how can we develop, what can we do more of to be the best we can possibly be?

That was the culture we had and that's always been my mindset.

If I'd have brought Daley up to Preston when I first arrived he'd have asked me what the hell I was doing there.

The attitude was so far away from one that he'd want to be involved with that I wouldn't even have insulted him by asking him.

It was so far removed from what I'd come from and that was difficult, very difficult. But of course, you can't always see things from the outside looking in.

I remember after we lost 3-1 at home to Brentford, the fans were really having a go at me as I walked off the pitch.

I was the manager so I took it on the chin. I actually enjoyed the passion they had - even if those passions were anger and frustration.

You've got to walk right into the corner to get to the tunnel at Deepdale and by the time I got there, the Town End was in full voice, letting me know exactly what they thought. And do you know what?

I loved it.

I didn't love the fact we'd got beat - I hated that.

But I loved the passion of those Preston fans. I actually slowed down to take it all in. They gave me absolute pelters; people were throwing coins and all sorts of abuse was coming in.

When that happens, you've just got to take it, lock it away and use it as motivation to turn it around. Down the line, when you give these people success, that low point could be used positively as a marker.

I went away and had a long, hard look at myself, but I knew deep down I wasn't the problem.

There was a much bigger picture that not everyone could see.

So I had to stay strong in that first season. I had to do a lot of thinking outside the box, to try and steady the ship and get results.

For example, we brought Aaron Brown in on a free transfer from Aldershot and he played a few games for us at centre half; a big strong athletic lad, very good in the air. The Saturday after that game I took got stick from the crowd, we played Sheffield Wednesday away and I decided to play him up front.

I can't remember my exact thought process going into that selection, but bear in mind we'd just been hammered at home in the previous game, so changes were perhaps inevitable.

It also probably had something to do with the fact Wednesday used a lot of set plays and his extra height would be useful to us at both ends of the pitch.

Now, for some people, playing a defender up front was a *no-no.*

For me, there's no such thing as a *no-no.*

I look at what I think will help us win the game and I act on it.

It wasn't that long before the game at Hillsborough that I'd played Darius Charles - a defender, who is still playing in the Championship - up front for Stevenage in a play-off final and he'd set up John Mousinho for the winner that clinched promotion.

Trust me, no-one was complaining about a defender playing up front that day!

The other thing that happened at Hillsborough, as everyone reading this will probably remember, is that the Wednesday staff told me they had heard about our team selection the day before - from a member of our own squad.

Well . . . that says it all doesn't it?

I think it summed up how things were. You can't have that in a football club can you? It's just wrong on every single level.

Whether I should have put it out there after the match depends on your view, but I wanted to be transparent with the supporters about the issues I was dealing with. I wanted the fans to understand the situation and see some of the reasons why the team wasn't winning.

Lads that weren't involved in it didn't get upset about it. Their feelings were the same as mine. It's just not on and we couldn't have it.

As a club, we didn't even try to find out who was behind it. I think it spoke for itself. There was no action taken. It was what it was.

It wasn't anything anyone could ever take pride in - just the opposite in fact.

It was just something else that we had to move past, yet another illustration of the situation at the club. So you've got to tackle these things in phases.

Obviously, everything was interlinked, but the thing that was most pressing was sorting the wage bill out. That was made very clear to me; we had to reduce it by sixty to seventy per cent. Once we'd stayed up in that first season and I'd got to the summer, it was then a question of moving people on.

I think out of 37 players, we kept the goalkeeper, a kid and Bailey Wright.

That's a hell of a task, but it needed to be done.

There were some players we wanted to move on and they just wouldn't move.

We put them away from the squad and made it clear to them that for the sake of their careers, they had to go. Their future lay elsewhere, but they were still hanging around.

It wasn't ideal, but it had to be done. We were bringing in good players and I wanted a clean break with what had gone before.

Aside from the balance between athleticism and ability on the ball that I mentioned earlier, a mistake in the summer recruitment was that I ended up with a squad where there was almost too much competition in every position.

In a way, we were almost too successful.

That was a real mistake by me and I only came to realise it later on.

For example, if you've got two good left backs - Scott Laird and Dave Buchanan - they BOTH want to play football.

Whichever one you don't select is going to have the needle.

And I didn't just have that in one position, I had positions all over the pitch where there was very little between Player A and Player B.

They say having to pick one is a 'good problem' for a manager to have, but there are repercussions to whatever decision you make.

When you've got too many senior players around, there are too many players who deserve to be playing but they're not, so a bit of resentment starts to creep in.

The way I recruited my squad over that summer, in hindsight, I got the balance wrong.

I got good lads in, good players in, but I probably lost a few of them along the way, not because of anything personal, but just because they wanted to play football and I couldn't give them the number of games that they wanted to play.

I felt for them, I really did. I knew in my heart that it was wrong that they weren't getting first team football.

Now, I hadn't actually promised them a shirt when I recruited them, but they were joining on the basis that they were going to get in the side. I understand that.

When they didn't get in the side, you've got a lot of good players in the background who are becoming unhappy.

You think to yourself that having good players in reserve is a nice position to have, but when eventually there's an injury and you call these lads in, you can detect a little bit of a grimace behind the joy of getting in the team. Yes, they always wanted to be professional and do a good job, but if their heart isn't in it because they're not quite believing in you because you've not quite believed in them, that can cause problems.

Admittedly it sounds counter-intuitive, but I recruited too many good players who expected to be playing, who I then couldn't give games to, because you can only put eleven out on the pitch. So that was a mistake.

I was at Preston, a big club, so I had the ability to attract players - good players - and I probably recruited too many at that senior level. I should have relied a little bit more on the youth and up-and-coming lads to fill out my squad.

That way you avoid the resentment that can maybe build up when senior experienced professionals aren't getting a game.

Let me pause here to mention one senior professional who epitomised everything good about Preston North End.

Graham Alexander had been brought in by Phil Brown and was right at the end of his brilliant career. He'd been out injured for a long time and probably thought he'd played his last game months earlier, before I'd arrived at the club.

But I just thought it was fitting and right for him to bow out at Deepdale in front of the Preston fans who absolutely adored him. Graham had been superb behind the scenes ever since I arrived and for him to go on in that game against Charlton and score that free kick right at the end . . . *wow*.

I mean, it's just the stuff of fairy tales and I was absolutely delighted.

Getting Graham out there that day was all about him, not me, and I could not have been happier with the way it worked out.

He's a tremendous professional, a tremendous man and it was fitting that he got that send-off that day. It also says a lot that he was physically ready to go out there, in good enough shape to still go on and not look out of place, despite being out injured for so long.

When I'd gone to Preston, I thought it was the right thing to do to bring my coaching team from Stevenage with me; we all had the same goal, we'd worked together very well and having your own backroom team obviously helps get your message across.

But when I arrived I was so, so impressed with Graham's coaching. I knew straight away that he was going to go on and be a successful manager in his own right. He had a way with the players and his sessions were so interesting. I used to go out after First Team training and watch him working with a few of the lads who weren't in the squad and it was always worth watching.

Those sessions kept me interested, as a bystander, so clearly the players were going to be taking his work on board. I've got a huge respect for Graham as a man and as a coach and I could see exactly where his career was going to take him. It's no surprise to see he's gone on and had success and I hope it continues.

Back on the transfer front, we missed out on a couple of players, but that happens to every manager and I never worry about signings that don't happen.

I don't have any regrets about players we didn't sign. You just get on with it and move on. In general, I was happy with the players we brought in that summer.

When you think lads like Jack King and Keith Keane played 60 or 70 games for the club and always did well, Scotty Laird played more than 100 games, Nicky

Wroe had a couple of good seasons, Stuart Beavon played 60-odd games and was a good player - all these lads were brought in for either free transfers (or a very low fee for Bevs) so there was plenty of good business in there.

No manager has a 100 per cent success rate with transfers and there were one or two that didn't come off as well as we would have liked, but those players weren't around for long.

Compare that with John Welsh, 160-odd appearances and a Player of the Year, Joe Garner another Player of the Year and Paul Huntington, still playing all these years later with 300-plus appearances and another Player of the Year.

These were all huge assets for Preston North End Football Club that I brought in over a very short space of time.

And they were all signed on frees. A few years later, Joe went to Rangers for £1 million -plus, so there were some good deals done over that period.

There's a lot said about recruitment, but look at the big picture and there's another story there, if people choose to see things objectively.

And we started that next season well. I think we were hard to beat and you could see the side taking on this new identity. We only lost two of our first ten games and although we were a work in progress, we were taking shape quite well. But the night it all changed for me was towards the end of November.

Scott Laird got injured right at the end of a game against Notts County at Deepdale and I walked off that night with two dreads; firstly that Scotty had broken his leg.

Now, he was 24 at the time, playing superbly and maybe on the cusp of a Scotland call-up. He'd been brilliant since he arrived - another one on a free - and was cut down in a poor challenge that deservedly got a red card.

It was devastating because Scotty had the quality to drive an entire team forward from left-back; that's how good he was.

His impact from that position could be felt all over the pitch because of his quality, his vision and the range of his passing.

His set plays were brilliant at one end and his marking was outstanding at the other; so in an attacking and a defensive style, Lairdy gave us something extra.

The game ended 0-0 and, as well as my concern for Scott, I knew that this left me without both my first choice full-backs for the foreseeable future.

Keith Keane was the other full-back and he'd come off in that game too, so I could see that was a massive problem for us. Keano was a midfielder playing at full-back, but he had the quality and the physical attributes to perform in either position, no problem at all.

On a points per game indices, those two were absolutely vital.

With them out, I felt their influence would be missed and I was right. The new team had been progressing well and was starting to really come together as a unit.

In that team, Keith and Scott were two cornerstones that I really didn't want to lose. As I walked off the pitch that night, I just knew there were going to be difficulties ahead.

That was down to me to find a solution of course and I had some good players to bring in, but that night was the start of things going wrong.

The team wasn't resilient enough to cope with the substantial change of losing those two at that point.

That's not about individuals, it's more the team as a unit hadn't had time to build up the strength to cope with the loss of those two key components.

The dynamic of a team evolves over time and that night knocked us off our axis to a degree.

We'd had some great results up to that point; we'd beaten Huddersfield who had just been promoted to the Championship, we'd beaten Palace 4-1 in a game where Wilfried Zaha played for them, we'd tonked Hartlepool 5-0 at Deepdale.

We'd gone down to Stevenage and put four past them, we'd put four past Swindon, so there were some good things going on.

Another problem was that John Mousinho, my captain, was out at the time too, so he wasn't there to hold things together.

So we became a little bit ragged; we were a new team, now missing several key elements and it doesn't always run smoothly when you're starting out.

I'd have got it back on track in time, absolutely no question about that.

But when you're a football manager, time is always a precious commodity.

After that Notts County game, we went on a run where we drew quite a few matches, then went out of the FA Cup narrowly at Millwall 1-0 before losing a crazy Johnstone's Paint Trophy game at Coventry where we were 2-1 up after 89 minutes and ended up losing 3-2.

That was Joe Garner's first game for us, having arrived from Watford and the following week, I freshened things up again by giving Ben Davies his debut in a league game when we played Coventry (again) at Deepdale.

It was a bit of a gamble on a 17-year-old lad, but I knew the team needed that injection and he was clearly such a good player it was a calculated risk.

You could argue that gamble didn't pay off straight away, but further down the line, I'm pretty sure the club is glad that I blooded Ben's talent at a young age.

For me, he was always going to succeed because of his drive and his attitude as well as his ability. He had absolutely everything right and he's worked hard to improve and get to the point where he's another one that came through during my time who has been the club's Player of the Year and a huge asset for the club.

At the time though, in his second game, Ben gave away an injury time penalty at home to Shrewsbury that ended up with us losing 2-1 at Deepdale in a game we'd been winning at half-time.

By that point, the crowd had started to turn on me and that defeat was a real hammer blow. The atmosphere as I was walking off the pitch was pretty toxic to say the least. It was like the Brentford game all over again.

But I have no complaints about the crowd that day - or any day.

That's Preston, that's passion.

In a way, that's what I'd signed up for - just not in that sense!

I'd brought in Declan Rudd on loan from Norwich towards the end of January and he was another nice young kid with great ability, who has since returned to the club and played 200-plus games. He'd been on the bench for a couple of games before we went down to Yeovil for a midweek game.

Thorsten Stuckmann had been Number 1 and was a good keeper, but Dec came in for his debut that night and I had no worries about him at all.

I didn't think it was make or break that night, because at no point did I think I wouldn't be able to turn things round.

I never doubted that we would get there in the end and I thought there was general acknowledgement that getting through that initial phase was going to be the most difficult period. I'd only been at the club just over a year and I think we had made progress in that time.

The only thing that stands in my mind from that night at Yeovil was something that happened before the game. I saw Peter and another director Kevin Abbott at the hotel before the game and I remember them exchanging some cryptic words.

Kevin said something like 'I hope you know what you're doing' and Peter replied: 'Well, I hope so.'

I looked at Peter and he was sort of staring into space and I remember thinking: 'That's odd.'

It wasn't like Peter at all. No more was said and obviously, we lost the game 3-1 having been leading with about 20 minutes to go.

It was a disappointing result, but it wasn't a terrible performance and they got a goal in injury time that put more of a gloss on what had been a fairly tight match.

My son was at the game, so he gave me a lift back to London afterwards and I got a text message from Peter asking to meet up the following morning.

So the next day, we sat down in Carluccio's in Waterloo Station and Peter told me that, effectively, the owner had lost patience. I said 'OK' and that was that, really.

It reminded me a bit of when Wilf McGuinness was called in by the Manchester United board and told: 'You work so hard, we don't know what we'd do without you.' Before he could say 'thanks' the chairman said: ' . . . but we're going to give it a try.'

So that was the end, on the 13th of February, thirteen months after I joined the club on Friday the 13th. Look, I understand that the results weren't there in the short term, I get that. I'm not naive - football is a results business.

But we were putting down foundations and these things happen in stages; you don't build a solid house overnight.

I never believe I'm going to fail in anything I'm doing - I always believe I will find the answers. And I could see the answers at Preston.

I knew that things weren't good enough when the end came, but I also knew that I was only a season into being there; half a season at the back end of the previous one and then half a season again.

I knew that a 37 per cent loss record over that period wasn't good enough, but I knew it was better than what had gone before and it had been achieved against a challenging backdrop where we'd put a lot of things right behind the scenes.

I'd cut the budget, moved a lot of players on and brought a lot of good players in. Injuries had hindered progress however and in the short-term, the results hadn't been there.

So there were a lot of mixed emotions when we had that meeting at Waterloo.

I knew where we needed to go, so I was gutted that I didn't have the chance to crack on and see the job through.

There was this huge sense of disappointment that this thing that I'd loved, that I'd devoted so much time and energy to, wasn't going to be part of my life any more.

It wasn't so much a sense of disappointment at the club for sacking me, more a sense that I wasn't going to be able to be part of the journey the club was going to take. But there was also great pride in having been part of this great club and the job that I'd done.

Previously, Peter and I had talked about Preston North End in the Premier League and the long, hard slog on the road ahead.

I wanted to be on that journey every step of the way, to be at the club forever and give those fans what they deserved. Sadly, it wasn't to be.

No complaints though; I can't say I wasn't given a fair crack at it because I knew the parameters I would have to work with from the start.

We had to take £4 million to £5 million off the wage bill and we achieved that, but it was never going to be easy. I look back and think maybe there were one or two things I could have done differently, as I've outlined here.

Would they have made things a little bit different for me in the end?

Who knows?

What I do know is that I can look myself in the mirror and say I gave it my all.

That's what I ask of my players and that's what I ask of myself.

What I also know is that Simon Grayson after me and then Alex Neil were able to build on the foundations that were put in place while I was there.

They inherited a platform where a lot of the dirty work had been done.

If there's a legacy I left the club with, it's the work that they've been able to build promotion on and then maintain a very good standard in the Championship.

Someone had to build the foundations and I think I certainly played my part in that. Bolton slipped into League 2 before they started their upward climb.

Preston didn't. Because somebody stopped the rot.

I know that I played my part in Preston's resurgence. And despite the negativity towards me, I would run from London to Deepdale to sit in that hot seat again.

I loved the job, I loved the people, I loved the club.

CHAPTER 11

RICKY HEPPOLETTE: HAVING A BALL

When I was a young lad growing up in Bolton, I saw a spaceman - a creature from another planet. (I bet that's not how you expected a chapter in a football book to start, did you?)

But it's true. Well, sort of.

I was on a bus going past Burnden Park, the old Bolton Wanderers ground, and there he was. A man mountain, a beast, something out of this world . . . it was Nat Lofthouse himself.

More than that, he was waiting for the bus - *my bus!* - and the next thing I knew, he was getting on. The driver took one look at him and said: 'Nat, you don't need to pay - have this one on me.'

Nat thanked the fella and then came and sat just a few feet in front of me while I just stared, open-mouthed. I daren't speak to him of course. I just marvelled.

To be up close to THE Nat Lofthouse, England's centre forward, the Lion of Vienna, well, I remember it to this day. It might sound funny now, but back then the world's best footballers were playing in front of 53,000 on a Saturday and getting on the bus with us 'normal folk' during the week.

If you'd have said 'Lamborghini' to them they'd have thought it was Italian food!

I heard Tom Finney would sometimes walk to the ground with the Preston supporters - it was a different world. My dad would take us to watch Bolton and when the ground got too full, there would be an announcement over the Tannoy: 'Would parents please pass all the small children to the front.'

And us kids would be lifted up over the crowd to the cinder track round the pitch. It was idyllic really and I loved growing up in those times, even if my start in life was somewhere a long way away.

I was born in Bhusawal, India, into an Anglo-Indian family in 1949 - we had English relatives on my mother's side. It was a turbulent time in Indian history and when I was four, my parents thought it would be better - and safer - to move to England, so we came over as a family to Bolton.

I started playing football at school and made it into the school team and then the Bolton boys team. Not only was I the only Asian lad in the side, I was probably one of a very small number in the town. But I never had any problems from people about that. I was just one of the young lads and treated the same as everyone else - it was never a problem for me as a child.

(Years later I was interviewed by the legendary sports writer Brian Glanville who was amazed to hear I'd not suffered racism growing up. In the end I just

said: 'Well, maybe one or two people were nasty to me, Brian . . . but I was just too thick to notice!')

As I got older, I started getting offers for trials up and down the country - the first one being down at Southampton, where the legendary Ted Bates was manager. They wanted to sign me, but I was only 14 or 15 and I'd gone down on my own. I wasn't there that long and I was homesick - it was just so far away; where were the mills, the factories, the chimney pots?

So I declined that and went back home to beautiful Bolton.

Other clubs came in for me - Sheffield Wednesday and Manchester City - but all I really wanted was a call from Bolton Wanderers that never came.

Nevertheless, all this attention convinced me that when I left school, I would be a footballer - there was no doubt in my mind. I didn't have a back-up plan, I knew it was going to be football.

Football was my life. I used to eat standing up so I could get out of the house quicker to get to school and start playing.

We'd be there at 7am and play until the bell went at 8.30am, by which time, we'd often be wet through - this was Lancashire weather don't forget (and 1950s coats). In the end, they stopped us going to school until 8am so that we wouldn't be quite so drenched, but it didn't really stop us playing every minute we could.

Preston North End had been watching me and, with no word from Bolton still, Deepdale was close to home and PNE was a very good club.

So when they got in touch, I jumped at the offer - and never regretted it. I joined in the summer of 1964, just a few weeks after they'd lost in the FA Cup Final.

Jimmy Milne was the manager; a nice man, quite quiet and often smoking a pipe when he spoke to you, big clouds of tobacco smoke following him around.

Not that we saw much of him, of course, the First Team was still a dream for us youngsters starting out as apprentices and we had to know our place. We'd do any job that needed doing; cleaning toilets, sweeping up - you name it, we did it.

One time, the old curved West Stand roof needed tarring so we were sent up there on ladders with these big buckets of tar and brushes and told to get on with it. (And, no, there wasn't much health and safety around back then!)

None of us ever complained - it was just normal. We were lucky to be at a football club and whatever they told you to do, you did it, no questions asked.

It was great. We were playing football for a living and life was wonderful. We got paid £7-a-week and that was a decent wage.

I was lucky because there was a First Team player called Malcolm Woods who lived in Bolton and he used to give me a lift every day.

At 17 I'd saved up a bit of money and got a car, so I used to pick John McMahon up at Bolton station (he lived in Manchester) and take him into training. Everyone mucked in together and there was a real spirit about the place.

Howard Kendall was there and he was only a couple of years older than us boys.

Even though he was in the First Team and had played at Wembley, he was great with us and he'd buy us apprentices a bottle of milk each after training when we'd sit around talking.

Occasionally, we'd see Tom Finney around the place and again, he was so nice to us. We were absolutely in awe of him, of course, so whenever he spoke, we just listened - and stared at him wide-eyed, like he was from a different planet. (Nat Lofthouse all over again!) Like I say, they were great days - but it wasn't all plain sailing.

I thought I was doing well, but as I came towards the end of my apprenticeship, the manager (it was Bobby Seith by then) called me into his office. He didn't say anything at first, so I just sat there wondering what was going on. He was looking down at these bits of paper on his desk and shaking his head, not looking very pleased at all.

'Ahhhh Ricky,' he said, 'I don't think we're going to keep you on.'

I didn't know where to put myself. I just sat there, stunned.

Meanwhile, he carried on like he was agonising over this decision: *'Ohhhh . . . Mmmm . . . No, I don't think you've done enough . . . I just can't do it . . . You've not got the height . . . You've not got the speed . . . Not enough skill . . . I don't think we're going to take you on.'*

And so it went on, telling me all this stuff about how I wasn't good enough. I just sat there, not saying a word, but churning up inside.

I thought I'd been doing well! I couldn't believe it and went home and told my dad they wanted to get rid of me.

Now, my Dad was brilliant with me all through my childhood; him and Mum came to every game and that carried on into my professional career. He was my Number One fan and he was as taken aback as I was.

He said: 'Well son, you've still got about five months left on your apprenticeship, give it everything you've got and let's see what happens.'

Well, that's what I did and five months later, I got called in again.

There on the desk was a professional contract for me to sign.

I was absolutely thrilled and I asked Bobby Seith what had changed his mind.

'Oh, I didn't change my mind really,' he said. 'I give that little talk to lots of young lads to see how they react.

'Some let it crush them and then I know they haven't got what it takes, whereas others push themselves even harder and they're the ones we take on.' That was an early lesson in football managers' psychology at the time - make of it what you will!

Part of the contract was the wonderful bonuses on offer; £4 for a win, £2 for a draw. The big time!

It went up a bit over the years, but North End started putting clauses in that meant bonuses depended on where we were in the league, which was fair enough, I suppose. It was about the same as everywhere else.

What I remember is that you got a £10 signing-on fee - and it was £10 for a reason.

Because when you became a professional, you had to have a club blazer, with this beautiful embroidered PNE badge on it.

It really was smart and you felt like the bee's knees wearing it, but the club didn't buy the blazer for you - you had to pay for it yourself.

Guess how much it cost?

Not long after that, Bobby gave me my debut, coming on as a substitute against Middlesbrough at Deepdale in 1967.

George Lyall came off just after half-time and I went on - I can't remember much about it other than we drew 2-2, I think. It was just great to get out there and play at such a young age. It must have been around the 1967/68 season and I'd only have been about 18 years old.

North End were in the old Second Division then - Championship level now - and Bobby was very good to me. He was very articulate as a manager; a deep thinker. When he spoke, you listened.

He was a Scot who had played for Dundee in the European Cup semi-final against AC Milan *(yes, Dundee!)*.

He was always well dressed and I always felt like I was learning from him. He played me quite a bit after I'd made my debut so I racked up plenty of games at a young age - not bad for someone 'too small, too slow and not enough skill', eh boss?

I had to pick things up fast though - and it was a tough learning curve at times. Sometimes, VERY tough.

In 1969, we played Chelsea in the FA Cup and drew 0-0 at Deepdale. They had a hell of a team; Peter 'The Cat' Bonetti, Ron 'Chopper' Harris, Peter Osgood, Charlie Cooke - all top players and Chelsea legends still.

In the replay at Stamford Bridge, we were losing 2-0 and it could have been 30-0 - we were heading for a right hammering. Anyway, as luck would have it, a fire broke out in a floodlight box and all the lights went out. Complete darkness - match abandoned and a real let-off for us.

They couldn't fix the lights so we had to play the following Tuesday afternoon at 2pm (36,000 still turned up to watch). This time, we were much better and went 1-0 up. Well, the pitch was atrocious and it was in the days when you could do slide tackles from about 20 yards away, clear out the ball *and* the man and the ref would just say: 'Play on!'

If you did catch someone badly, the ref might say: 'Don't do that again.'

'Sorry, ref.'

And that was that. No yellow cards in those days. You had to do something really bad to get sent off and if someone was given their marching orders, it was headline news: *'Player sent off in football match.'*

(Not like today where they give red cards for the slightest touch.)

Anyway, I was only 19 or so and had no fear, so I went in for this slide tackle and slid and slid until - *bam!* - I got the ball.

A great tackle I thought, and as a bonus, I'd got the defender as well.

He went flying up in the air and as he came down to earth with a splat I suddenly realised: 'Oh blimey - it's Chopper Harris!'

Now, for younger readers, Ron Harris wasn't known as 'Chopper' for his sweet and forgiving nature. The clue really is in the name.

He wasn't happy and he just looked at me like I was his dinner. Brave (or stupid) me, I just stood there and looked back at him. His head swivelled side to side as he had a quick glance to see if anyone was watching and then - *bang!* - he punched me right in the nose.

It didn't half hurt, but I still stood up to him and he said: 'Son, you don't mess with Ron Harris.' Or words to that effect!

I think I was that taken aback I even apologised to HIM before slinking away. I couldn't believe that no-one had seen it, but the game had just carried on. Anyway, Chelsea scored two right at the very end and we went out after giving them a right scare.

Afterwards, I met up with my parents who'd gone down for the game and my mum was furious: 'He hit you didn't he!'

She was the only person who saw it in the whole ground and luckily the Chelsea man wasn't around after the game. You might not mess with Ron Harris - but you definitely didn't mess with my mum!

Funnily enough, I met Ron quite a few times later on in life and he was always very nice off the pitch.

I reminded him about the day he punched me, but he said: *'I'm sorry Ricky, I hit so many people in my career, I can't remember them all!'*

Either way, North End started to struggle a bit and despite having a team featuring Alan Kelly, George Ross, Alan Spavin and Graham Hawkins, we were relegated to the Third Division for the first time in the club's history in 1970.

Bobby Seith went and at the start of the new decade, Alan Ball Senior took over. To call Bally 'a bit of a character' doesn't do the term justice - at all.

Bally was also the father of World Cup winner Alan Ball and if you ever met him, he may have mentioned this once or twice (in the first five minutes!).

Right from the minute he walked through the door at Deepdale he sat us down as a team and told us: 'Right, you are going to win the Third Division title this year.'

There was no messing about - he was convinced that we were going to do it. Our end of the bargain was just to do everything he said. One of the first things he did was bring in Arthur Cox as trainer and that was a masterstroke.

Arthur was hard as nails and a real Sergeant Major for us; very strict, short cropped hair, very tough. Small, but fearsome. As a person, he was a lovely man and very knowledgeable, too - going on to manage Newcastle United and Derby County (he signed me later on in my career for Chesterfield).

But he used to wear the tightest tracksuit bottoms you've ever seen - anyone who remembers the comedian Max Wall will know what I mean - and the lads used to take the mickey out of him for that. Just not in his earshot though!

He took most of the training and Bally was more of a tactician, a motivator and another exponent of football's mind games.

He was like a classic bloke you'd meet in the pub in many ways; he loved to tell a story, he loved to chase women and he liked a drink.

I don't know how it started, but a bottle of whisky appeared in the dressing room before every match and everyone had a tot just before we went out. Now, I didn't drink at all in those days so I was in a bit of a quandary.

So I used to take a swig, but hold it in my mouth and as we came out of the tunnel and the fans roared, I used to gulp it down - then the heat of the whisky and the noise of the crowd really gave me a lift before kick-off.

It's funny really, when you think about it now, but it was a ritual for the team at the time. I don't know if it helped me a lot, because I was always uptight before games. I'd laugh and joke at the ground, but the moment I went in the dressing room, no-one could speak to me. I was getting ready for battle.

The manager could talk directly to me and I'd just nod. I didn't want to talk or have anything upset my mindset. Going up the little tunnel at Deepdale was like a boxer getting into the ring. The fans leaning over the side, the sun behind the Town End, the smells, the shouts, I loved it all.

I remember not long after Bally came in, my contract was up and in those days, you had to go to the manager to see about it. I was in the First Team by then and thought I was doing OK, so I thought I'd ask for a rise. I knocked on his door and Bally bawled: *'Who is it? Come in. What do you want?'*

All very sharp. Just like that. He was quite blunt at times.

I went in and he was there at this big desk and right behind him was this huge photograph of Alan Ball Junior in his playing kit. I mentioned that my contract was up and I might be due a rise, as I was playing so often.

I could tell he wasn't impressed. He pointedly looked at the poster of his son, then turned to me and asked: 'What have you done in your career?'

Before I could answer, he went on: 'By the time my son was your age he'd played in the First Division, been a club captain, played for England, etc etc.'

I thought 'OK' and said nothing.

Bally leaned forward and went on: 'So tell me - what have *you* done?'

I was stumped: 'When you put it like that . . . nothing, boss.'

'Well, sod off then.'

(Only he didn't say 'sod off' - it was a bit stronger than that!)

And that was that. Contract talks over.

A couple of weeks later, a new deal arrived through the post with a £5 rise and I was just glad to sign it. Clearly, it was non-negotiable!

Don't get me wrong, I liked Bally a lot. He was a character that could fill a room as soon as he walked in and we kept in touch long after I finished playing at Preston. Some people couldn't take to him, but I don't tend to fall out with people and we got on well. Of course, I had run-ins with him at times, over little things in games, but he didn't mind that.

If you had an opinion and could back it up, he'd listen. (If it was a good idea, he would use it. Then, of course, it would become *his* good idea!)

But if you ever had a row with him, once everything was over, it was done with, forgotten about.

On the pitch, his first season was one of the most enjoyable of my entire career. He lived in Bolton and if ever there were any functions to go to, I'd pick him and young Alan and drive them across, so I got to know him quite well.

Bally used to take me, George Lyall and Archie Gemmill to Everton if North End didn't have a game and get us to watch Howard Kendall, Colin Harvey and his son play in midfield.

He'd say: 'See that, lads? THAT'S how to play football.'

Well, we *wanted* to play like that - nice neat passes and movement - but when it came to Preston, it wasn't that straightforward.

Back then, the emphasis for defenders was always 'clear your lines' so they would hoof the ball up the pitch as far as they could. Job done.

Willie Cunningham was reserve team coach and had been a hard-as-nails full-back - thou shall not pass at any cost.

As soon as you got it, he'd shout: 'Kick it! Get rid!'

And that's what you had to do. This approach made its way into the First Team and most teams we played against were exactly the same.

Well, Alan Spavin wasn't having any of that. He rebelled. He wanted to take a touch. Get the ball down. Pick a pass. Find a man.

At first, Bally took Willie Cunningham's side and suddenly there was a lot of criticism coming Spavvy's way: 'He's no pace. He slows us down. He doesn't fit in, etc.'

It was a load of rubbish, but we played the first few matches and he wasn't getting a game. But then someone got injured and Spavvy came into the side.

Would he do what he'd been told? Would he heck.

He did it his way; receiving the ball, turning, passing, keeping possession, starting attacks - he was absolutely brilliant.

He had this way of pushing the ball, caressing it rather than kicking it and we started knocking it about sweetly.

After that, Bally saw the light and Spavvy was fantastic throughout that season; Graham Hawkins was captain but Alan was our little general on and off the pitch. He was years - *maybe decades* - ahead of his time.

Before games, Bally would say a few words, but so would Spav. Even though he wasn't a big bloke, when he spoke, everyone listened. He'd say: 'We're playing in white today lads. The ball is our friend, just give it to another white shirt and don't let the other lot touch it.'

As we were winning, the manager had done such a U-turn, that he would now say: 'Lads, if you're in any trouble, give it to Spav.'

Only as a last resort should the defenders kick it down the pitch.

For me in midfield, that was great, because I wanted the ball to feet - I didn't want a crick in my neck from seeing it fly past 30 feet up in the air.

Suddenly, giving the ball away became almost a crime in the dressing room. Spav wasn't a fighter, but he'd physically get hold of people and tell them: 'Don't do it!'

I think we were playing the best football in the league that season and we always fancied ourselves in all the matches.

I was also learning a lot from Spavvy about always making yourself available for the ball, keep moving, keep showing, look for space; all these things came naturally to him and I just watched and learned.

If you ask any North End fans from that generation who saw him play, they'll say the same thing - he was just a brilliant footballer. He was the master and we were his apprentices. You couldn't ask for a better football education, but I was also doing everything else right that I thought would help me.

I barely drank and I lived at home (so I ate well). My Dad was a disciplinarian and would make sure I was in bed at the right time, getting my rest and I was always in good shape physically, so I never got tired in games. I don't like blowing my own trumpet, but I was brave on the pitch.

I wasn't the biggest, but I liked the physical side of the game and getting stuck in - a typical busy midfielder.

After matches, Spavvy and Alan Kelly would always insist that everyone went for a drink - you didn't really have a choice, it was team bonding and that was that. Even if you had a date lined up with a girl, it was: 'No, we're a team, we have a drink together, then you can go.'

I didn't really mind it of course, because they were such great lads and someone would always be telling funny stories, so us young lads would just sit and listen.

On top of that, mum and dad came to every match and sometimes if I'd had a bad game I didn't relish the post-match inquest back at the house, going over every kick!

What I remember most about that season is that we were hard to beat. Gerry Ingram was top scorer in the entire division that year and was a great target for us up front. He'd actually been Blackpool's top scorer a few years earlier but Preston pinched him from them. Not many people make that journey, do they?

He liked a pint did Gerry, and you could tell if he'd been to the pub the night before, because he'd be running round like a whirling dervish the following day in training, working it off. But he was a great lad, naturally fit and brilliant for us.

I think we went from October to April and only lost one game in the league. We drew quite a lot, but it was only two points for a win back then, so going to some tough places and coming away with a draw was a good result.

We'd been up and about the top for a while, but there were no play-offs in those days - the top two went up and that was that. No second chances.

Fulham had been top for months as we went into the tail end of the season and it looked like a formality for them to go up as Champions. The other promotion place was a bit of a fight between us, Halifax Town (Bally's old team) and Aston Villa - and yes, Halifax finished above Villa in the end.

At the worst possible time, we'd hit a bad run and not won for a month by the time we arrived to play Fulham at Craven Cottage on May Day.

I think they thought it was going to be a formality; it was their last game of the season, they were already promoted and only needed a draw to be champions.

The Third Division trophy was in the stand ready to be presented to them and there was even a picture of it on the front of the programme.

We thought: 'Oh, really? We'll see about that.'

We knew we had to win because we weren't sure of promotion if we'd lost. We had a game in hand on Fulham though and knew if we beat them at their place and won against Rotherham, we'd be champions. Easy, eh?!

Before the game, there wasn't much said about tactics; Sergeant Major Cox was ordering us to out-battle them, Bally was doing his one-on-one motivational stuff and Spavvy was saying the same thing as he always did (except this time it was 'pass to a red shirt', as we were in the change strip).

There were Preston fans all around the ground. You'd have this sea of London home fans and then a Lancastrian voice would shout from the middle of them: 'Come on Rickeh!'

The manager had nicknamed the Preston supporters 'The Gentry' because they were so well behaved and they'd started dressing up in bowler hats and smart suits - a great sight.

I know they still do it to this day for special games, so Bally's influence is still there 50 years later! *(I tell you what - he'd love that.)*

It was great to see so many down there because it was a fair old journey to London in those days. Quite early on, we got a corner and it gave us a chance for a routine from the training ground.

We didn't really do much set-piece practice, but that one was one we'd worked on for a long time. Nobby Clark put the corner into the near post area, where Graham Hawkins had the toughest task, because he had to flick it on - that's a really difficult skill, but he got it just right.

Me? I had the easy part. I had to come in with a late run, throw myself at it full length, ignore any defenders' boots and let it come off my forehead. (To be honest, putting your head in where it hurt never bothered me - if you 'took one for the team' but you scored a goal, I saw it as a fair trade and I've got quite a few scars in exchange.)

Anyway, we'd practised the move over and over again and nine times out of ten it didn't work in matches. But you've got to be ready for that time when it does - that one moment in your life when it all goes right.

And that day, it did.

It was absolutely perfect; a picture-book goal.

If I could score one goal over again in my career, it would be that one.

We were delighted to go in front in such a big game but I think we were equally chuffed that a set-piece had finally come off in a game!

Now then, how long left ref? About an hour (!) and Fulham knew what they had to do: one goal and they'd be up - as Champions. *Oh my days!* You can imagine the crowd, the players, the pressure . . . it was a hell of a game after that.

Thankfully, Alan Kelly was unbelievable for us that day. The whole team played well, but Kel was magnificent - what a brilliant keeper he was. It's funny but if someone scored against him, Alan would always take it personally.

He hated conceding, even in training. He'd get angry - he was genuinely insulted that someone had the cheek to score past him.

Early on in my career, if we conceded, I would always go and retrieve the ball from the net, to get kicked off as soon as possible and get back at it. But then I realised that if you went near Alan after a goal had gone in, you'd get a right mouthful: 'How the hell did you let that happen? What are you lot doing out there?! You - that's your fault!'

I quickly learned to keep my distance and if ever the ball went in our net, I put my head down and walked away sharpish - just like everybody else!

Anyway, that day he was brilliant; Fulham kept coming at us and we fell into the trap of sitting back, which we shouldn't have done.

We should have tried to play our normal game, but even so, we kept the ball well, kept working, kept giving it to Spavvy, Kel kept making saves . . . how long ref? How long?? 'Five minutes, son.'

Bally was waving his fingers at us: 'FIVE MINUTES LADS!!!'

Come on ref!

I can honestly say it was the longest five minutes of my life and then - peep, peep, peeeeep. Final whistle! We'd done it.

Everywhere you looked people were overjoyed - apart from the Fulham lot, of course. Bally came running on and hugged us all, but in the next breath he said we still had to finish the job.

Some Preston fans were on the pitch - they thought it was all over - but we had one more hurdle in our way.

We were now one point behind Fulham, with our game in hand to play against Rotherham at Deepdale on the Tuesday.

There was no big celebration among the lads when we got back from London, but I was giving Bally his usual lift back to Bolton.

In a nice way, he insisted I went to the pub with him; I wasn't a big drinker, so I had a quick half and then left Bally to it.

He was in his element, holding court about our brilliant win, and I'm not sure what time he left the pub that night . . !

Back in Preston, the whole town was electric for the next few days. Everywhere you went, people were talking about the game. I think there's always something special about a night match too, especially at Deepdale.

The floodlights give it a sense of theatre and there were people queuing to get in before the players even got to the ground.

They announced the crowd as 28,000 but I'm pretty sure there were more than that on that night - it was absolutely packed.

The best thing about it from our point of view was that we started well.

When you've got to win, you've got to assert yourselves right from the start - make the other team think they haven't got a chance. Rotherham weren't a bad side so we couldn't let them get a foothold in the game, we had to knock any belief out of them right from the off.

If they sensed we were nervous or the crowd was getting edgy, they would have capitalised on that. As it was, they were never in it. We scared them from the kick-off; pace, passing, moving, Spavvy pulling the strings, everyone up for it throughout the entire team.

The crowd was magnificent. If you made a pass, you got a cheer. If you headed the ball, you got a cheer.

If you fell over your own feet - you still got a cheer!

Rotherham had nothing to play for and you could see them thinking: 'Blimey, if we have a go at this lot, it's going to be a right hammering.'

Spavvy got two and Nobby Clark got the other as we ran out 3-0 winners.

It could have been four or five and I think Rotherham knew that. They were happy to keep the score down to three.

And when the final whistle went and we were champions - well, the roof came off. The loudest cheer I'd *ever* heard. I can hear it echo now.

The fans were on the pitch, chairing people off - something that happens once in a lifetime and just scenes that you never, ever forget.

They say your first love is always the best and that's what it was like for me and North End. I look back on those days and that night and just think how lucky I was to have been part of it.

I'm sure any supporters that were around then will think the same as me; it seems like yesterday and if you were there at Fulham, or at Deepdale that night, then I know you'll have a smile on your face reading this. I have, that's for sure.

We then had an open top bus parade and a big reception in the Flag Market where there were thousands upon thousands of Preston fans; banners, scarves, rosettes, just a sea of smiling faces.

Then there was us lot in our best suits (or £10 blazers) on the steps, trying to act cool, but really blown away by the whole day - just amazing, a proper football day in a proper football town. Perfect Preston.

And, of course, who was front and centre, waving the trophy to the crowd and lapping it up? Bally, of course - and deservedly so. He really was made for days like that.

The following season we were back in the old Second Division, Championship level now. We started quite well at home by beating Fulham (again) at Deepdale and in our second home match, there was a 27,000 crowd on for the local derby with Burnley, which we lost 3-1.

After that, we bumped around a bit, winning a couple, losing a few and really we were taking our time getting used to the higher standard.

The FA Cup was to test us even further that year. After beating Bristol City, we faced Manchester United in the Fourth Round at Deepdale; George Best, Bobby Charlton, Denis Law, the lot. What a team - and what an occasion it was.

Again they announced the crowd at 37,000 - just under the all-time record at Deepdale - but I'm pretty sure that it was a total full house.

There were people everywhere - you couldn't see a single seat or a foot of terracing that was empty. The ground was as full as it could possibly be.Brian Kidd was playing for them, David Sadler, all European Champions from a few years before.

And of course, Bestie, Charlton and Law - three of the greatest players of all-time, no exaggeration.

I tried to tackle George a few times in that game and he was like will-o'-the-wisp; he'd show you the ball almost at walking pace and you'd think: 'Oh, I've got this off him.' Then as you made your move, he wasn't there any more - and neither was the ball. They were just gone.

You were looking around thinking: 'Where did he go? How the hell did he do that?' You couldn't even get near him to kick him, let alone tackle him. (It must have been like marking Tom Finney a few years earlier.) Bestie was a magician, all the stories you've heard about him are probably true - on and off the pitch.

There were times when me and John McMahon would have a night out in Manchester and end up in the same club as George.

He'd be there with the Champagne flowing and have dozens - *literally dozens* - of beautiful young ladies crowding around him. He was good looking, had loads of money and he was a genuine superstar.

Women wouldn't leave him alone - not that I think he wanted them to.

It got to the point where me and John (both single young men at the time) would tap him on the shoulder and say: 'George, for goodness' sake, choose a girl - we haven't got a chance while you're still here!'

He was always good natured about it and I met him quite a few times throughout his career - he was always very friendly and a lovely fella to talk to. What happened to him in the end was sad, but there were so many temptations and no-one to guide him really.

Back on the pitch against United that day, we were heading for a draw and a replay until five minutes to go when United scored two in two minutes at the Town End.

Alan Gowling, who later went on to play for PNE, got both and although we'd been beaten, we had done well against a top side.

At the final whistle, hundreds of fans piled on looking for autographs (Bobby Charlton's, not mine!) but those who stayed in the stands applauded us off and we hadn't been disgraced.

In November we got our first - and only - away win that season at Middlesbrough and towards the end we went on a terrible run, winning only one of our last 11 games (ironically also against Boro).

There was a 4-1 defeat at home to Blackpool in that run, too. We don't like to talk about that. I know it was 50 years ago, but it's still too soon.

Thankfully, we just about stayed up, that year finishing fifth from bottom. Only two teams went down in those days and we ended up with a few points to spare. It wasn't great, but we'd had a few injuries and struggled a bit in front of goal.

Harry Hubbick was the trainer and he was a lovely bloke - but he didn't have any medical credentials at all. If the old 'magic sponge' didn't fix it, he was stumped. He'd be giving you a massage on your left ankle sometimes and after about 20 minutes, you'd have to stop him and say: 'This is lovely Harry, but the problem is with the right ankle.'

It would be there all swollen and Harry would just look at it all surprised and go: *'Really?? Hmmm.'*

There were never any calls for Bally's head while I was there and the following season started off roughly about the same; win a few, draw a few, lose a few.

We couldn't really get on a long unbeaten run like we'd had in the Third Division days.

I was playing every week and I was confident we'd come good. Neil Young had signed by then and some ginger kid called Alex Bruce had started banging in a few goals.

What a player Brucie was; you could always see that he rarely blasted goals in, they were mainly slotted right in the corner.

He had that rare knack of always having time in the box to pick his spot - a brilliant finisher as North End saw for many years after that.

Me? I was just ploughing on, doing everything I could and I felt like I was getting better all the time. North End was my club and the thought of leaving never crossed my mind.

It was a magical time for me and I was loving it.

So it was a bolt out of the blue when I got called into the office and was told: 'Ricky, we're selling you to Orient. The Secretary has booked you a train ticket. Get yourself down to London and sign the forms, lad.'

That was it - just like that.

I couldn't believe it. I was genuinely speechless for a minute before I managed to get some words out: 'But I don't want to go.'

'Well, we need the money. And not only that, we need it now, so get down there and get it done.'

I was absolutely gobsmacked and again said I didn't want to leave.

My dad spoke to the Chairman, but there was no budging. I don't know the state of the club's finances, but it was made quite clear to me that I had to go 'for the good of the club'. It got to the point where a couple of the directors were talking about coming down with me to make sure I signed.

Even though I was a Lancashire lad, settled up North, I didn't have any say in the matter whatsoever. That's the way it was back then. Players were just employees who were told what to do.

If you got to the end of the season and you didn't sign the contract in front of you, well, you were in a sticky spot.

The club still owned your registration, so they could stop you going elsewhere until someone paid for it.

And if someone didn't . . . well, you were stuck.

You couldn't fight your corner - the manager would just say: 'OK, you don't sign, you don't play and we won't let you go anywhere else.'

Players were in a really weak position and, of course, many years later the Bosman ruling changed all that and turned it on its head really.

Maybe if I'd have been a married man with a family, the directors might have looked at it differently.

But I was a young, single man, they were getting a decent fee (about £55,000) and it was taken for granted that I'd go.

I was still quite naive and when I got to Orient, again it was all sorted in about five minutes: 'This is what we'll give you. Sign here and here.'

It was scary, to be honest. I'd never been to London, other than to play matches and it was big and brash - a real culture shock. Preston had been a real family club, lovely people in the town and suddenly I was in this big city.

To be fair, the manager there George Petchey, was a good man and I enjoyed my time at the club. I lived in Southend and Bally would sometimes pop in if he fancied a visit to the seaside.

Orient had some good young players coming through and even though I wasn't that old, I think they saw me as a calming influence. I was single but I was a clean-living lad.

At the time, they had this young winger who was absolutely outstanding, but the club thought I might be able to show him the ropes and look after him a bit.

And that's how Laurie Cunningham came to live with me.

What a player and what a lovely lad. But he was a free spirit. I think he saw a ten o'clock start for training as a recommendation rather than an instruction - he'd get there when he could.

He'd be out late at times, but he wasn't a drinker - Laurie was a dancer. All 1970s fashion and smart suits, he was as stylish off the pitch as he was on it. So living with me near Southend wasn't really doing it for Laurie and he only lasted two weeks before moving out back to London.

I don't think moving out did his career any harm in the long run . . !

I enjoyed my time at Orient, but really I wanted to come back up north - and Preston would have been ideal. I would have walked up the motorway to get back to Deepdale. Instead, Terry Venables came in for me at Crystal Palace and I ended up going there.

Terry was a real character; exactly the same as he came across on TV and in the press. That Cockney wide-boy image was all true and he knew some 'interesting' characters in London, let's put it that way.

He was a bit of a villain I think, but he was a likeable villain. He'd think nothing of grabbing the microphone and belting out a Sinatra song after matches, telling jokes as he went - he just had this incredible aura about him. I think the press knew a bit too much about him in the end when he was England manager and that's why he went. But if he'd have stayed, I'm convinced we would have won things under him.

As a coach, he was a class above. Tactics, preparation, man-management; he had the lot. He was the best manager I played under tactically, because he would analyse absolutely everything - years ahead of his time.

And where did I make my debut for Palace? Deepdale.

The Preston fans were very good to me and again it was a nice welcome back. I thought: 'Bally was right again - they really are the Gentry.'

I didn't stay at Palace very long, but I was there when they got promoted from the Third Division, so it was a good time to be around the club.

Arthur Cox (and his amazingly tight pants) took me to Chesterfield and it was great to be working with him again - he really was a lovely man beneath that tough exterior. I then went to Peterborough under Noel Cantwell and he was another real character - I seemed to attract them!

Noel was an Irish player who had played for West Ham and Manchester United so he knew everyone; that's where I got to know Bobby Moore a bit. Bestie was a big mate of his so you'd have all these legends popping into Peterborough and again it was great to just sit and listen to these legends talk.

After that, I went out to Hong Kong, where I was one of the first Europeans to go and play over there.

I played for a team called Eastern FC and we had a successful time, winning the Hong Kong FA Cup, the Shield, all the big trophies. It went well and I was named Player of the Year for the entire league, which was a real honour.

There was big money out there - in fact, I earned more in three years in Hong Kong than I did in the previous 30 years in England.

The chap who owned the club also owned Panasonic so he was a big money man and he was a lovely guy. We'd always have full houses for every match but he was looking for something special.

He said: 'Ricky, what we need is a superstar to come out and set the whole of Hong Kong alight. Do you know anyone?'

Well, the biggest name I could think of was Bobby Moore. He was retired by then, but I'd give it a go and managed to get in touch with him.

The idea was that if we were winning quite comfortably, we'd bring Bobby on for the last ten minutes and he'd just swan about, the crowd would love it and everyone would be happy.

So that's what we did. You'd hear this almighty, excited roar and you'd know he'd taken his tracksuit top off and then when he came on I was thinking: 'Blimey, I'm on the same team as Bobby Moore!'

He could still play. No tackling really - he didn't need to. He'd just get the ball, play a five-yard pass and the crowd would go wild. It was perfect.

After the game, there'd be a reception and after that the players would go to a nightclub where we'd be treated like royalty.

Bobby would always have a great story to tell and one time I was sat right next to him - absolutely enthralled with these tales of Pele, Cruyff, Beckenbauer, the lot. And I suddenly realised I was getting so near to him, I was basically sitting in his lap, like a groupie!

Cool as you like, he said: 'Ricky, I think you're getting a bit too close.'

I thought: 'Oh blimey!'

Anyway, it was three or four o'clock in the morning by then, so we had a laugh about it and I thought it was time to go to bed and leave Bobby to it. I was with my girlfriend and we jumped in a taxi outside.

But as the car pulled away, I thought: 'What am I doing?'

I had this mental tussle: 'Girlfriend or Bobby Moore? Girlfriend or . . . Bobby Moore??'

A moment later, the winner was announced: 'Driver, pull over!'

I thought: 'Much as I love my girlfriend, how often do you get the chance to be with Bobby Moore in a Hong Kong nightclub at 4am?'

I raced back to the club, pulled up a chair and just carried on listening to the great man until the sun came up.

I've no idea what time we eventually got in the next day, but thankfully my girlfriend was very understanding - because she later became my wife.

It wasn't the first time I'd played in the same team as some all-time greats though. I remember George Ross's testimonial at Deepdale where a huge crowd turned out to pay tribute to a great guy.

It wasn't long after I'd left North End so I was playing for an 'All-Stars' team. Gordon Banks, Bobby Charlton, Geoff Hurst, Brian Kidd, Francis Lee, Peter Thompson . . . names that just rolled off the tongue.

I looked around the dressing room and thought: 'They genuinely are all stars - and then there's me!'

I think I was the only one who wasn't an international. India were aware of me but they just weren't very organised in the 1970s and football wasn't a big thing over there at all.

Even today there aren't as many Asian players as there should be really.

I think they are often very skilful, but they don't always enjoy the physical side of the game. Football has got bigger out there in recent years, but I think non-contact sports are still more popular in Asia.

I would have loved to have played for India, but I'm just proud to have been the first Asian player in the English league. People still ask me to talk about it now, but it was never a big thing for me, it was just natural. Yes, I was born in India, but I saw myself as just a normal lad in love with football - nothing out of the ordinary, other than I was quite good at it. And it is a love affair.

When you're playing, it's a perfect life. But as time goes on, you become aware that it won't last forever.

So a testimonial was a big thing back then and players used to stay with clubs if they knew they were in sniffing distance of getting one.

The thing is, when you finish playing, it hits you hard.

And most people aren't prepared for it. I certainly wasn't.

The money wasn't astronomical like it is now; if the ordinary bloke in the crowd was on £100 a week, a footballer might be on £110. That was the difference, ten per cent maybe, not a massive amount.

But you were a little tin god in the town where you played; you got all the attention and prestige - people treated you differently because you played for Preston North End. It was great.

But then when it ends - you're lost. It's a rude awakening, I can assure you. Outside of football, you've got no skills whatsoever.

You've done nothing at school, because you were always going to be a footballer. You're maybe worldly-wise, but you've got no education and nothing to go on to as a career. You've got a bit of money, but not a lot. You've got to come up with something to start earning a living.

So it might sound daft . . . but I started selling balloons on street corners.

It was a good life in the summer and I was always a good salesman, so it was fun - and, believe it or not, there's money to be made in balloons.

After a while, I was out selling one day when someone pointed out an empty shop nearby. So we moved into the shop. Then that went well, so we got another shop and we built up a party supplies business from there.

I wasn't a great businessman, but I could sell and things just kept growing. We were importing balloons and doing quite well.

So well in fact that in 1991 we were hired to do Princess Diana's 30th birthday party at the Ritz. We were there for seven days setting up all the decorations and it was just a fantastic experience.

When UEFA lifted the European ban on English teams, we were hired to mark the occasion when Manchester United played the first game back - releasing 10,000 balloons at Old Trafford and also at Villa Park, where Villa were back in Europe too. It was very spectacular and looked great.

Also, we were based in Peterborough, where the MP at the time was John Major, who then went on to be Prime Minister. That was another stroke of luck, because he was looking to put some business to a local company and we ended up with the contract to do events at 10 Downing Street.

All the way through his time as PM, we used to do all the parties and decorations down there for him. We'd get invited to Downing Street as part of the social team and it was all just wonderful.

To go from such small beginnings on street corners to doing these national events was fantastic.

So I was very lucky that when my playing career ended, I found something else that I could be successful at.

I know that doesn't happen to everyone and I've always been very grateful for the life I've had.

I'm lucky that all through my life, I've had a good family around me and even though I'm slowing down a bit these days, I'm desperate for knowledge and keen to learn new things. I still do college courses now, even though I'm in my 70s.

I've no regrets about my career, but I wish I'd have been able to stay at Preston longer.

It was my first love and - in the words of the song - first love never dies.

The old Deepdale was a magical place, but the new stands are fantastic and I'm proud to be in the PNE Former Players Association, so I keep an eye out for the results, of course.

I've been back on occasion and I always love the warmth of the Preston people - and the Northern humour.

One time I was up there and I was introduced to this fella as an ex-PNE player. I was playing down my career a bit and jokingly said to him: 'I bet you want your money back on me, don't you?'

'Yes I do,' he said, 'You were flaming crap.'

So I fished in my pocket and gave him 10p!

It was all good-natured and we had a laugh about it.

A few minutes later, he came over, tapped me on the shoulder and put 5p change back in my hand. I asked: 'What's this for?'

'Well,' he said, 'You were great in the warm-ups!'

CHAPTER 12

JON PARKIN: HAPPY DAYS

I was lucky in my career because I was never fussy with my clubs; if someone wanted me, that was it - I'd probably sign for them. I never had a big opinion of myself, so I was just glad to be wanted somewhere.

That gut feeling worked out well for me (most of the time) and definitely when I came to Preston. What a great call that was.

I was at Stoke at the time and we'd just been promoted to the Premier League under Tony Pulis, who was always alright with me. Hard but fair, so he was sound as a pound - apart from those baseball caps, obviously *(what's all that about gaffer? You're a 55-year-old man!).*

The season we got promoted at Stoke, I only started about half a dozen games, but I came on as sub most of the time. So I was part of it, but I knew that now we were in the top division, I was never going to play.

They'd just signed Dave Kitson for £4.5 million so I knew my chances were going to be even more limited. In the first game of the 2008/9 season, I wasn't involved at all as we got stuffed 4-0 at Bolton, but then I scored in the Carling Cup against Cheltenham on the Tuesday night.

We had Middlesbrough away at the weekend and I knew I'd be back on the bench at best, so things weren't looking good for me there in terms of playing games. I got on well with Tony and had a good contract, but I was never one to just sit and pick up my wages; money didn't mean that much to me - playing football did.

Anyway, on the Thursday I got a call from my agent saying Alan Irvine up at Preston wanted to speak to me in an Italian restaurant - would I go up to see him?

In a restaurant? Definitely, 100 per cent, just tell me when, where - and do they do garlic bread? So that night I went up to meet Alan and Derek Shaw at a nice little place in Preston.

I'd eaten at about half past twelve in Stoke but I don't think we met until about half eight, so I was absolutely starving by that point. I was thinking 'garlic bread, starter, main, the lot', but I thought I'd better just wait to see what the other two ordered before I piled in.

Alan went first: disaster - straight to a main, no bread, nothing.

I'm looking at Derek thinking: 'This lad looks like he enjoys a meal, come on mate, go for it!'

Nope. Same again. No bread, no starter. Just a main. I was gutted, but I thought: 'Well, it's a job interview really so I'll have to play along here.'

You can imagine what I was thinking as I said to the waiter: 'Oh, just a spaghetti bolognaise please . . .'

It was funny because I think Derek was trying to impress me and obviously I was trying to impress them back: 'Excuse me, is this pasta organic?' What I was really wondering was: 'Where's the nearest Maccies on the way home?'

Anyway, Alan was telling me what he thought I could do better and asking about what it was like at Stoke. I was saying stuff like 'well, I think we could do a bit more training' (we really couldn't, but it was job interview spiel, you know?).

The three of us hit it off straight away really; I liked Derek and he obviously had a massive feeling for the club.

But that voice, I mean, come on . . . he's got the biggest Preston accent you've ever heard, hasn't he? Where did he get that from? Preston, I suppose!

He was trying to sell me the club a bit, but he really didn't need to. As I mentioned at the top, I was never that confident to be thinking: 'I'll wait to see who else comes in for me'. If a club wanted me, I'd be pretty much up for going.

Alan was quite serious but very friendly and had this air of authority about him; you could see this guy knew what he was talking about and you don't always get that with managers, trust me.

(I'd already played for Phil Brown at Hull, don't forget. And later on, Graham Westley at Newport - thank God I wasn't at Deepdale when he was there!)

Anyway, fair play to Alan, because I imagine there were certain managers who would look at me and think: 'I can't sign him because he can't do this and he can't do that and look at the size of him, he's too fat and whatnot.'

But Alan wasn't like that; he pointed out things I could do better, fair enough, but he told me all about how many times he'd watched me, good things I'd done in games, goals I'd scored, he was very positive.

So straight away, I knew that I wanted to play for him.

It was a great introduction and after a happy meal at the Italian place, I stopped off for a cheeky McDonald's on the way back too. Win-win.

The following day, I got a call from my agent saying North End wanted to put an offer in, but I was due to travel up to Middlesbrough that day with Stoke.

I had to arrange to take my car up there, just in case I needed to get over to Preston pronto. So that's what I did and in the afternoon, I grabbed Tony Pulis for a quick word in the hotel.

I said: 'You probably know Preston are putting an offer in - and I'd like to go.'

He hadn't been picking me, so I thought he'd be fine about it, but he just said: 'Nah, no chance, you're not going.'

I said: 'What do you mean I'm not going? I wasn't in the team last year in the Championship so I'm not going to get much of a kick in the Prem.'

But Tony was adamant: 'Look Parky, I like having you around the place, you're a good lad and you're great for morale.'

Now, that may be the case and I know he meant well, but I'm a footballer first and foremost.

I said: 'Gaffer, I'm 27 - I need to be playing football. I'm not just going to hang around to be the class joker and keep everyone entertained.'

He 'ummed and ahhed' a bit and in the end said: 'Leave it with me.'

That evening we had a team meeting at about seven o'clock and half way through I got a text from my agent saying Stoke had accepted a bid and I needed to get over to Preston ASAP.

I felt bad because you're not supposed to have phones in those meetings, but I knew something might happen, so in the end, I had to put my hand up like a schoolboy in class and just say: 'Excuse me gaffer, but I've got to go.'

Tony gave me a quick smile, wished me all the best and that was that, I jumped in the car and legged it over to Deepdale.

That's where I met the physio Matt 'Cue Ball' Radcliffe, for a bit of a medical then went and checked into the Marriott.

It was all a late-night job, but Derek was at my door at half past nine the next morning with a contract and papers for me to sign and that was that.

Luckily, they got it all through in time for me to make my debut that afternoon against Charlton at Deepdale - I think it must have been one of the fastest transfers on record; meal Thursday night, hotel with Stoke Friday afternoon, hotel in Preston Saturday morning then debut a few hours later.

The fee was about £400,000 and it was absolutely manic, when you think about it, so fair play to them for sorting the paperwork so quickly.

In hindsight, I should have probably tried to sign on loan for the rest of that season because I took quite a big pay cut to come to North End - about 25 per cent, in fact.

Obviously, my money had gone up at Stoke when we got promoted so if I'd have signed on loan, I'd have been on the same salary.

After the season I then had, maybe I could have got a better contract at Deepdale. Ah, well. Who knows? It's only money isn't it.

And on the other hand, Preston might have wanted to send me back at the start of December, because I was crap in the first few months! But, as I mentioned, money wasn't a massive thing for me, I just wanted to be at a decent club and play football with a good set of lads - and that's what happened.

The funny thing on that first day was that I didn't even have anything to wear so I think I turned up at Deepdale wearing my Stoke gear.

It was a case of waiting in the dressing room and meeting the lads for the first time as they came in for the game.

I hadn't played regularly for quite a while at Stoke and I could see the look on Paul McKenna's face saying: 'What the hell have we signed here?'

Kenna was never one for hiding what he was thinking, he'd just say it out loud. I don't know if it's better or worse to go straight into a game, but I remember sitting there just praying that I was decent and could hit the ground running.

As it was, I did OK and, most importantly, we won 2-1, so I was chuffed with that and the Town End gave me a right good round of applause at the end, which gave me another bit of a lift. It was a good result and I thought: 'Hey, we're not bad here, this is a decent team.'

The thing was though, I hadn't really played regularly for a year and I was one of those players who wants to be playing. Saturday/Tuesday worked better for me than Saturday/Saturday because that's how I kept sharp.

As for training, well, there's a lot of myths said about me, but ask anyone and they'll tell you I used to work hard in training.

If I'm honest though, I just couldn't get my head round it.

I didn't really like it, it was just a means to an end for me to build up to the weekend.

However, Alan's sessions were brilliant and all the lads loved them; well organised, clear, you could see the purpose behind them all.

They weren't just thrown together to give you something to do like some are.

And the thing that was really special about Alan was the way he was with you. He treated everyone equally and fairly. For example, if you weren't in the first team, you didn't have to play in the reserves. He'd say: 'You're not reserve team players - you're first team players who just aren't being picked at the moment.'

We trained that hard under him that we were fit enough with reserve games anyway, even if you weren't playing week-in, week-out. He wasn't a ranter or a raver but he was probably the only manager that I was really scared of in my career.

Preston was a two-hour drive from Barnsley and I remember one morning for some reason my dad was taking me into training. Now, I was late maybe once a week, but never too late, if you know what I mean.

We had to be there for ten o'clock and I'd be there at maybe five or ten past; a little bit of a fine but still in time for the start at 10.30am.

Callum Davidson used to collect the fines and I'd see him laughing his head off sometimes as I came racing into the car park at 10.01am: 'Too late Parky - just missed it mate!'

Anyway, that day with my dad driving we got caught in horrendous traffic and I was bricking it in the car thinking: 'I'm going to be in some serious bother here.'

Turns out we didn't get there until ten to eleven and then I always had to have my ankle strapped up every day, so that made it even worse.

When I came out onto the training pitch, Big Al didn't say a word.

He just stared at me . . . and that was enough.

Other managers would have had a right scene with me, gone off on one and, even though I was in the wrong, it would have put my back up.

No . . . he just stared at me with a look that could turn you to stone.

And I tell you what, I got the message.

He didn't need to say anything - no matter what the backstory was, I'd let him down and he wasn't having it.

Don't get me wrong, he could lose his rag, but he always did it at the right time.

One time, we played on the Saturday and I got a bit of a knock, so I had to go in for treatment on the Sunday if I was going to miss training on Monday.

But I'd got a night out on the Saturday so I didn't go in on the Sunday, which I knew was wrong. I then didn't train on the Monday and he was furious with me, absolutely fuming.

He never said much to me, but we were away at Southampton on the Saturday and we were 3-0 down at half-time. I was horrendous, horrific, really, really bad.

And I swear for 14 minutes of the 15 minute break, he absolutely slaughtered me; tore strips off me and I just had to sit there and take it - because he was right: 'You've not done this, you've not done that, you've been a shambles!'

If I'd have gone in on the Sunday, or trained on the Monday, he wouldn't have been as harsh, but because I'd done wrong, he absolutely hammered me.

He'd stop for a moment to catch his breath and give me THAT stare again - and I swear that was worse than being shouted at.

I think because everyone respected him that much, no-one wanted to let him down or step out of line, so because I'd done that, it had really wound him up.

Anyway, that day I was sat next to Chris Sedgwick, just taking this absolute hammering and then at the end, Big Al said: 'Right, sod it, you've been that bad, I can't even take you off. You can only get better. Sorry Sedg, you're off son!'

Well, Chris is a great lad but he was a right moaner at the best of times, so when he heard that he was like: 'What the . . ! You've just annihilated him for 14 minutes and I'm the one coming off?! Cheers Parky!'

Sedg was probably the funniest lad in that dressing room - he always made me laugh, but he was even funnier when he was moaning. The more miserable he got, the funnier it was. But that day was no laughing matter and I couldn't really complain because I was in the wrong, so I just had to take it.

I wasn't always like that though; if there was an instance where I thought what the manager was saying was wrong, I'd be like 'Err, hold on a minute . . .' and have my say.

At the end of the day, I know they're your manager, but we're still grown men and we can all have an opinion, as long as it's done in a respectful way.

There's been plenty of times I've told managers 'I think you're wrong' but if you do that, you've got to be able to back it up. (If you're reading this and thinking of going into work and having a pop at your boss tomorrow, remember that second bit: you've got to back it up - don't go getting sacked on my account!)

You might have a bit of a barney after the game, but come Monday morning you'll look at the video and work out who was right.

Good managers are big enough to take other people's opinions on board, it's the duff ones who just think they're always right.

Alan had made some good signings already when I arrived and Stephen 'Sleaze' Elliott came around the same time as me. Chris Brown was there but he was injured and Neil Mellor was there too, so we had really good options up front and at no point did I think I was going to walk into the team.

Youl Mawene was at the back with Sean St Ledger and they were two top class defenders at that level. I love Youl and I used to love winding him up even more and when *'Frenchie'* went . . . he really went!

In nets we had Andy Flappergan, sorry, Lonergan (!) and he was another one I had some right laughs with. To see how Lonners' career has gone is brilliant though and shows that if you work hard and stick at it, you get your rewards, so well done Flappers!

I used to room with Andy and he's a top guy, straight as a die and another proper Preston lad who'd be on the terraces if he wasn't a footballer. Same with Kenna - a brilliant footballer and someone who was never afraid to have his say.

So yeah, I doubt he was impressed with the state of me when I signed, especially as I think the shirt they dug out for me was XXL. I had to win him over and show that even if I liked a joke, I was serious about playing football.

Because I tell you what, Kenna had so much focus - he wanted the club to be pushing for promotion all the time, he wasn't interested in mid table, or just doing OK. We had to be pushing all the time, or else.

I'd played at Deepdale a couple of times before and been impressed with it, but I was never one of those who cared that much about things like that.

When players say they come and look round the club and are impressed and all that sort of stuff, fair enough, but that was never my approach.

I wasn't really bothered what the stadium was like - or the training facilities, which was a good job when I saw Springfields!

There's a lot said about it and it was a bit ropey, but I never cared about that, I just wanted to get through training and play as many games as I could and start scoring. That last bit was the trickiest and it took me ages to get going.

I never doubted myself though, because I never had much of an opinion of myself to doubt! However, if you've not scored for a new club, and you miss a chance you do think: 'Oh flaming hell, here we go again.'

But you've just got to keep plugging away.

I was playing alright but I'd been bought to score goals and I wasn't doing that, so by November, I was out of the team and I could have no complaints.

I was still on the bench though and I came on for the last 15 minutes against Doncaster and finally got off the mark with a header.

The next game, I came on again and scored the winner against Birmingham, when Ross Wallace put over a great ball that I chested down and leathered in at the Town End. The Donny celebration had been a quiet one, partly because I was embarrassed it had taken so long to break my duck, but the Brum one . . . I think I nearly took Ledge's head off with it!

The good thing about that was that we were off on our Christmas do to Dublin that weekend, so at least I could relax a bit after finally hitting the back of the net.

I knew then that something had just clicked and I was up and running for real.

I scored again when we beat Derby on Boxing Day and after that, I was in the team for pretty much the rest of the season.

It was more of a relief than anything to start getting goals; when you're missing chances or coming off after not scoring, you're just frustrated with it all.

It's true what they say that you need one to go in off someone's backside or a keeper to drop one on your toe - anything to get you off the mark and set you off on a bit of a run.

Around New Year, we had that massive FA Cup game against Liverpool and, yes, that was a time when I thought the stadium looked fantastic; packed to the rafters and an unbelievable atmosphere. They went in front through a cracking strike but it was 1-0 for a long time and we did well against them to be fair.

In the second half, the ball was pinging around after a corner and Ledge got it at the back post to make it 1-1.

The place was going mad, but unfortunately the ref had spotted someone holding Jamie Carragher in the box. *Who would do such a thing?!* To be fair, it was one that I thought I'd get away with - sometimes you do. I definitely held him down but I was trying to be subtle with it and just give him a little tug. When I saw it on the replay though, yeah, it was a bit obvious wasn't it? Sorry.

We were pushing for an equaliser right to the end when they broke away and Lonners was left with a two-on-one.

How he never saved it, I do not know - it was only Fernando Torres and Steven Gerrard, what was he playing at?

To be fair, they had some great players out that day and I bet Torres must have been looking at me thinking: 'What on earth is that?'

But looks are deceptive (hopefully!) and I think a lot is made about me being fat this and overweight that.

Do you know what? If I'd have lost a stone and a half, I don't think I'd have been the same player.

I would not suddenly have got loads quicker, my touch would be the same, my positioning wouldn't change and I might lose something from the other side of my game like taking on big defenders.

Maybe that's just me making excuses, or being optimistic, but I really don't think I'd have been the same player if I'd slimmed down a bit.

My pre-match meal if I stayed in the hotel before a game was always a full English and it worked for me. There's a few myths out there about my eating habits, but at the end of the day, you do what works for you.

Managers and dieticians tried a few times to change me, but if a packet of crisps works, at the time you're thinking: 'Why change it?'

Now I've retired, I look back and I can see that throughout my career, I didn't eat right and I went out drinking too much. The price I paid for that is that it possibly stopped me playing higher, for longer.

You make your decisions and you come to terms with them and the consequences, but I think the vast majority of players have things that they look back on and say: 'If I'd have done this or that differently . . .'

The fact is, you'll never know. You can't deal with what might have been, only with what was.

You can't turn back time. Even Cher couldn't do that.

The big game that everyone talks about is the Cardiff one at Deepdale that got us into the play-offs. I'd scored quite a few by then and the team was really clicking into gear in the second half of the season, but I don't think we thought we had a realistic chance at that point.

Cardiff had been at the top of the league all season and before the match I bumped into Jay Bothroyd, who was playing for them. He'd had a brief spell at Stoke so I knew him from there - and I also knew he was a prat.

Normally before a game, you're just making small talk if you know someone, but he was giving it: 'Yeah, we'll do you lads today, then that'll set us up for the play-offs and we can relax a bit.'

I was thinking: 'Oh reet, pal. We'll see about that.'

I think I must have mentioned it to the lads, but to be fair, they never needed any extra motivation, they were always fired up for games anyway - especially at Deepdale. We were unbelievable at home that season and time and time again, we'd come back to win games in the second half.

The crowd got right behind us, lads were flying into tackles, Kenna was keeping everything ticking along and it was just relentless.

That Cardiff game summed it up; we weren't really thinking about goal difference at that point, we just wanted to win by as many as we could. And as it turned out, it was one of the best team performances I've ever been involved in.

Fair enough, everything went for us on the day, but that's because we were right at it all over the pitch. Mells' first goal bobbled in and then the second one took a massive deflection off a Kenna shot that hit Mells and went in.

I love Mells, he was such a good player and an absolute legend with the lads, not just because he used to wear his shorts so high up like something out of the 1980s. But I tell you what, he was ALWAYS going to claim that goal - the standing joke was that if anything went anywhere near him, Mells would try to claim it, even in the warm-up!

Billy Jones tried to get them back into it by giving away a penalty, but Lonners made a brilliant save and Cardiff must have been thinking: 'It's not our day here.'

They must definitely have thought that when I outpaced the defence to score a third just after half-time.

By the time Mark Kennedy scored one of the best own goals you'll ever see to make it four, I bet they were just wanting to get on the bus and go.

It was that bad even Brownie scored to make it five - just kidding, obviously, Chris is a massive mate and what a player for Preston. He'd do all the running, take all the knocks and pop up with some great goals too; he was a dream to play with - anyone would tell you the same.

Lee Williamson made it six towards the end and Willo was another one who was brilliant for us in that second half of the season. We still had two tough games coming up and overall Cardiff were still massively in the driving seat, but you just sensed they might crack if we kept at them.

After the game, I just happened to be in the corridor when I heard Dave Jones giving them both barrels about me and Mells: 'You've let those two fat b******* bully you all day!' He was absolutely caning them about *'fat this and fat that'* and I thought: 'Oh aye?'

A moment later, him and Peter Ridsdale (who was at Cardiff at the time) stormed out and went into one of the little kit rooms for the type of manager/chairman chat you have after getting pumped 6-0. Things were obviously tense but, you know me, I thought: 'I'll have a bit of this for a laugh.'

I took my top off and as I flung the door open they just looked at me as if to say: 'Seriously? What the hell are you doing in here?'

Me? I was all: 'Oh, sorry to interrupt gentlemen, very sorry . . . I'm just looking for my diet sheet.'

I had a poke around a bit and just about managed to keep a straight face as I left them to it. Cheers for the three points and the 12-goal swing lads!

The following week we went down to Birmingham and I think they expected us to roll over a bit, especially when they went 1-0 up. Willo got sent off for some handbags with Lee Bowyer and that was a ridiculous decision, really bad.

But then Kenna scored a worldie and Ross Wallace pinged in an unbelievable free-kick to win it right at the end. I felt a bit guilty because we had our Player of the Year do the following day and my goal against Birmingham at home won it.

Now, it was a decent goal, but I'd just chested it down and knocked it in from six yards out.

If it had been up against those two from the previous day, I wouldn't have stood a chance.

In fact, there were probably about ten better than mine and I was a bit embarrassed when I went up to collect the award, especially as Kenna (who else?) was moaning loudly: 'Flaming hell, how has that won Goal of the Season?!'

The only bad news from that game at St Andrews was that Rosco had been sent off for taking his shirt off in his celebrations - it's a rubbish rule, that, made up by people who have never scored last-minute winners.

It was a massive loss though because Ross had been possibly our best player that year - he was unbelievable out wide and for me in the middle, seeing those crosses coming in was like food and drink. We still had to beat QPR though and it wasn't a 'gimme' by any stretch - they had a decent side.

The thing is, our confidence was through the roof. You get that feeling sometimes don't you - this is our year. Everything had fallen into place for us, Cardiff were crumbling and we were bang on form.

You can see that from the first goal when I got it in from a ridiculous angle. I should never have been trying that, to be honest, as I could have squared it to Mells for a tap-in. But when you're on a run, you just do things by instinct and that goal summed things up - it actually skimmed the near post on the way in.

Good job too, otherwise Mells would have crucified me! It was one of those: 'You greedy . . . oh, great goal mate!'

As for the winner in the second half, people talk about the long-throw but I swear it's something we'd never worked on. The lads were in the gym the previous day and I wasn't a regular visitor - I only ever really went in there for the crack. There just happened to be this ball there and someone said: 'Parky, see how far you can throw that.'

I threw it and it went quite a long way so when we got that throw in the game I just thought: 'Why not?' I was waving Ledge and Youl forward and I could see Frenchie thinking: 'Vat ees he doing now?'

I just wanged it in, Browny got a touch in front of the keeper and Ledge bullied their lad at the far post put us back in front.

Next thing, the stadium's gone berserk and the last 15 minutes were just panic stations. Credit to QPR, they had nothing to play for, but they kept right at us and Darren Carter got one off the line with the last kick of the game.

Everything just seemed to transpire for us to get in the play-offs which was quite an achievement BUT . . . if we'd been half decent away from home, we'd have had a chance to be challenging for the automatics that year.

Like I said before, we were brilliant at home, we had this amazing team spirit and defended that pitch like our lives depended on it. But for some reason, we struggled away from home.

I don't know why. It's not like we lacked character. In fact, we had a great set of lads - it's not very often you get in a dressing room and there's no prats. There's normally one or two (sometimes more than that) and you're thinking: 'Oh, here we go.' But we didn't have any.

Even the ones who weren't playing, they were all great lads. And that was down to Alan as well; because he treated everyone the same there was no great moaning behind the scenes, which happens at 95 per cent of clubs.

We were fit, so we could always finish games strongly, and we looked after each other. You didn't want to let the manager down, your teammates, the supporters. People might think that's the same everywhere, but again, trust me, it isn't. Alan had done his homework on people and made sure that anyone coming in was going to fit in with the group, not start causing trouble.

He'd always ask about players and find out what they were like as people before letting them in. Again, you'd think that was just common sense, but you'd be amazed how many clubs don't check things out properly.

We were up against Sheffield United in the play-offs and over the two legs, there wasn't much in it. We had the better of them in the first half at Deepdale when Ledge scored and then I hit the post, but their goal straight after half-time knocked us back a bit. It finished 1-1 and, given our away form, we probably needed more than that to take to their place.

It was always a tough place to go; I remember one time we were there and I was up against David Unsworth and Chris Morgan - it was like playing against Max and Paddy.

To be fair to those pair though, if you smashed either of them, caught them with an elbow or whatever, they'd be fine. And if they banged you with one, well, you had to take it on the chin - literally sometimes!

But after the game, you'd shake hands and then have a pint with them in the bar, no problem at all. That's the way it should be, if you ask me.

None of this rolling around on the floor nonsense you see so much of today. Without the fans in during lockdown, you could hear these lads squealing when they had barely been touched and it's embarrassing.

You're watching it thinking: 'Really?? You should try having Chris Morgan up your backside for 90 minutes.' *(Hang on, let me re-phrase that!)*

Anyway, in that Sheffield United second leg, we made a few changes and went with a slightly different formation, which was unusual for the gaffer, but maybe he was trying to catch them out. Ross was in the hole behind me and Brownie and, really, it left us a bit exposed down the flanks.

They had Kyle Naughton and Kyle Walker as full-backs bombing on and they took advantage of the space all night, really. Greg Halford got the winner with a ridiculous header from the edge of the box, but not before I'd caught him with a high boot, somewhere above the knee and just below the neck.

It was outrageous really - probably assault in the real world.

It looked bad, but I was genuinely just trying to look after myself and you know when people say *'he's not that type of player'*, well I genuinely wasn't.

At the time, I knew straight away it could easily have been a red card so I just turned round, tried to look as innocent as possible and said: 'I got the ball ref!'

You'll say anything in that moment when you're thinking 'Oh crap!', but I think what got me out of the mire was that his foot was up high too.

Thankfully the ref only gave me a yellow and although people tell me it was Alan Wiley, I wouldn't know his name. I don't get this 'celebrity refs' thing, I never knew any of their names and they probably didn't know mine - well, I hope not anyway. I tried to keep on their right side during games, but all this being on 'first-name terms' business in the Premier League doesn't sit very well with me.

They're not your pals, they're officials.

Anyway, we never really got into the game massively at Bramall Lane, but even so, Billy Jones had a great chance in the last minute to get us level.

I love Bill to bits, he's one of the nicest lads you could ever wish to meet, and he was a brilliant player everywhere he went.

But I always cane him for that miss every time I see him even now. There was a bit of a scuffle in the box and it dropped to him about ten yards out - he's hit it and it's gone just wide.

Every time I see him I say: 'That was my chance to play in the Premier League and you blew it for me Bill. It's alright for you, you got there in the end, but me? Nope. Cheers pal!'

At the end of the game, we were all gutted, as we really thought everything had lined up for us to do it over the past few months. What can you say? It's better to have got there and lost than not to have got there at all.

You've given yourself a shot and then it's down to who plays best or how things drop for you in those games. You've just got to pick yourselves up and go again, that's football, that's life, crack on.

One thing that gave me a lift was being named Player of the Year and to be honest, my overriding emotion was relief if I'm honest. Up until I'd started scoring in December, I'd deemed my performances as a bit crap really so I was just relieved that I'd made up for it in the second half of the season. It's all very well doing alright, but ultimately my job was to score goals and I wasn't doing that. So I was chuffed, but relieved more than anything.

It was also a self-justification that I'd done the right thing moving from Stoke, taking a pay cut and coming to the right club. North End had put faith in me, gave me a shot and in the end, I'd had a good season.

The worst thing about that summer was losing Kenna to Forest and then later on Ledge went to Boro as well, so there were two key players we were missing going into the next season.

But before we even got to that we had to go through a pre-season with Alan and it was . . . horrendous.

I think it was Moyesie's pre-season that he'd brought with him from Everton and, if it's not THE hardest, it's up there with the top three I've ever had to do.

But I keep saying this, the great thing about Alan was that he was fair with you. Now, let's not kid ourselves, I couldn't really run distances - anything over 90 seconds, my thighs just started screaming.

Big Al knew that I couldn't do it, but he also knew that I was trying my best and that was good enough for him. If I didn't make times or whatever, he wouldn't be on my case because he knew that I was trying as hard as I could.

He used to tell me that Yobo at Everton was the same; he couldn't run any sort of distance, but he was great in games. Alan looked at everyone as individuals and he worked with you on stuff like that one-to-one.

Sometimes, he'd drop back to jolly me along a bit, then run off and leave me. I'd be thinking: 'Hang on, he's in his forties and he can do all this running better than me!' But some people are just like that - they can do it, no problem.

What used to naff me off though was when we were doing, for example, six 1,000-metre runs one after the other with say a 30-second break in between.

I used to hate it, I was always tailed off behind everyone else, but I was knocking myself out - doing the best I could. So it really got my goat when the coaches would shout 'Come on, last 500 metres - step it up!' and lads would do it - they'd speed up and give it a big finish.

To me, that was wrong. By that time, you should be that knackered that you shouldn't be able to speed up. If lads still had something in the tank for the sixth one, they clearly weren't busting their balls for the first five. If they asked me to step it up , I couldn't - I was doing the best I could from the start.

The good thing was that Alan accepted that and said: 'As long as you're giving it all you've got, that's enough for me.'

And, as ever, he was true to his word. First game of the season, we played Bristol City at Deepdale and I started - happy days.

With about 10 minutes to go, we were 2-0 down. Not-so-happy days.

But then I scored on about 82 minutes and Callum Davidson got the equaliser right at the death, so I might not have been at the front of those long distance runs, but I was still fit enough to score against a good Championship team in the 82nd minute.

The point is, it didn't really matter what you did on the first of July, it was what you did on the eighth of August that mattered. I always felt I did my bit up top in terms of closing down, splitting the defence, etc.

I don't think fans of any of the teams I played at would ever question my work rate, and for me that's one of the biggest things throughout my career. I think people would say: 'He wasn't the most mobile lad, but he'd bust his balls in every game.'

That's all you can ask really, but a big part of it is knowing when NOT to close people down. They might have two lads at the back; one can pass, one can't. So it's common sense just to sit on the passer and let the other one have it.

You can see them panic sometimes when they're thinking: 'Someone come and take this ball off me!'

No mate, you crack on. Then it's a big hoof. In the stand. Job done.

Also, what's the point of chasing down a long ball that's obviously going to reach the keeper?

Sometimes people do it and get a big cheer from the crowd, but really you're just wasting energy - especially as you've then got to leg it back to avoid being offside. You see lads who then walk back because they're knackered and are still offside when their team's won the ball back.

Then they stand there with their hands up because they can't get involved. It's pointless. There's no point running round like a headless chicken, you've got to be ready when the time comes, not on your last legs from chasing a dozen daft through balls.

(Sometimes you do get players who were that good they could get away with not doing much off the ball. I played with Ricardo Fuller at Stoke and he was just incredible. He'd go missing for 85 minutes, then do something outrageous to win you the game, but those types of players are few and far between. The other ten would have to carry him in games, but nobody minded because he was that good.)

At the start of my second season at Deepdale, we only lost one of the first nine games in the league - and that was when we got beat at home by Reading.

I scored a penalty in that game but to be honest, I didn't like taking them. Always in the back of my mind, I had this little voice going: 'You're going to look a right prat if you miss this.'

But I took them because it was a free shot on goal and I was the centre forward. If the striker can't do it, who can? (Callum Davidson actually, but we'll come onto that later!)

I didn't really have much of a technique if I'm honest; I started off placing them to the keeper's left but as I got older, I just used to run up and lash it.

Anyway, that Reading game was the start of a run where we only won one in ten, but there were four draws in there as well.

Things weren't great, but we were still in touch with the play-off places and no-one had any inkling that they were going to sack Alan, but - *yup* - that's what happened. Football clubs, eh?

We were on a day off when Sedg rang and said: 'You're not going to believe this, Big Al's been potted.' I thought he was winding me up. All the lads were gutted, we couldn't believe it.

It was just surreal. Why would you sack a manager who'd just got into the play-offs and was looking like he might do it again?

We'd lost the captain in the summer, but Ledge had just come back and things were looking up. It made no sense at the time and it still doesn't, does it? Stupid.

On the Saturday, Rob Kelly took temporary charge as we played Colchester in the FA Cup and I remember it well - because if Alan had still been there, I wouldn't have been playing at all.

Before every game in Preston, I used to stop in a hotel but that game was just after New Year and I'd got family up from Weymouth.

So I decided to stay at home then travel over on the morning of the game. Coming over the tops, M62, in January - you can see what's coming can't you?

I woke up and it was snowing. Brilliant. I jumped straight in my car but it was chaos, slipping and sliding everywhere.

By 12.30pm I was bumper to bumper at that house in the middle of the M62 in snow - and we had to be in for 1.30pm. I'd have been pushing it to get there with no snow, so I phoned Rob and told him.

He was great about it and said: 'Look, the team sheet's got to be in at 2pm. If you can get here by then, you're playing.'

I drove like a crazy person and ran into the stadium at 1.58pm, the team sheet went in a minute later and we went on to win 7-0.

I think everyone was fired up by what had happened to Alan and I scored a hat-trick that I dedicated to him.

The funny thing is though, if he'd still been there, he wouldn't have had me anywhere near the team. He was a stickler for being on time so I'd have been up in the stands and facing a fine.

I remember one time, we were playing a midweek game at Derby and I set off early from Barnsley to meet the lads at the hotel by 12.00pm.

About 200 yards from the motorway junction, there was an accident and everything just stopped dead - solid, nothing moving, air ambulance, the lot.

I was sat there with my indicator on and could see the exit, I just couldn't get to it - about two miles away from the hotel.

I phoned Rob to tell him but it was about 2pm when I got to the hotel, not bad I thought and still nearly six hours before kick off. I went straight to my room but when I came down for the pre-match meal at 4.30pm, Alan pulled me to one side and said: 'You're not playing tonight.'

'Why?'

'You were two hours late to the hotel.' I explained the full story and I don't think he didn't believe me, but it didn't make any difference. I think I got fined £500 too, but there wasn't a lot I could say and the thing is, with any other manager, I'd have kicked off. But with Alan, I took it, even though I wasn't happy. That's the authority and respect we all had for the man.

It was crazy to sack him, it really was.

Rob Kelly's a great guy and a top coach (he does well everywhere he goes, doesn't he Rob?) but the powers that be brought in Darren Ferguson and to be honest, he had a blank slate with the players when he arrived.

He'd done well at Peterborough and was seen as a rising talent, so it didn't look a bad appointment. But I think as time went on, he was stitched up at North End.

I had about 18 months left on my contract so I was just hoping he would take to me and keep me in the team really - there's always that uncertainty when a new man comes in, so everyone is on their toes to make a good impression.

In his first season, we did OK but weren't pulling any trees up and it became one of those where we weren't going up or down, a bit of a nothing season really.

You could see that he was weighing things up and would probably start to make changes in the summer, but I don't think anyone expected them to be so big and so quick. I think Maurice Lindsay took over from Derek around that time and Fergie got told to cut wages.

They probably told him that if he chopped thirty grand a week off the bill, he'd get twenty back to spend on his own players, but I don't think that ever happened.

He'd obviously identified people he wanted to get rid of, whether that was because of wages or he didn't fancy them as players only he would know.

But he alienated them and ostracised them - they had a separate dressing room and were training with the kids.

Now, you just don't do that. People like Mells, Sedg, Richard Chaplow - he was trying to naff them off just to get them out of the club.

Let's be honest, loads of managers at loads of clubs try that, but these were people who we'd played with for two years, we'd been in a good dressing room with them and had some success with them.

They were our mates and they were all good lads, they shouldn't have been treated like that - they were just cast aside. It created a divide, not among the players, but between players and the manager.

The thing is, if you're a player and you've got 18 months left on your contract but the club wants to get rid of you . . . you've got to have a club willing to take you.

You're not just going to sign for another club on seventy per cent of the money you're on now - you just wouldn't do it. You can't do it.

He should have just come in and said: 'Right, I've got to slash the wage bill so I'm going to use you until you get yourselves sorted out somewhere else.'

Now, as a player, you'd then think: 'OK, that's fair enough.'

You can't really have a complaint with that; the manager doesn't want me, but he's going to be alright with me.

The lads would probably have got shipped on quicker by doing that as well, because if you're in or around the team other clubs are far more likely to take you than if you've been completely bombed out and haven't kicked a ball for months.

So naturally, it took time for everyone to get sorted out; I don't know if lads got pay-ups to leave, or had wages subsidised or whatever, but it was a messy business and it could easily have been avoided.

If I'd have been in that group of 'rejects', I'd have made Fergie's life hell. He was lucky that they didn't really kick off and disrupt things for the rest of us.

Look, if a manager doesn't want you, trust me, you want to move on as much as he wants you out.

But it's all got to work hasn't it? If you're on, for example, ten grand a week and someone's offering you six, as long as Preston make the difference up, then fine.

They can't be naive enough to think someone's just going to walk away from a chunk of money like that, because they're not.

Obviously Maurice had been in Rugby League, which is a different world, and Fergie had managed at Wrexham and Peterborough, where it wasn't like that.

We're talking about experienced Championship players, not kids who would take any old rubbish.

That just wasn't going to happen and I think that summed up Darren's problem. He came in and made his decisions on players, fair enough, but the way it was done was totally wrong. Yes, there was a new chairman and one or two things were changing upstairs, but let me tell you this - when teams talk about unrest in the boardroom, players don't care.

It's all a load of rubbish - players don't give a toss what's happening up there.

As long as you're in the team and you get paid at the end of the month, no-one gives a flying fig. Anyone who tells you that they do is talking rubbish - it's an excuse sometimes and that's about it. You hardly see the chairman or directors (if you're lucky) apart from when it's contract time.

Beyond that, they're not involved and that's the way it should be.

So I think Darren's reign got off to a shaky start but to be fair, he was a good coach and his pre-season was tough - though not quite as bad as Alan's.

He took us off to Spain somewhere and I was rooming with Lonners at the time West Brom put a bid in for him. It was a good offer of around £1.5 million and life-changing money for Andy, but the club were saying no.

He asked me what he should do and I gave him some advice from an old pro. I said: 'You go down to training tomorrow, you knock the cones over, kick every ball as far as possible, you be the biggest pain in the backside you can be.'

Lonners being Lonners, he said: 'I can't do that!'

I put it to him that this deal could change his life and he needed to do what was best for his family. People might say *'greedy this'* and *'greedy that'* but it's a short career playing football and clubs will shaft you as soon as look at you if the boot's on the other foot.

I said: 'Look, none of the lads will think you're a prat - they'll know the situation and understand.

'Fergie won't like it, but he will understand, too. They've brought this situation about, not you.'

But, of course, Andy wouldn't do it and in the end I think he left for a lot less money a year or so later when Phil Brown came in - so that was a great piece of business by the club, wasn't it? Not.

Back on that pre-season trip in Spain, we did quite a lot of work with the ball, but it was still a tough week physically - really hard work and I don't think anyone would say we weren't fit enough under Fergie.

It's a strange one, because he was always alright with me, even when I had a bit of drama myself that summer. I'd had a minor knee operation at the end of the season and was having a bit of physio on it.

But also around that time, my mate was having his stag do in Krakow one weekend, so I was torn a bit, you know?

I was due in for more physio on the Monday morning and the club had made it quite clear - I was not to go on the stag do.

Time for a cunning plan. Dead simple; I'd fly home on the Sunday night and Bob's your uncle - I'd go on the do AND make it to the physio.

All sorted. The return flight was booked - what could possibly go wrong?

Well, I don't know if you've ever been on a stag do with a load of lads from Barnsley . . . but needless to say, come Sunday afternoon, I was in no mood to knock it on the head early.

I did ring Jacko the physio to leave a message, saying I wouldn't be in the following day, but then I turned my phone off to cover my tracks.

As expected, when the club tried to call me back they got a message saying 'this number is unavailable'.

The only problem was, it was in Polish!

When I turned the phone back on the next day there was a message from Fergie: 'Call me ASAP.'

'Hi gaffer, are you OK?'

'Better than you,' he said, 'Good weekend in Krakow?'

He said he wanted to see me the next day and I thought I'd get fined or something. Deservedly so, I suppose.

Instead when I went in, he told me Barnsley had come in for me with a bid of £300,000 but, fair play to Fergie, despite what had just gone on, he wanted me to stay. Me? I'll be honest, when I heard about it, I wanted to go.

Nothing against Preston, but I wanted to play for my hometown club again.

I'd cocked it up earlier in my career by going out too much when I was still a teenager. I'm a Barnsley fan, I live in the town, so it was a real tug on my heartstrings more than anything else.

We had talks and the contract was all sorted, but when it came down to it, they could only offer £300,000 and North End wanted £500,000.

I think that £200,000 gap was too big to bridge, because I'll be honest, if Preston had wanted £375,000 and were turning it down over a relatively small sum, I'd probably have kicked up a fuss. Not in a disrespectful way because I thought too much of the club, my teammates and the supporters to rock the boat, but I would have been a lot firmer with Fergie about trying to make the move happen. I'd got a year left at Preston and I didn't know what was going to happen after that. Barnsley were offering three years, the contract was fine and it was all perfect for me. But once it didn't happen, no problem, I just put it to the back of my mind and cracked on. That's football.

Unfortunately, we came out for the first game of the season away at Swansea and got stuffed 4-0. We were 3-0 down at half-time and that defeat set the tone really, I think we lost six out of the first seven and were rock bottom.

I was largely coming off the bench but made my first start in the derby against Burnley at Turf Moor, live on Sky. I think Adam Barton made his debut that day and for most of the match we absolutely terrorised them.

Adam scored, Keith Treacy got a cracker and I got the third right in front of the North End fans, 3-1 up - everything was looking good.

Then with about ten minutes to go, Billy Jones got sent off for time-wasting - it was a joke of a decision, shocking. They got back into it almost straight away - 3-2 - then, unbelievably, they got an equaliser, 3-3.

You know the rest don't you? 4-3 in injury time and we'd fallen apart.

Afterwards, we were low in the dressing room, just stunned by it. Three-one up with six minutes to go and you lose 4-3; how the heck has that happened?

That day summed things up really - under Fergie we never had any problem scoring goals, we just used to ship too many at the other end.

I don't think we were miles away, if we could just tighten things up a bit.

If it carried on like this, we were going to end up beating someone 6-4. Oh, hold on . . !

Leeds away. Probably the game that everyone remembers me for most in Preston and if you're going to be remembered for something, make it something special. What a night that was. Iain Hume had come in and he was brilliant; a real gem of a player and an all-round good guy in the dressing room.

But the game itself was the same old pattern - I scored to put us 1-0 up and then on 32 minutes we were 4-1 down: 'Flaming hell, we're here again! What's happening here?'

I can just remember thinking: 'Blimey, we've got to chase around here for another 60 minutes after half-time - this could get embarrassing. It could be six or seven.'

But then just before half time we got the big turning point when I got another one to make it 4-2.

Paul Coutts played a brilliant pass and watch out for the dirty step-over before the finish - I should have celebrated more looking back, but when you're 4-2 down you just want to get on with it.

We came in at half-time and when it's a crazy scoreline like that, we genuinely thought we could get something out of it - they weren't brilliant at the back. Quite early on in that second half, Keith Treacy scored direct from a corner (which was the type of thing Keith could do, by the way, what a natural talent he was.)

Then Couttsy got brought down for the clearest penalty you'll ever see.

I remember going for the ball to take the pen, but Callum was the designated penalty taker and he came over to take it off me.

I said: 'Are you joking? I'm on a hat-trick here!'

He said: 'I couldn't give a toss, give me the ball.'

And that was that. Cal blasted it in and suddenly at 4-4 we were thinking: 'We can win this!' You get that feeling and I think everyone does; our fans, their fans, their players, the momentum just swings behind you and it's like a force of nature. You can feel it coming.

We were going for it like there was no tomorrow and piling forward when Ledge clipped a great ball forward.

I managed to roll the defender, hit it low and hard and . . . *Booom! Get in!*

Celebrations? *CEL-EB-BRA-TIONS??!!! Oh my God.*

I mean, it was surreal wasn't it. Three fingers in the air on each hand, biggest smile on my face ever and right in the corner where the North End lot were going wild. And when I say wild I mean flipping *WILD*.

Credit to them, they'd gone over to Leeds for a night game, a tough place to go, we'd been 4-1 down but they hadn't slaughtered us - and then this . . !

All those Leeds fans silent and the Preston fans going absolutely crazy. That feeling . . . you can't put it into words, you just can't.

I bet if you asked the North End fans who were there they wouldn't have the words for it either. But they'll never forget it. It's just one of those football nights that pays everything off for the supporters. The travelling, the money, the time - it suddenly all becomes worth it. A life-long memory. You can't put a price on that.

The mad thing was, there was still quite a bit of time left so it wasn't until Humey got the sixth - *six at Elland Road!* - that we could really start to relax a little bit.

For a lad of his size, Humey was brilliant in the air and he was brave too, especially after what had gone on with that head injury he suffered a few years earlier. Some people might protect themselves a bit more after a knock like that, but he would still put his head in anywhere, bless him - a top man.

We got back in the dressing room and amid all the celebrations, there were looks of disbelief. It was like: 'Did that really just happen?'

Barnsley had played at home that night so I arranged to meet a couple of pals and have a night round the town in my Preston tracksuit, ditching the car and having a celebratory drink or two.

I don't think anyone would have minded after a game like that.

It's when you're drinking at the wrong time that things start to catch up with you. I think Keith Treacy was one of the best players I ever played with, who should have done so, so much better with his talent. Left foot, right foot, there wasn't much he couldn't do, but he just couldn't get his head straight.

Obviously, he liked a drink - and don't get me wrong, I can't preach here - but he needed someone to just get hold of him and look after him.

It's a crying shame really, because it was such a waste of talent and he was a lovely lad, but he just went the wrong way in his career. Really sad.

Even though the team was struggling, I was still doing OK with seven goals in our first 12 games.

But things weren't great and after we beat Crystal Palace 4-3 a couple of weeks later, we tightened up at the back, but we stopped scoring too.

It wasn't a great time and I tweaked my knee again around then too, so I was struggling a bit.

My contract was up at the end of the season, but I hadn't put any feelers out when both Cardiff and Sheffield Wednesday came in for me around Christmas.

There had been no mention of a new contract from North End at that point so I had to sort myself out. Both clubs had offered £100,000 and both bids had been accepted.

So just think about that for a second; the club had turned down £300,000 from Barnsley for me a few months earlier and now they'd said yes to £100,000

And on top of that, they were about to let Lonners leave for a fraction of what West Brom had offered.

That's more than £1 million lost on two deals by my reckoning - for a club that was talking about needing money. Absolute madness.

When I weighed it up, Alan Irvine was at Wednesday and it was only 25 minutes from my house. Yes, Barnsley fans would give me stick, but I couldn't care less about stuff like that.

However, they were in League 1 at the time and Cardiff were pushing for promotion to the Premier League.

It was a tough call because I would have loved to work with Alan again, but Dave Jones really wanted me at Cardiff too - I must have made a good impression on him after that game at Deepdale.

Cardiff were offering a lot more in wages and in the end my thought process was: sign for them and hopefully they will get promoted, at which point my money will double, they'll realise I'm not good enough for the Prem and they'll loan me back up north somewhere. Everybody's happy.

I spoke to Fergie about it and, again, even though the club had accepted the offers he wanted me to stay.

At that point, there was finally some talk of a new contract but things had clearly changed at the club and Fergie made it clear that it wouldn't be anywhere near what I'd been getting previously.

It was also nowhere near what the other offers were and so I said: 'Thanks, but with all due respect, I can't do that. I'm going to have to go.'

It might have been different if we'd have been at the top of the league and flying with a chance of promotion, but it was just the opposite in fact - we weren't great, we were in trouble and we were looking like we might go down, which is sadly what happened in the end.

You get a feeling about the way things are going and it wasn't through lack of effort on anyone's part. It was just that downward spiral that's very hard to get out of once you're in it. You could see how the club was going at that time.

In all honesty, I've no regrets about leaving - I think it was time to move on. The old team had been broken up and I think things never really recovered from sacking Big Al for quite a long time, even after I left.

As it turned out, Cardiff didn't get promoted, Dave Jones got fired and things didn't work out as planned.

I missed Preston like mad, but there was no chance of me coming back under Phil Brown (we had history from my Hull City days) and I wouldn't have signed for Graham Westley for a gold pig.

Funnily enough, right at the end of my time, I ended up getting him as manager at Newport a few years later when I was 35. It didn't go well.

I lasted two games - I tweaked my hamstring and was then out for six weeks. I was watching the lads doing his training and I thought: 'Nah, this isn't for me.'

I left the next day. It really was as bad as they say, but to be fair to him, he's actually a nice fella as a person. And he signed some good players for Preston; Scott Laird, Joe Garner, Paul Huntington.

If you sign for him knowing what to expect then you can't complain, but with me, he came in when I was already there, so I wasn't having it - it would have been too much for me at 25, let alone 35.

I was nearing the end of my career then but undoubtedly the first 18 months of my time at Preston was the happiest of my playing days.

Going in there with Kenna, Mells, Browny, Youl - every one of the lads really, they were all great. The fans were top, Alan was the best manager I ever played for and it was just a really great place to be.

Obviously when things started changing, it was sad to see North End get relegated and I was absolutely chuffed when they won those play-offs to come back up. Was it the tenth attempt? The celebrations must have been brilliant and I was buzzing for everyone, I really was.

I want all my ex-clubs to do well and I think if North End get into the play-offs, they've had a successful season. I don't think anyone is expecting them to get up there most years, but similarly - *touch wood* - there's no real chance of them going down again in the foreseeable future.

They're established as a consistent Championship club, unless they have an absolute shocker or an incredible season. One extreme or the other.

Me? I'm keeping busy with the Undr The Cosh podcast and one or two bits and bobs. We have a good laugh doing it and if you ever wonder why we dropped the 'e' from 'Under' it's because there's a Canadian podcast that uses that name.

I think we've got away with it now and it's going really well - it just gets bigger and bigger. When we first started it, I didn't even know what a podcast was.

Someone said that if we could get to 10,000 listens per episode that would be brilliant. But it's grown so much now we're getting about 100,000 so it's mind-blowing really, especially as we're basically winging it every time!

Paul McKenna summed it up when he came on the podcast and said that no matter how well they were doing, he never thought North End were going to give it that extra push to get over the line.

Preston fans will know what he means, but hopefully they can crack it at some point. Bolton, Wigan, Blackpool and all those other Lancashire clubs have been in the Premier League and it's a joke really that North End haven't.

It's got to happen at some point and, trust me, dreams do come true.

Just look at me. When I was young, I used to stand in the mirror getting ready for a big night out, playing my favourite song and dreaming of becoming a professional footballer.

Some people might have thought it would never happen for a fat lad from Barnsley, just like they don't think Preston will get to the Premier League.

Don't listen to them. Put a bit of Journey on - and don't stop believing.

CHAPTER 13

TEPI MOILANEN: OUTSIDER

Winning and excitement; that's what I was looking for from football. The kicks, the thrills, the intensity, the adrenaline rush. And I found it all in Preston, a long way from my home in Finland.

I loved the people, I loved the club and I loved those times.

Did I always fit in? No, of course not. And without being harsh, I didn't really care about that - I didn't come to make friends. I came for the winning.

I didn't come to build a football career. I didn't come to study the game. I didn't come for money or adulation. I just came to win the next game and the championship. If that made me a bit of an outsider, I accepted that and so did everyone else, I think.

That was me, that was who I was and this is how it all came about.

I grew up being passionate about playing football, but not really watching it - that didn't interest me very much. I wanted to be out there, playing. I'd watch the World Cup and Euros, but - and this will become more important as my story goes on - I didn't study the game religiously.

Ice hockey is the biggest sport in Finland and when all us kids were outside, we'd be playing street hockey, not football.

Luckily, when I was six I joined a junior football team as an outfield player, just running around like a crazy person at that age. But the following year a load of the older kids left and the boy who went in goal was terrible. I was tall so I volunteered to have a go and that was that - suddenly I was a goalkeeper. I did really well at school and was all set to take up a place at university, where my career path was to study and probably go on to become a teacher. So far, so normal, I guess.

But my football career was also taking off and at 18 I was playing fairly regularly for my local team, Ilves (Tampere). I'm not sure you'd call it professional, as the wages were tiny - and about 18 months late!

It wasn't really full-time either, so I was able to do my studies and still have a path laid out; university, Finnish football, job.

Nothing wrong with that - but not too much excitement, either.

And you know when you're young, you're a little bit restless - you do things your parents don't always agree with. So there was a fair bit of family criticism when I left university and moved to the West Coast to join a team called Jaro, where the wages were even less, but at least they were on time!

It was a town of about 20,000 people and the crowds were less than 2,000, but it was known as a football town and when you're young, playing sports, who needs lots of money? Enjoy life.

I certainly enjoyed it and got called up to the Finland Under-21 squad, where we did well and nearly qualified for the European Championships.

Occasionally, my roommate was Sami Hyypia who went on to play for Liverpool and you could see right from a young age that he was a student of the game, always analysing tactics, his position. Same with Jari Litmanen, who I played with in the national squad; those guys immersed themselves in football from a really young age and learned everything about it.

Me? I didn't want to be in a classroom, I wanted to be out in the thick of things. I had some talent, but my progression was more instinctive and not as straightforward as it might have been if I'd been brought up in England.

It's a different culture in Finland and here is a big example: One of the things you have to do growing up is National Service - for 11 months.

So when I was 18, I had to go in the army along with my pals from the national team - no exceptions. We went into the officer training class and it was really physically hard; runs, marches, drills - all that army stuff.

We were in a reconnaissance unit and we learned how to fire all sorts of weapons and set off explosives and things. We would take command of squads of eight and go out on exercise, setting up tents, looking for enemy movement, maybe call in artillery - then get back and have time for football training, too.

So it was full-on but we were kept together as a football team, so that made it a bit better. It's a good example of the life and culture I was coming from when I arrived in England. I'm not sure what some of the Preston guys would have thought if you'd told them they had to go in the army for almost a year at 18.

For me, that was normal.

My path to Preston began with a guy about my age who wanted to make it as a sports agent. He was casting around for footballers who would let him represent them.

Well, no-one else had ever asked me if they could be my agent, so of course I said 'yes' and he arranged a trial for me at this English Fourth Division side I'd never heard of - Preston North End. There was talk of somewhere in Belgium, but Preston was the first one lined up and I came over for a trial under Gary Peters.

I can't remember much about it, but it must have gone well because an actual fee was agreed - I think it was about £150,000, maybe a bit higher.

So everything was going great . . . until I failed the medical.

I'd had a problem from childhood; I have osteochondritis which affected the bone in my left knee (it still does) and at 16 I'd had quite a big operation on it.

The club could easily have called the deal off and my whole future could have looked very different.

But instead Gary pushed it through and re-arranged the fee to be based on appearances, so I had a lucky escape and two days before my 22nd birthday in December 1995, I signed for PNE. So far, so good. But the reality was that I wasn't prepared at all for the move - in fact, I was totally overwhelmed by it.

The step up from everything in Finland was huge.

The pace of the game in England, the stadium, the size of the fanbase at PNE, the passion, the expectation, everything was different and, honestly, I was intimidated by it.

I'd come from a fairly laid-back culture into a country where football is a national obsession. I remember being introduced to the crowd at a first team game at Deepdale - I wasn't playing, so I just had to walk on and wave.

All very straightforward, but when I turned to go back down the old tunnel, there were these away fans on one side going crazy at me.

I didn't even know they were opposition supporters, so I gave them a little wave and a smile back. I was genuinely being friendly, but - *oh, man!* - these guys started going crazy, calling me all these names and getting very wound up. I hadn't even played a game yet! I'd not been brought up on the terraces, so this was a whole new world for me, an intimidating world. And I had to learn fast.

The tempo, the training, the tactics - all of it was a huge step up for me.

There was just a lot more structure than I'd been used to and I wasn't ready for it. I wasn't one of those guys who had been planning to be a professional footballer from a long way back.

I hadn't been coached for it - and now here I was.

Preston may have been in the lowest division in the English league, but Saturday afternoon at 3pm was a bit like entering the Colosseum in Rome. You had the old Town End with that low roof and the fans packed inside it and the noise - *wow!* You could see that it *really* mattered to these people.

Then there was the media, too . . . it was all a big surprise to me - a real culture shock. Luckily, English had been my strongest subject at school, so I spoke the language very well.

Mind you, I still learned some new words - *'minging'* was a favourite among the lads that I always found funny.

John Vaughan was the goalkeeper when I arrived and physically he couldn't have been more different to me; he was smaller, super agile.

The fans called him *The Cat* and you could see why.

I shared a terraced house in Tulketh Brow with John; he had the apartment upstairs and I had the one downstairs and we got on well.

I found the British people really friendly and welcoming - you have a great way of dealing with getting to know new people. There are unwritten rules; no religion, no politics, no complicated subjects - just football, weather and general chit-chat. Use the word *'minging'* in every sentence and you'll fit in just fine.

Anyway, a couple of weeks after arriving, I made my debut away at Lincoln in a minging 0-0 draw.

I had David Moyes and Russ Wilcox in front of me and Ian Bryson in midfield, so I looked at them and thought: 'Wow - this is great, these guys really know what they're doing.' It was second nature to them and Moyesie never stopped talking all game. The whole thing was brilliant for me, the fans gave me a good reception and it was all going well. Too well.

The next game was away at Darlington and in the warm-up, Vaughany was banging the balls at me as hard as he could - really belting them.

A bouncing ball hit me right on the end of my middle finger and that was it - I had ligament damage right before the kick-off. It was strapped up and we went on to win 2-1 but really, that was a nightmare injury and my hopes of a good start at the club were ruined from that moment, especially as they later found a fracture.

For the rest of the season, my hand wasn't right so it was really frustrating not to be able to play, especially as the team won the league that year. I was part of the celebrations, but with only a couple of games to my name, I wasn't a very big part of it at all.

Still, it was great for the club to be promoted and there were nearly 19,000 fans at the last game, so I felt my desire to join a winning team was going in the right direction.

Speaking of which, I'd also cut my hair by that point after realising that maybe a Finnish mullet doesn't fit the English game so much. *(Also, I was starting to go thin on top already and trust me, there's not very much of it left at all now.)*

Anyway, going into the next season, I was first choice at the start, but I was very wobbly at that time. I was still getting over the injury, so wasn't playing well and it wasn't a surprise when the manager brought in a young David Lucas for his debut in a League Cup game against Wigan.

Dave kept the score down to four that night (!) and understandably, Gary then brought a more experienced goalkeeper in - Bobby Mimms.

Bobby was great with me and Dave and it was the right decision to bring someone like him in - he was a safe pair of hands in every sense.

He had bags of games under his belt and was still a very good goalkeeper, so I couldn't really argue with it.

Instead, I went out on loan to Scarborough and then Darlington to try to get some experience of my own.

To be honest, I didn't really know what to expect. I'd arrived at PNE without much experience, I hadn't played well at times, I had no agent by then and now I was sent out on my own to the other side of the country.

Frankly, I wasn't sure if I was going to be sold, so it was a tough time but I just had to get on with it and learn as much as I could.

My stay in Scarborough was only very brief and they got a bit angry with me when they asked about a permanent transfer. I said something like: 'Oh no, I'm not staying here for long - I want to get back to Preston!'

That didn't go down too well and about a week later, I was packing my bags. I enjoyed my time at Darlington much more.

The manager was the old Liverpool striker David Hodgson and he was great with coaching me and I felt I learned a lot there, getting used to the surroundings of the English game. He wanted me to join permanently and looking back, I don't think it would have been a bad thing to have gone there and got really settled at that level.

At Preston, I felt it was always necessary to play well to stay in the side and I thrived on that excitement. Darlington might have been a safer option and a better environment to slowly develop my game, but I didn't want that.

Some players have more patience and think more long term. Not me - I just wanted to get to the top as quickly as possible.

Deep down, I felt I was good enough and I could do anything. You always do when you're young, don't you?

Of course, looking back now, I realise I still had a lot to learn.

The reality was that I'd been in England for 18 months and it was starting to be 'make or break'.

I'd only played a handful of games, I'd not been brilliant, and I knew that the 1997/98 season was going to be huge - *now or never,* you know?

By that time, Dave Lucas and me were the only two goalkeepers in the squad and I started as first choice. I did OK, but results were patchy and you could feel the pressure building on Gary.

We lost 6-0 to Blackburn in the League Cup at Ewood Park and had a bad run around Christmas in the league. I don't think performances were that bad, but every manager knows you live or die by results.

You got the feeling change was coming, but in terms of Gary stepping down and Moyesie taking over, I didn't see that as anything dramatic.

I don't remember any big bust-ups behind the scenes, beyond the normal discussions we'd have as a group.

The change made sense to me; it was a natural progression for David and a good use of Gary's skills with younger players.

The biggest change when the new boss took over was the physicality. Now, Gary wasn't soft - *far from it* - but Moyesie was physically more demanding and upped the intensity in training even more. We were a young side so we were naturally fit, but the work we did on stamina was now huge.

In Gary's time, there was the old approach that if you win, you get days off and if you don't win, you get called in for more training.

Moyesie wasn't so much into that sort of thinking - he just made us work harder and harder every week and we spent more time on the training ground almost without realising it.

One of the differences from then to now is that there wasn't a full-time goalkeeping coach until Kelham O'Hanlon arrived.

Before that, the PNE legend Roy Tunks would come in and help out part time with us, so it was good to learn from his experience.

Goalkeepers still had to do the long runs in pre-season though - even though I sucked at it, always at the back and lagging. The rest of the guys were running twice a day, whereas the goalkeepers would train separately in the morning then just do the second running session in the afternoon.

For me that was still way too much - I could sprint, but I had no stamina at all.

There's a reason why I became a goalkeeper in Finland and not a cross-country skier, you know!

What we did have was a brilliant team spirit and everyone got on together. Sean Gregan was probably the master of the banter; so quick-witted and funny - he could slaughter people, but always with a smile on his face and never nasty.

Greegs was just a naturally funny guy and a big, big leader in the dressing room, on the pitch and off it too.

We were young guys, in a fairly small town, with free time on our hands - and, crucially, there was no social media in those days.

So we had a lot of fun, a lot of big nights out, some big days out, and people in Preston were fine with it. You weren't in a goldfish bowl like you might be at a bigger club and if fans saw you out - they just joined in. They loved the way the team was out in the same pubs they were in and there wasn't this distance between them and us. We weren't in a roped-off VIP area drinking Champagne - we were playing darts and pool in The Sumners or the Withy Trees, just like everyone else.

That team spirit off the pitch is priceless. There is so much to be said for having that bond and everyone being united when you're grinding out a result on a cold and windy night at a tough away ground.

And I include the supporters in that too - they knew that we knew we were representing them and we wouldn't stop fighting right to the final whistle. *(Is it too soon to mention the Birmingham game yet?)*

Once Moyesie took over, it took a while for results to improve but when they did, you could see that the future was looking good. We'd turned a corner and instead of looking down the league table, we were now always looking up. Who could we reel in next? Where will three points on Saturday take us?

That was the mentality.

I ended up playing 48 games that year and was very proud - *incredibly proud* - to be named Player of the Year. I'd challenged myself by coming back to Preston and shown I could perform at that level - I'd proved a point.

The next year was Moyesie's first full season in charge and, with a hell of a pre-season behind us, we picked up right from the start.

I remember that night we beat Manchester City at their old stadium. The surrounding area in Moss Side was crazy - it looked like we'd come to a different country and I was thinking: *'What the hell is this?'*

Concrete all over the place, all the windows boarded up and barbed wire everywhere. But there were thousands of people walking to the game from miles away and you knew this was a big club, so to go there and win was a great night.

It's funny - and this is going to sound selfish - but I learned to use the crowd at games as a facilitator to get in the right mental 'zone'. The more intense the crowd and the fans the easier I found it to get where I wanted to be.

I always acknowledged the Preston fans' support and thought their loyalty was incredible, to see them hundreds of miles away, watching a midweek game somewhere.

But if I'm honest, I didn't seek to have a strong personal connection with them in the 90 minutes; I wanted to use them, feed off their energy. It didn't matter if that energy was good or bad, because I would use it to fuel my performance either way. The more noise, the better I would play.

As a result, I struggled a bit during pre-season and Moyesie often made the point that I was a slow starter in the first few weeks of the season.

Anyway a few games after that big win at City, I got injured at Northampton in a crazy game where there was trouble between the players at the end and even the police got involved.

If I'm honest, I can't remember what went on because when you're in games, you get caught up in the moment and afterwards, it's not always easy to recall.

Games where I was on the bench, I can remember much better, because you're not a part of it and you're a lot more analytical. I probably should remember that Northampton game because after that I was out for the season.

I injured my sternum when their striker slid into me - late, studs first - so that was really disappointing and really, really painful.

Lucs came in and did brilliantly though and I had to watch from the sidelines while we played Arsenal in that great FA Cup match and then made the play-offs against Gillingham, where we just lost out narrowly.

Dave started the next season as first choice and was doing well until we played Wigan at home on a beautiful sunny day at Deepdale.

There was a short back pass and he came out, caught the guy's leg and got sent off. I quickly had to get on to face the penalty and that situation was something I wasn't very good at.

If I wasn't involved from the start, getting into the zone wasn't easy for me.

You go from one minute on the bench to the next trying to save a penalty in front of 15,000 people . . . I found that hard.

So unsurprisingly, my first touch that game was picking the ball out of the net.

Goalkeeping is a technical position and Lucs, for example, was brilliant technically, a superb goalkeeper, who had been brought up living and breathing football. Because I had limited exposure to football growing up, I was probably the opposite. I was intuitive - I handled situations as they came up, I didn't really prepare for them.

If I could go back and do it all again, I would study much harder.

As it was, I went out and immersed myself in every game to see what it would bring, what saves I would make and what kicks I would get out of it.

When I say kicks, I mean 'thrills'; a big save, a good catch, a big punch, a one-on-one - that adrenaline rush you get. Remember, I was looking for winning and excitement? Well, that Wigan game is one where I probably had too much excitement, because in the second half, I came out to clear a long ball, got the sun in my eyes and, yep, missed it completely.

A swing and a miss - I didn't have the ball in my hands, I had my head in my hands.

Their guy walked the ball into the empty net and it stings for a couple of days, for sure. If I had a bad game, or made a mistake like that, it bothered me. This was because I didn't have a strong enough process to be resilient. That wasn't an aspect that you can prepare for, it affects your life.

One miss for a striker, one mistake for a goalkeeper, one moment has a big impact. You go home and it sucks, really unpleasant, and it's something players have to handle. Some people might be able to block it out, but the reality for me was that I couldn't.

Luckily that year, we had a very good team and a very good season. I stayed in the line-up as we won the Championship and kept a record of 23 clean sheets, which again, is something to be proud of. But it's the whole team that keeps clean sheets, not just the goalkeeper. The defence, midfield, even the strikers when they came back, everyone protected our goal like their lives depended on it.

After that Wigan game (or maybe *because* of that Wigan game), I really got into the zone and the team was like a freight train - once we got rolling, we were very hard to stop.

We had Graham Alexander, Ryan Kidd, Michael Jackson, Sean Gregan, Jon Macken . . . you could go through the entire line-up and they are Preston greats.

We went out expecting to win every game, we treated it like it was inevitable because we had so much talent and we worked so hard.

The manager drove and drove and drove us on - it was relentless. Once we got into our rhythm, the games couldn't come fast enough for us. We harassed teams to death, we didn't drop too deep, we were right at them from the start.

It was really, really impressive and I was proud to be a part of it. I'd watch the guys going from start to finish and be stood there thinking: 'Wow! I'm glad I'm not on the receiving end of that.'

I keep using the word '*intensity*' because that's what our game plan was. The only issue was that if that didn't work, we didn't really have a back-up plan to deal with a slow game. If we slowed things down and fell into the tempo of the opposition we weren't as effective.

Back then, Fulham under Jean Tigana were really the only ones who could counteract us and they played us off the park at Craven Cottage.

These days, I think probably more teams would.

I don't really watch football now, but when I do, I watch it in an analytical way, which I suppose makes it less entertaining in a way.

The other thing that was happening back then was the stadium development was taking shape and we now had two new stands, as well as the old Town End, so it was the best of both worlds really; comfort for those who wanted it and craziness for the guys behind the goal.

I remember we played Blackpool on a Friday night at Deepdale and beat them 3-0 and it was just insane. The emotion and the scenes from the supporters to win a derby game like that . . . all the boys understood it and afterwards there was so much celebration in the dressing room - that was a BIG result.

By that time I'd moved to Cottam, so I was still right in among the supporters and they'd stop me in the street - I wasn't exactly hard to spot I suppose!

So I knew the rivalries and knew what it meant to everyone. Looking back, I suppose a more professional decision would have been to live outside the town, to be away from that intensity so that you weren't always in among it. But I enjoyed being right in the heart of things, talking to people and feeling their passion.

It all added to the excitement and feeling that you were a part of something special.

When I was away with the Finnish Under-21 team I used to prepare for games by almost isolating myself. I'd have my hood up, headphones on, playing heavy metal music and just get myself in the 'zone' away from everyone else.

What's strange is that I never really did that at Preston. There was a different vibe and being out on your own wasn't really the done thing.

I'm not saying we weren't all together with the Finland team, but the Preston players had this creed that everyone was involved with everything.

It was kind of unwritten, you just knew it.

That's what the culture was - and it worked because we won the title that year.

Ironically, probably my best game came in that run-in when we beat Wigan 1-0.

It was at their stadium, but the number of Preston fans made it feel like it was ours that night - incredible support.

A couple of weeks later, we played away at Cambridge; a really small ground, a long way away, but still there were thousands of PNE fans there.

We were probably expecting to win but we were rubbish and deservedly got beat 2-0. At the end, I was feeling terrible because we'd played so badly, but then the results came in that we were promoted - and not only that but league champions too!Suddenly, everyone went crazy and the celebrations were long and hard that night.

But it's a sign of the team that on the bus going home, amid all the cheers and beers, the result on the day wasn't forgotten and there were discussions about how we could improve. That was Moyesie all over - we'd just won the league, but that didn't mean we could forget a bad performance.

When we got back, it was amazing again how freely we were able to celebrate with the fans and the people in Preston. There was less money in the game back then, so the distance between players and supporters was much closer.

So it was a great night, but to be honest, there were so many great nights round the town while I was there, they're hard to remember all these years later!

Not that it was all partying, of course. We were now going into the Championship and by this point Moyesie's pre-seasons were harder than ever.

His mentality was always 15 per cent more, 15 per cent more, you can do more, you can do more again . . . maybe we couldn't!

Same with post-match analysis. Even when we won, it wasn't just: 'Here's what you did well, guys.' It was: 'Here's what you can do MORE.'

Running up all the sand dunes, literally everything we did was increased year after year. There was all the mandatory throwing up and puking but luckily, I benefited from having long legs so I could get up the dunes easier.

For sure, when we went into that first Championship season, we were all crazy fit - well, the ones who had survived anyway!

I was in the team, but if I'm honest, I wasn't always a consistent performer.

There were times when I was poor and I think it all comes back to not having a proper football education right from the start.

It's a theme I keep mentioning because there were good habits and things I could have picked up sooner if I'd studied the game more, but it wasn't until much later that I realised this. You pick up positioning, patterns of play and especially, *stance*, which is massively important for a goalkeeper.

It sounds so obvious now, but at the time, I didn't think about it. I had good reactions and great agility, but my centre of gravity was too high and my goalkeeping stance was resulting in a poor balance at times. I could be explosive from a standing position and it was easier to make spectacular saves in the top corner from that starting point, as I had a good leap and a long reach.

But that uprightness was also a weakness with handling the ball around my body and especially around my feet. And, again, it wasn't until much later that I came to realise this.

I looked at Craig Gordon when I went to Hearts and he always had a wide stance, forward leaning posture, great balance and brilliant handling of the ball.

Lucs was like that, too; he was miles ahead of me, technique-wise. He had a very similar stance and positioning awareness to Craig. My narrow stance and upright posture required more footwork and timing and more reflexes.

It can be flashier, but it's also fragile. And the higher up the leagues we went, the bigger a problem it became for me. As a result, I was not consistent enough.

So in that season, it was a case of me playing sometimes, Lucs sometimes and that was no problem for us personally - we got on really well and he's a great guy; a proper Preston 'lad' as you'd call it. He was super funny and laid back and I loved spending time with him and Kelham as goalkeepers.

Same with Paul McKenna, local guys who really understood what it meant to play for their hometown team.

What can you say about Kenna that hasn't been said before? He just made the game look easy and was a top, top player - the epitome of consistency.

We were so lucky to have him and in the dressing room he was so laid back on the surface, but underneath that . . . different levels of intensity and determination.

We'd done well so far in that first season up, but we went on a bad run around New Year and lost four games on the trot with Dave in the team. The last game of that run was away at Wimbledon and we lost 3-1.

Now, there was always analysis after games, but after that one, there was a full-on inquest.

Everyone was having their say but to me, it was all just going round in circles.

I was getting fed up with hearing it all, so I just stood up and said we need to get the *intensity* back - it was as simple as that.

I don't know what happened after that, but suddenly in the week, the training was sharper, the boys were spikier and the mood had turned around.

I was really pleased with that reaction, but I was still thinking: 'Either I've blown it here and I won't play again - or I'll be in the team on Saturday.'

Thankfully, when the team was named, the gaffer had made quite a few changes and I was back in.

So that was a relief - and even more pressure than usual after my little outburst!

We went down to Portsmouth and won 1-0, then beat QPR 5-0 at Deepdale, then beat Stockport away and you could see the mood was: 'OK, we've had our wobble, now we're back on track.'

By that point I think we really were surprising people. We'd just come up and now we were beating these teams that had been in the Premier League or in the Championship for quite a while. There wasn't much media attention on us, so we were kind of under the radar - no big stars, just a great team ethic.

So it was all going well for me again, but I should have known there would be something around the corner - there always was.

We played away at Burnley in April and after about half an hour this through ball came down the pitch.

I flew out to clear it and, really, I was a bit naive. I got there first and cleared the ball with the inside of my foot, but the guy (Gareth Taylor) absolutely clattered me right on my ankle with his follow-through.

A more savvy keeper could have got the ball away, won a free-kick, got the guy a yellow card and not be injured. But I wasn't that player sadly, and I feared my season was over - the pain told me that!

To this day, my right foot still drops from that injury. The inside of the ankle ligaments are very weak and it just tilts.

It was infuriating because I knew the team was going to fly for the rest of the season and now I wasn't going to be a big part of it.

And the worst thing of all? I missed the flaming Birmingham play-off match, which was just THE best game of football ever. You will not show me a better game than that.

Luckily, if you're not going to play, I had the next best thing - I was on the bench and it was just one of the best nights of my life.

I was close to Moyesie and I remember he could get really fidgety and tense on the bench. That night he was excited, but calm; team - spot on, tactics - spot on, substitutions - spot on. He got everything right and as I mentioned earlier, we had a team that would fight, fight, FIGHT to the very end.

For me, that game was the signature performance of that side; skill, passion, spirit, teamwork, how many words do you want? It just summed up everything.

Once the subs were made I knew I wasn't going on - so I became a pure supporter. I was a fan sitting on the bench, enjoying the intensity of the match, just drinking it all in.

If you asked any Preston fan if they could go back and relive a game it would be that one.

The crowd, the noise, the atmosphere - it's giving me goosebumps to talk about that Mark Rankine goal now. You could feel it coming. The guys were out on their feet, they'd given everything, the ref should have blown, but one last attack and then . . . wow! *Ohhhhhh, WOW!*

Talk about emotion, talk about celebration. *THAT* was football at its finest. Those moments are what makes people support teams for the rest of their lives.

Adventure? Excitement? That game was more than that - it was an intense experience. I was like an adrenaline junkie with it. Did it make me want to study and learn the game? Hell, no - I just wanted more nights like that!

As for the final against Bolton . . . anti-climax. That's all I can say. Complete opposite to the semi-final and somehow flat by comparison.

Nobody's fault, maybe we just ran out of juice. On the other hand, you've got to give credit to Bolton - they dictated the game and didn't let us play the way we wanted to. Not many teams could do that to us.

But, yes, gutted on the day, gutted the week after, the year after and still gutted now.

On another day, we win that game, we go up and the whole history of Preston football is different.

But you can't turn back the clock. You can only deal with what happened. Life goes on and we went on.

On a personal level, that summer reached a low point for me with an incident in Austria which I can only sum up in one word - *indiscipline*. We were out there on pre-season that summer and had lost a couple of friendlies, one against a German team and the other a Turkish side.

Again, maybe I was too intuitive - *or not intuitive enough* - but you know by now that I have a passionate approach to life . . .

Anyway, the '*indiscipline'*. We were in a bar late on and there was something that Kenna thought was an injustice with him and Moyesie.

Something had gone on, or something was said that was incorrect, I can't remember exactly what sparked it.

What I do know is that if I saw something that I felt was wrong or an injustice, I would react in an instinctive way, but also probably an unprofessional way.

That's what happened, really.

There was a little bit of pushing and shoving between me and Moyesie - voices were raised and we basically ended up having a bit of a wrestling match.

No punches were thrown but, yes, it got out of hand. It was definitely my instigation and I was in the wrong, I know that.

I'm not making excuses, but you can look at it as part of a bigger picture to a degree. Our dressing room was built on that intensity and those types of backlashes weren't unheard of.

It was unusual because the manager was involved and somehow the press found out. It doesn't mean people didn't get on - in fact, we all got on great in the group.

That intensity is what you'd have in the week and on a Saturday it would fuel you - there was an energy to it.

That Austria incident was easily the most public, because the media got hold of it and made it a much bigger thing than it was.

To give you an example, on a Friday before games we used to play young against old and those games were often the hardest, most physical parts of the week - full-on matches. You always wore your strongest shin pads.

Moyesie would get under your skin about it and make it really, really competitive.

I mention that just as an example of the intensity and the culture, because - coming back to that Austria incident - mentally, I was really getting tired.

The combination of my approach with Gary and Moyesie's dressing rooms had really taken it out of me over the years.

The training was fighting for your life, young against old, every Friday. It drains you over a period of time and I think that tiredness played a part in my reaction that night.

And from a playing perspective, there's only so far you can take your game on intensity alone. As you get older, it's normally someone's 'footballing brain' that kicks in and players compensate for their physical deterioration by employing what they've learned over the years.

But, as I keep saying, I didn't have that football learning to replace it.

I had started doubting that intensity in my own approach, so suddenly there was this backlash within me, which maybe contributed to what happened in Austria.

I was no longer a young player and this full-on dressing room environment that had carried me so far, was now turning from a positive strength, to something that was increasingly negative.

The intensity wasn't powering me anymore, it was draining me.

Intensity was at the heart of English football and everything that we did at Preston, too. Just to give a contrast, when I went to Hearts the approach was totally the opposite. Credit to Craig Levein there because it was very successful for Hearts and as a learning experience it turned out to be amazing for me in the end. On the Friday before games, we would play the youth team; eleven against eleven, half tempo, with the manager Craig watching from the stands.

He would constantly interrupt about exact distances between people, shape and positions and those games would take ages.

It opened my eyes to another way of doing things and it worked for Hearts, but the intensity level for me was absolutely zero compared to Preston.

At North End, if you were injured and in the physio's room, there was no respite - Moyesie would be on you all the time.

What injury is it? How often were you injured? When were you coming back? If you weren't back when you said you would be - why not?

It was the whole package, all the time. But let me make this clear - for a very long time, it was the absolutely right environment for me.

It was giving me the experiences that I craved - the winning, the excitement - and I have no complaints at all.

While you're riding that horse and you can keep up with it, it's fantastic.

But towards the end, I was getting tired and the balance between rest and work was off. That came down to a personal lack of a long-term game plan.

I think also with English football generally, there are no slow parts tactically - it's frenetic from start to finish. One side attacks, then the other side attacks. If you switch the play three times from left to right, the crowd starts to boo. There's no patience, no respite - you attack, then they attack.

The national side and the top teams have developed in recent years and maybe Preston has too, but I haven't really seen games for a long time. Maybe things have changed and maybe the style would be better for me now, less draining.

Back in 2001, we started the next season badly and didn't win for the first five games. Lucs was in goal to start with, but then I got called in against Millwall and we finally won.

We then picked up (Jon Macken scored that unbelievable goal as we beat Man City 2-1 at Deepdale) and I stayed in the side until we beat Stockport 6-0 in November, when this time, I injured my thigh.

So I was out again for a while before regaining my place in the New Year, just in time for some big games again, against Man City in the league and Chelsea in the FA Cup - both great experiences, even though we got beat.

What wasn't so great was Norwich away at Carrow Road where Graham Alexander rolled a simple back pass to me with about ten minutes to go.

Being a goalkeeper is tough for many reasons, but mainly because 95 per cent of the time, the game happens away from you. You don't have an influence on when you're going to be involved, so you have to make sure you are always prepared.

That day was one of those crazy moments where my preparedness dropped, Grezza rolled a simple back pass to me and it went straight under my foot.

It was just bad technique on my part and then it was in the back of the net - right in front of 6,000 Norwich fans laughing their heads off.

You'll see it on those blooper reels on YouTube and most of the time, it's goalkeepers making the mistakes. That's the position we're in and those are the risks that come with it. It might make 30 seconds on a blooper video and everyone laughs, but it wasn't funny for me. I dwelled on it and once I was out of that mental zone, it was hard to get back in.

And there were other consequences too; I was dropped the next game and didn't play again for about seven matches. So you know that one mistake can cost you your place - especially under Moyesie.

However, around that time the stories about him leaving were getting louder and louder. Every time a big job came up, the papers would be full of it and in the end, it wasn't a big surprise when he went to Everton.

David leaving was a huge departure for the club, and for me personally, it was shattering. I just wanted to keep winning and it was the end of an era.

To be fair, Kelham O'Hanlon took over and did really well for the rest of that season, but something was missing.

By that time we'd lost Jon Macken too, but I think Kel kept things going right to the end and we were unlucky to miss out on the play-offs again that year.

It showed what a good side we were that we could lose a great manager and the top scorer and still keep going. That was in our DNA and everyone was keen to see who the new boss would be, because they had big shoes to fill.

If I'm honest though, when Craig Brown came in, I found it very difficult and my game was off. With the changes taking place and a new manager coming in, I disconnected at some level. Maybe it was disappointment, maybe the feeling that the team had gone as far as it could.

Would we still have the excitement? Was the journey over? It all affected me.

I can't explain it, other than to say my connection to the club at that point meant I was acting more like a fan - I was too emotional about the changes taking place. Supporters are allowed to think like that, to feel those emotions, but as a performer you have to be more detached, more professional.

I wasn't and I shouldn't have been that way. I know that now.

Craig Brown and Billy Davies did a decent job with the 'good cop/bad cop' routine, but I was frustrated. Even with the brilliant Ricardo Fuller in the team, we were not getting results like we used to.

I started as first choice and played most of the games until October, when Lucs came back in for me. I had no complaints. I was really flat and disappointed with my own form, if I'm honest. I was becoming more and more aware of the inconsistency in my game and that ate away at me even more.

I produced some really low performances and you get on a vicious circle.

I hadn't checked out mentally and was still trying my best, but I knew instinctively it was coming to an end for me at Preston.

My last game was in the FA Cup against Rochdale at Deepdale when we lost 2-1. I didn't realise it was my final appearance at the time, but I just remember being really disappointed with my form and my performance in general.

Previously, I'd been reliant on intuition and intensity.

When I lost that *intensity*, it was too big a part of my game gone.

I couldn't get into the zone properly and that's always the test of a player; how does he do when things aren't right for him - he could be out of position, out of form, something in the dressing room not right, the opponent gets the better of him, the weather is wrong. It could be anything. How does he handle that and perform on those days? Someone like Graham Alexander or Paul McKenna? No problem - they were super consistent.

Someone like me? Not so consistent - and I knew that.

I remember one season, we played Grimsby away in the first game of the season and the day before in training, I had a big row with Moyesie.

I felt he was questioning my positioning and, hey, I was the goalkeeper so I had my say. Going into the game, I was still angry, really fired up, but I drew on that anger and used it as an energy. I remember the ball came over the top and I raced out of my area to clear it with my head.

I got there first, made the clearance and felt this huge adrenaline rush because THAT is what we'd been arguing about the day before. I let out this big roar. It was exhilarating - I'd used that row to get me in the zone.

Now, I didn't have that any more and, in all honesty, some of my performances were crap.

My positioning would be off, my posture would be wrong, my stance would go, it was all just wrong. Probably, if you'd asked me at the time, I would have blamed Craig Brown for not creating the right atmosphere.

But looking back now, it was *my* fault for not being able to adapt to a new type of management approach. When you think about it, *'getting in the zone'* is not a high-quality game plan.

The bottom line is, we were rebuilding and you are going to lose games along the way. But I didn't accept that at the time and it got into my head.

You can maybe tell from reading this, the anguish I was going through as a footballer - it's not all fun and games at times.

It all weighed on me and I remember conceding a goal from a really tight angle in that last match. It wasn't a very fitting way to end things, but it kind of summed things up.

I wasn't right for the club any more and, painful as it was, the club wasn't right for me.

Jonathan Gould was around by then and Andy Lonergan was also coming through, so from being first choice, I was getting pushed further down the chain.

I was out of contract at the end of the season and the chances of me getting more games were slim. By that time, I'd finally got a proper agent and Hearts got in touch with him because they had an injury crisis and needed a keeper on loan for the rest of the season.

It all happened pretty quickly - the deal was done, goodbyes were said and I don't think Craig Brown was sorry to see me go.

I played well, but Hearts were looking at other keepers before eventually signing me at the end of the summer on a permanent deal.

As time went on, I found myself back-up to the incredible young Craig Gordon and even though I didn't play that often, it was good for me in terms of learning about goalkeeping. I spent two-and-a-half years there and, no longer at the centre of a football whirlwind, I grew up a lot. It was a vital transition for going back to Finland and working in a normal office job, where you can't be fighting with your colleagues on a Friday morning and wrestling with your boss in a bar.

It really prepared me for working life back home and was a good stepping stone in that sense.

Because now I live a fairly football-free life.

When I came back to Finland, I took up my university place and gained a master's degree. My qualification is geared towards Human Resources and for a while I was working in recruitment.

After that I joined the government office for employment, helping organise educational training and other support for job seekers. From 2017, I've worked for the city of Tampere, working on metrics and statistics, business intelligence in the employment department and I really enjoy it.

Yes, I miss my days in English football - *who wouldn't?* - but life moves on and you've just got to move with it.

I haven't been back to Preston since I left, but that doesn't mean I don't have feelings for the town and especially the club - I do. I had a great time there and it will always be a huge, huge part of my life.

My wife and I have thought about going back with the children to show them where they were born. But we have limited time off and if you say to the kids *'you can visit Preston or have seven days on the beach in Spain'*, they give you a fairly obvious answer for a summer holiday!

It would be great for me to have a nostalgic visit, but not really fair on them. We live in Finland, you know - we want some sun on holiday!

I followed Preston's results for a few years but, if I'm honest, I don't anymore. That says more about my relationship with football than the club really, I was never a massive fan of watching the game.

It's also about my selfishness; I dived in, I got my kicks . . . and I buggered off!

The English game is a phenomenon and to be in the middle of it for so many years was amazing. It was exactly what I was after and I maximised my experience all the time, so I have no complaints, none whatsoever.

My main feeling when I stopped playing was pride, for sure, but mixed with regret.

I was proud of playing and winning things at such a great club, with such a super set of teammates, great supporters, lovely town.

It was a hell of a ride, like the biggest roller coaster in the fun park; you don't know which way you're going next, big highs, deep lows, darkness, bright lights, twists and turns and everything always at crazy speeds.

You cling on all the way round until it's over.

Then you get off and say: 'Wow, that was brilliant.

'What's next?'

CHAPTER 14

BRYAN GRAY: THE BOARD GAME

As a young boy growing up, there used to be a board game called 'Wembley'. It was a bit like a football version of Monopoly and the winner was the person who owned the team that won the FA Cup Final.

In among the Uniteds, Albions, Citys and Towns there was one name that always intrigued me: *Preston North End.*

It was a 'one and only' and stood out from all the other teams. What was this magical place? Why is it called Preston North End?

I don't know what I expected but a few years later, I visited Deepdale as a boyhood Barnsley supporter. Of course, one glimpse at the road atlas and the obvious geographical answer became clear.

My story is that I'm from a mining village called Brampton in the West Riding of Yorkshire. My parents were butchers and we lived over the shop. My brothers were much more sporty than I was, but between us we would support all of the local teams; Barnsley, Rotherham and Sheffield Wednesday.

After passing my Eleven-plus exam I attended grammar school where I became head boy, and then read chemistry at York University.

I worked for ICI for many years before joining BAXI in Preston in 1993 as Commercial Director. Within a year I was Chief Executive, with a brief to modernise the company and grow it from being primarily a UK-focused organisation to an international one.

So I had a major job on my hands and if you'd have asked me whether I fancied running a football club at the same time, I would have thought it highly unlikely.

But, of course, that's what happened.

Whether it was serendipity or a prepared mind, a lot of things came together over a short period of time and a great journey began.

Firstly, I got involved in a business initiative started by Prince Charles called *'Seeing is Believing'*, where he challenged people to look at their communities and see where they could intervene to improve things.

From that, a group of us were invited to St James's Palace where we had various discussions about problems we'd seen and ideas we'd subsequently had.

He listened, then basically issued us a challenge: 'You've all seen things, now what are you going to do about them?'

Of course, in the main, these were problems with youth unemployment, urban decay, that sort of thing. I don't think anyone said *'we need to restore the local football club'*. But I went away looking for some way to get involved and basically the 'first cat to cross the street in front of me' was Ben Casey.

Ben was the owner of a design business called The Chase in Manchester. They did design work for BAXI and he was a lifelong Preston supporter.

We got talking and in the course of one conversation, he said to me: 'Why doesn't BAXI sponsor North End? They're a grand old club in need of a bit of help at the moment.'

Partly because I remembered the name from the board game and partly because I had been there as a boy, I was intrigued and thought I'd find out a bit more about the club. So I contacted Derek Shaw who suggested I meet Malcolm Woodhouse, who was the major shareholder.

I had a look round the stadium and it was just like going into a time warp.

In one room there were what looked like khaki First World War stretchers hanging on the wall. *(Come to think of it, they might actually have been First World War stretchers.)*

The toilets were so open you could stand against the wall at the urinals and see the people buying their pies just a few feet away.

The old West Stand was still there of course, all wooden seats and that barrel roof, one of the oldest stands in England. I looked through the gaps in the floorboards and could see piles of cigarette butts - they were probably the oldest cigarette butts in England, too.

So my first thought was: 'Oh my goodness!' But after getting over the initial impression, I quickly came to the conclusion: 'We could do something with this.'

My view was that BAXI could help regenerate Preston North End as a community club. To a degree, it already was a community club; fans could hire out the pitch and things, but I thought we could do something more significant and permanent with the stadium.

We could regenerate Deepdale and bring new life, not just to the immediate area, but to the town itself.

So I wrote a memo to the BAXI board in September 1994 that said four things. Firstly, that unemployment is the root cause of many community and social problems.

Secondly, youth unemployment is bad and getting worse.

Thirdly, there are many well-meaning, but inefficient projects.

And finally, miracles ARE possible - they just take a little longer.

They were the bullet points I put to the board and I said: 'Why don't we develop Deepdale, both as a football club and a community enterprise?'

BAXI's role would be as a catalyst and strategist, we would sort out the money issues and manage the project. All credit to the board, they were very innovative and very supportive as was the company founder, Philip Baxendale.

He backed the idea and within a few weeks we were having a press conference to say that BAXI had effectively taken over Preston North End Football Club.

It all happened so quickly because Malcolm Woodhouse and Keith Leeming were such good men, who cared deeply for the club. Malcolm was a successful businessman up in Lancaster and Keith was the Chairman.

Malcolm, as major shareholder, said: 'I would never stand in the way of anyone who wants to take this club forward.' They'd been involved for many years and proved their commitment to keep things going over a long period of time.

Their dedication to the club was absolutely unquestionable, but collectively the board at the time did not have the sufficient finances to make progress in the way we were now looking at. I said to them: 'I think I've got a plan that can really take this club forward.' They looked at it and, thankfully, they agreed.

Also, another shareholder who really made it happen was Trevor Hemmings, who was and is a supporter in many, many ways. He persuaded other people who owned shares in the club at the time to facilitate the BAXI deal and we were always very grateful for his help.

In terms of taking the club over, it wasn't a huge financial commitment in the scheme of things. Moreover, the financial input came from implementing a business plan that would see the club become profitable in a very short period of time. Not hugely profitable, but enough to be a viable proposition. The Number One rule of business is to survive and then you can grow from there.

Actually, the club was in profit there or thereabouts, but it was only achieving that by selling its best players. Transfer revenue was being used to pay the bills and to keep the club going. I understood that policy because of the situation at the club, but there's no guarantee it's a sustainable strategy in the long term.

So my view was that we needed to raise money to fund our business plan - and that was going to cost about £10 million. My role as Chairman was to raise that money in a controlled and phased way. The thing that is often overlooked in business is that if you have a good idea, money is never the problem.

It's people that are the problem.

Later on, when I was in charge of the North West Development Agency, people would come to me with projects that required funding and I would always say: 'Show me the person that's going to deliver this project, then we will talk about the money.'

And the same rule applied back then at the football club. Money is always there to support the right people with the right ideas.

Looking back, I was probably naive, but I was confident that we could run North End as a profitable business and in those days, that was unusual for a football club. We never really discussed who should be Chairman, it just fell into place because it was my idea and I was the Chief Executive of BAXI.

So on the 28th of September 1994, I became Chairman of the club. At the time, there was a lot of scepticism in the town. There were some people who welcomed the involvement. But there were others who had never heard of me and were dubious about our intentions.

At the time, Preston Council owned the freehold to Deepdale, so they were involved in discussions and were very supportive, although a level of scrutiny was to be expected. That was understandable, given their public responsibility.

So I spent quite a lot of time building relationships with people who would then be able to trust us to deliver the shared dream of a rejuvenated Preston North End.

It wasn't quite *'if you build it, they will come'*, but people had to be shown that we were genuine in our intentions.

That physical construction process was absolutely vital and delivering the first steps would give people the tangible evidence that we were serious about what we were doing.

As has been seen elsewhere, once the stadium redevelopment began, achieving success would become easier. Better players would see the club as more attractive, investors and decision makers would see progress being made.

So in the early stages, it was all about getting the ball rolling, building relationships and showing everyone concerned - including the supporters - that we were serious.

We spoke to South Ribble Council and the MPs too and within six months we were able to acquire a 125-year lease from Preston Council.

Without that, we would not have been able to move the project forward. It was one of a number of fundamental issues that had to be overcome and obtaining that lease was absolutely critical. Without it, we wouldn't have been able to raise the money we subsequently did and the dream would have been dead in the water.

So it was an example of BAXI being the catalyst, but other bodies and organisations in the community doing their bit also. Those relationships were vital, both outside and inside the club.

At that point, John Beck was the manager and the team had just missed out on promotion at Wembley. The manager is critical to the success of the club and fundamentally the role of the Chairman is to support the manager.

My Number One task was to have a good football manager and to work closely with them. Given that I wasn't a football expert, I had no desire or intention of being a back-seat driver - that never crossed my mind.

Moreover, I knew I would need to work closely with someone who I could trust and respect. Looking around the club and seeing things in those early stages, it didn't take long to realise John Beck was not that person who I could have that working relationship with.

He'd achieved some good things in terms of raising attendances and interest in the club, but overall he did not have the right attitude for the way forward.

There wasn't a sense of us being 'in this together'. No feeling that we were a team. He wanted to do things the Beck way and it wasn't my way. Therefore, it was inevitable there would be a parting of those ways.

It was unfortunate, but these decisions have to be taken and as Chairman, you have a wider responsibility to everyone involved in the club.

When John departed, his assistant Gary Peters was the obvious choice. I liked him a lot and thought I could work with him. More importantly than that, I thought he spoke sense.

Appointing him as manager was my first big decision and I never, ever regretted it. Gary Peters was an exceptional manager, an exceptional man and Preston North End owes him a great deal.

He was incredibly knowledgeable about football, but he was also a learner. He listened to people and we had a great relationship.

Having my business background, I was keen to put in place a number of systems that would help me understand enough about what was happening on the football side to make better decisions when the time came.

We had to become more scientific and data-driven than I suspect many football clubs were at that point.

So we put in place some basic systems and Gary embraced this wholeheartedly, because he too was a very systematic person.

He prepared a squad assessment that listed each player in the squad, with the coaching staff's view on their strengths and weaknesses, potential to improve or possibly deteriorate with age.

It also looked at each section of the team, how good they were and whether they would need strengthening in the short or long term.

For example, I've still got Gary's assessments from 1996 when he wrote: 'The goalkeeping department is the only part of the team which is already good enough to get into the First Division (now the Championship).'

At the time we had Kelham O'Hanlon, Bobby Mimms, Tepi Moilanen and David Lucas, two of whom went on to play many games for us at that higher level. So that was an accurate assessment, several years before we achieved promotion.

Every player had sheets that listed their age, background, playing history, contract details, etc. Gary wrote down not only what he thought, but what the previous manager's thoughts had been also. We then updated these sheets twice a year and later on David Moyes continued with this system.

Another discipline that Gary put in place was to put a transfer value on the individuals. We agreed every season what the value of each player was - and we agreed at what price we would sell a player. I didn't want to argue with the manager over whether we should or shouldn't sell someone.

I wanted the manager to be in control of that process.

Therefore, he was able to say 'this is the value of that player to us, but if we're offered more than that we should consider selling'. That took away the conflict that often exists between managers and chairmen over player sales.

I wanted the manager to accept responsibility for that process. A very good example of this later on was the sale of Jon Macken. We put a value on him and declined various bids that didn't match our valuation. When Manchester City came in with a bid significantly above that figure, it was therefore a no-brainer and we took the decision based on assessments we already had in place.

From those early days, we weren't doing things off-the-cuff if bids came in. We were now making decisions based on long-term reports, taking into account a number of criteria that the manager had agreed upon. I think that stood us in good stead and removed a lot of the emotion from decisions.

Back in those early days, we knew we had to invest in both the squad and the stadium. It wasn't an either or. It couldn't be.

But the stadium was a pressing concern and that design process had already begun with Ben's concept drawings, which I still have to this day.

He had come to me and said that he wanted to design a new Deepdale. That was really music to my ears and I said: 'Great - go for it, Ben.' From the very start, it was done as a complete stadium, not a piecemeal approach.

As I reflect, I'm looking at the concept drawings based on the Stadio Luigi Ferraris in Genoa - and the finished construction of Deepdale is very similar to those initial illustrations; the floodlight towers, the angular roofing, the enclosed corners, it's all there.

Stating the obvious, the first stand had to have two floodlight towers to support the main structure. Thereafter it became cheaper, because you only needed one further tower for each end stand and then the fourth side came without the need for any towers at all.

The capacity would be an initial 24,000 with the potential to extend to 30,000, which could still be achieved if necessary.

The Sir Tom Finney stand was designed to take more weight than the others and extra seating could be accommodated in a second tier there. In addition, the Invincibles Pavilion isn't quite finished off yet, so there's a few more seats to go in there. In short, the capacity could be increased at some point in the future if required.

As it stands though, it is undoubtedly a fantastic football stadium. For everything to have come in place from those initial designs and to look so good is something I'm very proud of. Ben did an exceptional job and the finished stadium is a thing of football beauty - I think everyone recognises that.

I wanted it to be stunning and it is. I wanted good visibility and it's perfect.

And I wanted us to do it very cost effectively, which it was.

But what I believed - and again Ben is a star in this regard - is that good design doesn't have to be expensive. You just need to be creative and there are many, many little design details that are cheap, but effective. One of the main ones is the metal cladding on the structure; it is just an industrial product that was quite inexpensive, but all these years later, it still looks the part.

March 2021 was the 25th anniversary of the Sir Tom Finney Stand and it still looks clean and modern - it is a building everyone can be proud of.

Leading that redevelopment of the stadium was essentially my job, but I knew that unless the team was successful we wouldn't achieve our goal. It's stating the obvious, but that was the tricky part.

I was pretty sure we could build a football stadium - I wasn't sure we could build a winning football team that could get us where we needed to be.

The objective always was to be in Division One - which is Championship level now. Back in 1994, when we were close to the bottom of the fourth tier, it seemed to me that Division One was the natural landing point for the club.

And that's what we set out to achieve.

Once we were there, we could start to think about the Premier League.

In some ways it was quite simple; we had to have a good manager and we had to have a plan that wasn't just based on luck and intermittent good judgement.

It had to be built on solid principles applied on a consistent basis. Thankfully, Gary and then David Moyes felt exactly that way.

If you look at the evolution of the team that ultimately competed in the play-off final at Cardiff, you can see a thread of how that team was built up over time.

Each season we lost players who weren't going to take us to the next level and invested a certain amount in players who we thought could do that.

Obviously, we didn't get that right every time - no club ever does.

But due to the incredibly thorough way we went about signing new players, we were able to make progress - and I think huge credit for that goes to Gary and later David for their fastidiousness.

They didn't just see a player once or twice; they looked at them over and over again. How would the player cope in different conditions? Or in a slightly different position or formation? Or when their team went behind? What was their character like? All these things were noted and used to assess whether the player was right for us.

Perhaps at times the supporters got impatient for signings, but if so it was probably because Gary and David were doing their homework to ensure that the right people joined the club. It is much better to take your time and get it right than to rush in and find out it was the wrong decision - that's just common sense.

We were moving in the right direction on the pitch though and by the end of that first 1994/95 season, we reached the play-offs, losing out to Bury over two legs. I think, really, we weren't quite ready for promotion at that stage but you could see things were coming together on the playing front and we were happy with Gary and optimistic about the following year.

We'd secured the lease and began demolishing the old West Stand in July 1995.

That work actually began before we launched our share offer on the Alternative Investment Market, which was aimed at raising the capital required for the Tom Finney Stand. That share offer was very successful in two ways.

We never expected to raise all the money required, but it still brought in a significant amount. Moreover, it was something that got the message across to the fans, local businesses and the wider community that we weren't going to achieve our dream without everyone pulling together.

It was a two-way street and success depended on everyone doing their bit.

Therefore, the share offer was to raise money but also to raise awareness of our ambition. We launched it on August 8 and significantly, three days later we signed Steve Wilkinson and Andy Saville.

So it was clear to the supporters that the stadium and the playing side were developing hand in hand. There was a lot of interest in the share offer and because it was a new idea, a lot of people didn't fully understand what it was all about, so public 'question and answer' sessions were arranged.

There was a minimum share purchase of £400 for very practical reasons.

We were trying to raise a sizeable amount of money to do something practical. It wasn't about having lots of people pay £10 to put a share certificate on their bedroom wall. There was a serious business aim to the exercise - a lot of thought went into it. We based the float on one Celtic had done in Scotland and used the same company behind that process.

Two encounters from those public meetings stick with me all these years later.

A supporter came up to me and said: 'I've just withdrawn my life savings from the building society to buy these £400 shares.'

I looked at him and said: 'Really? Are you sure about this? That sounds like a big step.' And he replied: *'No it's not. This club is my life.*

'There's nothing more important to me than Preston North End so if I can help you deliver this dream, I'm going to do it.'

It just hit me, how much this club really impacted on people's lives.

It was that emotional connection. North End wasn't something he had as an interest, or a hobby - this was part of someone's life.

And there were lots of people like that. Another supporter came up to me and said: 'I haven't got £400, but I've just been to the club shop and bought a shirt, so at least I'm doing my bit for what you're doing.'

Those vignettes really brought home to me the huge responsibility of the task we'd taken on.

It's the old cliche about 'when Saturday comes', but it's true. Right on my doorstep at BAXI, many people worked in the factory throughout the week, dreaming of watching PNE win at the weekend.

As it was, the share offer was very successful and brought in something in the region of £4 million, which was enough to get the show on the road. Work then began on the new West Stand and at that point, we hadn't considered a name for it - we were more concerned with getting it built.

However, one day Ben came to me with one of his ideas (as he often did) and you could sense his excitement.

In his hand he had some graph paper - you might remember it from your schooldays. He also had some tracing paper and on it, he'd made this image of Tom Finney's face using the little graph squares.

'What do you think of that?' He asked.

I looked at it and said: 'That's amazing. What is it?'

He explained the plan for the seating and from that moment there was never any doubt it was going to be called the Tom Finney Stand.

Obviously, I ran the idea past the great man and he was appreciative, humbled, honoured - everything you'd expect Tom Finney to be. Stories about him on and off the pitch are legendary and he really was as nice as everyone says.

And he was wise too.

I'd often sit in front of him in the directors' box, so I had the privilege of hearing him talk about things going on on the pitch.

It wasn't a running commentary, but when he spoke, he had seen things that I would never have noticed in the game. It was an incredible eye-opener into someone who understood football on a different level to 99 per cent of the people in attendance and I had this incredible education, literally sitting at his knee.

They say being the manager of a football club is a very lonely position and that's absolutely correct. I saw it as part of my role to be part of the support network to the managers we had. But equally, being Chairman is lonely too - everything I said got picked up, repeated, churned about in the press, etc.

So there were very few people you could have a conversation with and know that it wouldn't go anywhere.

But Tom was that person for me; it was a bit like a Prime Minister meeting the monarch and I'll always be grateful for his wise counsel.

Speaking of football royalty, one player Gary was especially keen to bring in was a young lad from Manchester United. After the loan was arranged, he came to me and said: 'Chairman, this David Beckham is something special. He's going to be taking all the set pieces on Saturday.'

Not that I would ever interfere with a playing decision, but I said: 'Really? Are you sure about that Gary?'

I hadn't seen him in the flesh by then, but in the pictures I'd seen I thought he looked pretty weedy *(this was before the chiselled torso and tattoos!).*

Gary just smiled, gave a little nod and said: 'Trust me.'

Of course, in the game he scored a spectacular goal and I remember everything just going quiet for a split second - almost frozen in time before this almighty roar. Everyone was standing up and looking at each other going: *'Wow!'*

We always invited new players to come into the boardroom with their parents and they were generally starstruck by the trophy cabinet, the aura about the place, etc. It was a very nice boardroom up in the old Pavilion Stand.

David came in with his parents and I remember them as very nice and he was incredibly polite. What perhaps goes unnoticed is that the Beckham loan was fundamental to future success further down the line.

I don't think people can appreciate how important that loan was.

David went back to Old Trafford with good reports about his time with us and it kick-started a relationship with Sir Bobby Charlton and Sir Alex Ferguson that really helped the club subsequently.

Obviously, Sir Bobby had been Preston manager in the past and he became a great advocate for having the National Football Museum at Deepdale a few years later. And the link with Sir Alex helped us bring in Michael Appleton, Jon Macken and Colin Murdock on the playing side, too.

So it went a lot deeper than just having David Beckham on loan and again, that was down to Gary, his eye for a good player and the way he coached them when they arrived.

We did ask about whether United would consider selling Beckham to us, but even then we thought it would be a very long shot. Sir Alex just said: 'Bryan, I don't think any club in the world could afford to buy him right now.

'He is going to be one of the best players people have ever seen.'

And, of course, he was right.

But later on, it was the sale of Appleton and Macken that helped fund the development of Deepdale, so in a roundabout way, that brief Beckham deal helped build the stadium. (Thanks, David.)

Funnily enough, when we signed the three players from United, we got a call asking if Sir Alex and Sir Bobby could come to watch them in an away match.

On the evening in question, I'd just parked up when this big Mercedes pulled alongside and out popped these two giants of the game, amid lots of surprised onlookers in Rotherham for a Coca Cola Cup game on a Tuesday night.

To me, that visit demonstrated one of the reasons for their success. Alex and Bobby put the effort into relationships with their players and there they were coming to check on the progress of three young lads who had already left their club. They had that paternal - almost family - approach with these young men and their parents.

That was something I noted and we tried to instil down the years at Deepdale as well. If players knew that the club cared for them, they were much more likely to care for the club in return and I think we were successful in that.

Not just because it's good business, but it's the right thing to do as well, particularly for young players. They need to know there's support and progression and a solid base for their careers. That's what we always tried to give them.

When I read books like this with players of that era saying how much the club means to them all these years later, again it's something everyone can be proud of. Part of that comes from the care the club gave to the players.

We were all deeply concerned for the health and well-being of the squad, physically and emotionally. Both Gary and David were always concerned that our medical facilities were up to scratch and they were way ahead of what most clubs in our division were doing.Around that time, Chris Nelson approached me and said he would like to be club chaplain. I'm a Lay Minister myself and I thought this was a great move. Chris said: *'Look, I'm not going to preach sermons to them, but I'm a North Ender and I'll just be there if they need me.'*

So that was established and I think Chris was another important man behind the scenes who did a great job of providing support when it was required.

We didn't necessarily see it as a religious thing - we were supporting the whole person, not just the footballer. There were times when we'd have young players living away from home, in a B&B setting, and they needed someone to talk to.

The stereotypical image of footballers is not always the case and in my experience they are a wide and varied bunch - just like any other workplace.

For me and the management team, we had a duty of care mentally, emotionally and physically and I think the players responded to that.

Obviously football has changed dramatically since that time and clubs now have all sorts of liaison staff to ensure players are looked after, but I think we were ahead of our time with what we were doing.

Gary's first season (1995/96) in charge was also my first full season and the progress we made was huge. He put together a championship-winning squad on the pitch and we put together the new main stand off it.

It was all a bit of a blur at times, but I was always a confident person and to me things were just following the plan we had put in place.Saville and Wilkinson were scoring goals for fun, the sun was shining, the BAXI shirts seemed to be everywhere you looked around the town and everyone had smiles on their faces.

The new stand opened for the last game of the season, nearly 19,000 were inside the ground, with a significant number unable to get in and again, that day gave us belief that we were doing the right thing.

We weren't wasting our time - there was this huge affection and appreciation for North End. It was a glorious time and exactly what we'd gone into this venture for. It felt like we were at the start of a journey and we all had the belief that we were going to succeed.

We also made some symbolic changes behind the scenes.

When I arrived, I was surprised to learn that women were not allowed in the boardroom.

They had a little room under the stand with no windows, where they had egg sandwiches, while the men upstairs had this lovely old room with much nicer food, big cigars and a well-stocked bar, all very grand.

I thought: 'This is just wrong. *Very, very wrong.*'

So right from the start, I changed the rules so that women were allowed in and smoking was kicked out.

It was the mid-1990s, but we'd finally reached the 20th Century.

The other thing I set out to do was improve communications. Malcolm Woodhouse was a very private man and he didn't like talking to the press, which was entirely his prerogative.

But my view was that the Lancashire Evening Post was going to have a story on PNE every day. We were lucky to have such a fantastic newspaper on our doorstep and I wanted us to work together.

If we didn't help Brian Ellis and his colleagues to have a story, they'd still carry something, so I'd rather it was the stories we helped them with.

Obviously, they would always take their own line and have their own voice. At times, they said things I disagreed with, but that's part of a healthy relationship with a free press.

So I said the manager must always be available to the LEP and Radio Lancashire and I would do the same. There were times when I was listening to the BBC phone-in after a match and if I heard something I disagreed with, I'd ring Gary Hickson live on air and have my say.

I just wanted to set out a new way of doing things; I wanted to be open with the supporters and I wanted to build relationships with the local media.

I recognised that things wouldn't always go well and therefore when the bad times came (and they did) people would be more understanding because we'd been so open about the situation.

Financially, I had two golden rules - and they're not rocket science. People can over-complicate business at times, but certain fundamentals stare you in the face.

Primarily, we had to make a profit. It didn't need to be a big profit, but enough for us to survive. Clubs back then weren't run as any other businesses would be - I'm not sure they all are these days, come to think of it. But we set our stall out to run Preston North End like we would run any other business.

Unfortunately, we were up against people elsewhere in football who did the exact opposite.

Some owners just looked at it like it was their train set and they would do what they wanted. They were bad news for football and I think a lot of the subsequent problems - not at Deepdale - came from people whose egos wouldn't fit in their Rolls Royce.

It pains me to say that Jack Walker was part of that story with what he'd done at Blackburn a couple of years earlier. Don't get me wrong, Jack did lots of good things, but he saw no need or reason for operating Rovers like it was a conventional business.

And his success encouraged others to do the same, which caused all sorts of problems for the wider game. We didn't want to be like that. So we had a rule that the manager could spend 60 per cent of turnover on players' wages.

That left 40 per cent to spend on everything else; overheads, upkeep of the stadium, other bills, etc.

How the manager spent that 60 per cent was up to him. He could spend a big chunk of it on a few stars or he could spread it more evenly throughout the squad.

Gary and David understood that rationale and there was never any grey area.

The transfer budget was separate - that came out of the capital budget, the same as stadium development, so it was variable to a degree.

These rules were agreed upon and everyone knew where they stood. And I think that clarity was important to the success of the chairman/manager relationship too.

On that level, again there were three main rules (I apologise if I sound like a schoolmaster with all this, but in my career I've found this approach works).

Firstly, no surprises.

Secondly, if we agree we'll do something, we do it.

And *third*, if there's a problem, the sooner we talk about it, the sooner we can find a solution. I found that approach worked very well with Gary and David and throughout my time, we had very open and honest relationships.

In the 1996/97 season, we'd raised more money through a second round of funding to develop the old Fulwood End into the Bill Shankly Kop. (Saying it in one sentence like that makes it sound very easy, but it actually involved a lot of hard work.)

On the pitch, we learned a big lesson that year. We stayed loyal to the team that had won the championship the year before and that was a mistake.

We realised that and learned from it for next time. We stuck with the players without really thinking through the higher standard in the division we were now in. We had to correct that over the course of the season and at times it was painful. We lost Saville and Wilkinson - two key players for us at the lower level - and the fans didn't quite understand what we were doing.

They didn't agree with it and they didn't like it.

But we brought in a lot of players that season, Mark Rankine, Sean Gregan, Michael Jackson, David Reeves, Kurt Nogan - people who were very influential for us over the following years. Paul McKenna was also coming through the ranks and emerging as a real talent.

So there was a lot of change in the team and that was all down to Gary, helped by David, travelling miles and miles, night after night, week after week, to watch players, study them, find out all about them.

It got to the point where we'd discuss a player for so long I'd say: 'Can't you just make your minds up?'

But, of course, it was actually a good trait. When managers take one look and make a quick decision, that's when things go wrong.

So our recruitment was always spot on around that time and the foundations were laid for what was to come. We consolidated in the division above but still felt we were moving forward.

As it was, it turned out to be the calm before the storm.

We hadn't foreseen the problems that were to come the following season, which turned out to be another period of change.

That summer we sold Kevin Kilbane to West Bromwich Albion for a club record £1.1 million and that was above the agreed valuation the manager had put on the player.

We were balancing all the time between selling players, buying players and funding the stadium, which I think we generally handled very well.

We had serious discussions at times, but they never descended into arguments, partly because the manager had done the assessments.

So when bids like that came in, we could go through their comments and step through things in a methodical manner.

There were columns on the assessments which indicated which players were going to make it, which ones might and which ones definitely wouldn't.

So again, that informed the decision processing by that point, we'd got a bit of history we could refer back to about certain players. For example, buying Saville and Wilkinson was a good decision, but selling them was, too.

I think with Kevin Kilbane, the offer was above our valuation and everyone agreed it made sense. He went on to have an outstanding career and I'm pleased that we played a part in that.

We brought in the three young players from Manchester United, but they would have come in anyway.

Those deals were not dependent on Kevin being sold, because we were organised and we'd already got our budget set. Throughout my time, there was no set percentage of transfer fees received that went to buying new players.

Instead, it was a case of having a capital spending budget - for transfers, the stadium, etc - and then assessing on a year-by-year basis where that money needed to be spent. That's why the flotation was so important, because it was getting through to people the importance of understanding business.

If you go at things willy-nilly without a clear strategy and parameters, you're heading down a dangerous path and one that most likely won't be successful.

Most fans don't want to get into that of course, they just want the club to spend money. But it's got to come from somewhere and we didn't have a wealthy benefactor, we were doing it ourselves. So one of the things we consistently got right was having enough money to do the things we wanted to do.

We'd got out of the bottom division using a core of older players, but now we recognised that we were going to need younger players to take us forward.

That's a trickier proposition because you're investing in talent that isn't always proven at that stage.

That's why so much homework had to be done to be absolutely sure that these younger players would be up to the task of taking us on the next stage of the journey. The bonus for us was of course that if they were successful, not only would we benefit on the pitch, but their value would go up as well.

At times, it's a tough choice to stick or twist with a player in terms of selling him on. It's that point of knowing when he's reached his peak value to the team AND on the transfer market. That's what we were assessing all the time in terms of what was best for the club.

Having had a season where we put lots of building blocks in place, the 1997/98 season was one of momentous and dramatic change.

As the season started, the National Football Museum project started to gather pace and with the funding in place, we began demolition of the Kop.

On the pitch, we had the three new players from Manchester United as well as David Eyres and Gary Parkinson, two excellent, experienced professionals.

We'd lost Lee Ashcroft and David Reeves during the close season but we were in pretty good shape. So it should have been a good year, but it wasn't.

Instead, it was the most challenging period of my tenure.

It came down to results not going our way which led to Gary starting to feel pressure. It's stating the obvious to say being the manager is a very pressurised job. He had an incredible workrate and a huge commitment to the job and the club. If anything, he was overworking to put things right and as results took a downturn, he was struggling a bit.

There'd been a bit in the press and on the phone-ins and no matter what anyone says, it's very difficult to ignore that sort of thing when you're in such a high-profile role in the town. He came to see me towards the end of 1997 and suggested that he should maybe move to looking after the youth set-up and let David take over the First Team.

It was an interesting idea, but at that time I said it wasn't the right thing to do. I wanted him to carry on.

But I arranged to meet the pair of them at my house on December 30 to talk it through in more detail and at that point Gary was offering to resign.

The were both still very united, they were still working as closely as ever and the upshot of that meeting was that Gary would carry on.

David thought the manager was working too hard, if anything, and had become too intense during this run of results. That was understandable to a large degree, but it was having an effect on the players.

So, we agreed that Gary should 'chill out' a bit; his job wasn't in any danger and we were confident we had a good enough squad to turn things round.

I said I would talk to the press to take a bit of pressure off, which I did. But then a couple of weeks later, things deteriorated again when we lost 3-1 at home to Gillingham.

I'm not a football expert, but even I could look at the players and see their heads were down - there was no will to win. The crowd could see it and I thought: 'This is dangerous. Something's wrong here.'

Normally, we would talk on the phone the day after a game, usually around Sunday tea time when we'd had 24 hours to reflect on the game, win or lose, good or bad. I felt like I learned a lot from listening to the manager's assessment on the day after games.

That weekend however, instead of talking on the phone, we had another face-to-face meeting the day after that Gillingham game. Between us, we decided that the change Gary had proposed would take place after all. He would look after the youth set-up and David would take over the First Team.

When I'd parted company with John Beck, I'd thought at the time that we had to have a succession plan in place. Again, it's common in business to have contingencies and I thought it was very odd that football clubs didn't seem to do this. So in our case we were fortunate that we did have a plan; David was the heir apparent to Gary and so the mechanics of it were not as disruptive as they might otherwise have been.

David was disappointed for Gary, as they were still very close, but delighted to be getting the opportunity. However, he turned down a contract as permanent manager because he wanted to see how things went.

Gary stepped across to look after the youth development side of things and was subsequently a great success in that role, too.

His commitment to the club was absolute. For him, Preston North End came first and his future was secondary to that. He was an exceptional servant to the club. We were fortunate that we'd kept his expertise and experience, while also allowing David to continue his progression as a fledgling manager.

But before we announced this change at a press conference, there was one more thing I intended to do.

I said I wanted to meet the pair of them with Sean Gregan, in his role as club captain. So at 8.30am on the Monday morning in the BAXI offices, I spoke directly to the captain in a formal sense for the one and only time in my seven years at the club.

It never happened before or after.

He came in and I told him: *'You are responsible for this change. Nobody else - you and the players.*

'It's not going to happen again. From this minute, you support David and give him everything you've got.'

Possibly for the first time in his life I think, Sean was speechless.

I said: 'There's going to be a press conference in a few minutes, I want you to hear what I'm going to say and you are going to be part of it.'

I don't know whether he was embarrassed or overawed, or he thought I'd gone loony (!), but he basically just said: 'Yes.' So we had the press conference saying we had appointed David as manager and never looked back.

Lots of other people had been in touch around that time - it's a bit like vultures circling if they scent blood. There was talk in the papers about Ian Rush and he had indeed contacted us, but we politely informed him that we had a succession plan in place with David. There was no serious thought about anyone else.

That night, I phoned Gary and told him he'd have our full support in his new role and the following day I sent flowers to both Mrs Moyes and Mrs Peters.

We then played Macclesfield in David's first game and won 1-0 in an AutoWindscreens game.

The following day, I sat down to write a letter to David confirming his appointment. In it I said it was a privilege to be Chairman of this great club and I was sure he felt the same about being manager. I ended that letter by saying that for both of us: *'Preston expects.'*

And that was true.

OK, it was corny (!) but true.

It's fair to say it wasn't a universally-welcomed appointment and in fact I got a lot of stick for it at first. Some of the fans wanted a big name and I could never understand that. Big names are people who have generally failed somewhere else, then you pay a lot of money to get them to come and fail for you, too.

I had no doubt whatsoever that we'd done the right thing. We'd spent several years getting to this point, as I've outlined here.

I got some quite strong letters from people telling me I was wrong, but what was nice is that many of those people subsequently wrote back to me, admitting that in the end I was right and *they* had been wrong.

I didn't mind the correspondence because the people weren't abusive, they were just forthright - as football fans tend to be.

The reality was I knew that when things go well, the manager gets the credit and when things go badly, the chairman gets the blame. So that was a tough time, especially as we didn't win a league game under David for the first six weeks or so.

We lost 3-0 to Carlisle in February and there was a protest after the game, with 'Gray out' chants and things like that.

The LEP, in its own inimitable way, ran a poll about me carrying on and out of 1,000 votes, I think I scraped home with a majority of 37. So that was a relief!

In essence, I said at the time: 'If you don't want me to do this job and can find someone better, then fine.

'But think about what you are doing. We are on a journey here. If you throw away what's been achieved so far and dispense with the plan, is that really the future you want for the club?'

Don't misunderstand me - I felt that the fans had a right to say what they thought. In fact, I saw it as a strength, a sign of passion and caring for the club.

No-one ever stopped me in the street to talk about their boiler, but people stopped me all the time to talk about their football club.

As a business, you'd do anything to have that level of caring.

For people to tell you about your product and get their honest *(very honest!)* feedback is invaluable.

That's why I spent a lot of time at fans' forums, doing stuff in the press, attending supporters' meetings, etc.

Often there were informal meetings too. I've got three sons and we'd travel to away games and bump into fans at service stations just like everyone else.

In 1998, my lads were 16, 13 and 10 - passionate North Enders, decked out in their BAXI shirts and they saw the stick their dad was taking in Preston at times.

But what was really interesting was that the fans attending away games tended to be very thoughtful and respectful.

They'd talk to me, but they'd not overdo it, as I was with my family and they gave us space.

I remember one time we were on a London Underground train going to Fulham and virtually the entire carriage was full of North End fans.

We ended up having an impromptu fans' forum, talking about players, strategy, etc. I've no idea what the 'normal' passengers made of it, but it was a good experience actually - just being able to sit and talk directly to the supporters.

I loved that.

They could hear things straight from the horse's mouth, without the filter of a journalist or anything and it was great.

Being a relatively straight-talking Yorkshireman I said what I thought and, of course, there was no social media back then, so you didn't have to worry about things being filmed and taken out of context or whatever.

We could just talk openly and we did.

Obviously, as time went on, David's methods and new ways of thinking led to an improvement in results and we eventually finished 15th.

When you have periods like that where the position is ultimately disappointing, the important thing is to learn from it and move forward.

And, together, that's what we did.

The following season really got us back on the right track. I remember us going to Manchester City and winning in October and that put down a marker for us.

Gary Parkinson scored the winner and after the game the crowd was quite 'difficult' shall we say!

Well, OK, it was a bit frightening coming out into Moss Side at the old Maine Road stadium. But it was a measure of how far we'd come that we were able to go to places like that, not be overawed and get a result.

Safely back at Deepdale, the Bill Shankly Kop was opened and the question now was 'could we fill it?' In January, we played Arsenal in the FA Cup and it was absolutely packed to capacity. We went 2-0 up on the night and the TV commentator said: *'Deepdale is in dreamland.'*

And it really was. I looked around and just took it all in. To my mind, what that night said to me was: 'This is what we're all about. This is what we can achieve.'

The stadium wasn't finished, but particularly at night with the floodlights on, you could see what it could become. Even with just two sides completed, it was a vision of the future.

Only a few weeks after that game, David and I had a pre-arranged season review - we generally started to think about the following season around January/February.

We looked at who would stay, who would go, which areas needed strengthening, which targets had been identified - everything really that would help us move forward. Obviously at that stage we didn't know we were going to reach the play-offs, where we ultimately lost to Gillingham.

But timing is everything and if we had gone up that year, I don't think we'd have been quite ready. It was David's first full season in charge and we hadn't really got the squad where it needed to be. It sounds counter-intuitive, but you can go up too soon in the development process.

We'd have taken it if it had happened obviously, but I think it was better in the long term that we had another year at that level to get everything in place and to bring the squad up to a higher standard.

Because of that extra year when we stayed down, the following season was the simplest of all of them during my time. Everything was in place and the machine was well-oiled by then. We'd worked things out, knew what to do, we operated well, we built the squad up and really it just happened exactly as we'd planned.

I've got so few memories of interventions, because it all just went so smoothly.

Almost without a bump in the road, we'd now won two divisional titles in four years.

Everyone remembers the open-top bus celebrations and the scenes on the Harris Library steps - they truly are 'goosebump moments' that normally come once in a generation.

We'd had that twice in a few years and they were simply unforgettable moments and experiences. Truly incredible.

As much as anything, seeing those crowds and the joy about the town was fulfilling the mission statement we'd set out with five years earlier.

Deepdale was in dreamland, now Preston itself was in dreamland.

It was just breathtaking, really, and I still meet people who recognise me from that time (even though I'm now grey-haired) and we always talk fondly of those days. It could be anywhere; on trains, on holiday abroad, walking in Cumbria - people still come up to me and it's always nice to reminisce.

One of the proudest things to see are the North End BAXI shirts from back then that are still about, even now.

Branding was very important to me and I always wanted the simple white PNE shirt, with a classic look which we kept re-inventing season by season.

I've seen them all over the world - America, Canada, all over Europe - and had conversations about North End in all four corners of the globe.

I think people look back on that era as 'glory days' and in many ways they were. Having events from 20-odd years ago spark so much energy in people to this day is a very special thing.

I also look back with pride on some of the players who came with us right from the start of the journey.

Lee Cartwright, David Lucas, Ryan Kidd, Paul McKenna, for example, these were young men who grew with us and had a real connection to the club.

We invested as much as we could in the youth set-up and, again, Gary Peters played a huge part in that development. We all saw the need to bring our own players through, but also the obligation to do it.

Going right back to my 1994 bullet point about youth unemployment, we needed to create opportunities for young people, which we carry on to this day through the club's Community and Education Trust.

I saw that as fulfilling part of the vision of PNE as a community football club.

And when we did go up into Division 1 that following season, it was a fantastic year for Lancashire football; North End, Bolton, Burnley and Blackburn were all in there, which I think is the last time that happened.

We didn't go crazy in the transfer market that summer, because we'd already done our work in advance. We'd built the spine of the team with an eye on being ready for the next level; younger players coming into their prime, supported with experience where required.

Both David and Gary always had this view of building from the back, prioritising the foundations of a good goalkeeper and defence.

We made a great start in the first half of that season but eventually David decided we needed a little bit more up front, so we brought David Healy in from Manchester United.

It was a record fee at the time - about £1.8 million all told - but the manager had done his homework in his usual thorough manner and we felt it was a good investment. I didn't realise it was still the club's record purchase until recently, but in a way that's testament to the recruitment policy at the club over the years.

I've still got David's notes on all the players back then and the stricture was that he would do an assessment on the day they signed and then at regular intervals after that.

So six months after Healy signed, for example, David thought he had 'settled in well', was 'a good finisher' but 'needs to work on his pace and strength'.

And again, those notes were very useful for players' development.

Off the pitch that season, the stadium work continued with the demolition of the old Town End. I was sorry in one way to see it go, because it had played such a key part for the supporters over the years and was nationally-recognised for its atmosphere.

But we were achieving a vision and the all-seater stadium had to become a reality. The other significant aspect was that the new Town End created the fourth floodlight tower, which was a landmark development in more ways than one.

For me, nothing beats driving to Deepdale for a night game.

Coming in from Parbold on the motorway you can see it lit up like a football cathedral. It was just magical when that fourth tower went up and I still think the same now.

There's a sense of theatre and tradition and anticipation when you see those lights in the night sky. It's a special stadium and again, credit to Ben Casey for his vision in the first place.

That work was still taking place when we came to the play-off games against Birmingham City. Now, you obviously have feelings about local rivals and that's to be expected - it's all part of the sporting landscape.

But at that time, Birmingham were a club that were quite full of themselves. It's always interesting as a visiting chairman to see how clubs treat you.

Most clubs were absolutely great and very welcoming, but one or two stand out as not being quite so friendly.

I remember we played Tottenham Hotspur and Lord Sugar wouldn't meet the Preston directors. He was there, but we obviously weren't important enough.

It was the same at Fulham, where Mohammed Al Fayed wouldn't be in the same room as us. Charming.

On the other hand at Norwich, Delia Smith was lovely and served up wonderful fish and chips with homemade mayonnaise, as you might expect.

But Birmingham under Messrs Sullivan and Gold were a bit 'bling'.

Karren Brady was quite interesting too and tended to stand out at Football League meetings with her outfits, shall we say, where she always seems to be on the front row amid the sea of men in grey suits. (Incidentally, at those meetings, there were a small number of us who tried - and sadly failed - to restrict the amount of power going to players' agents. I think that has led to problems for the game, but at the time there were too many people who couldn't see the business implications of allowing agents to operate virtually unrestricted.)

Anyway, we'd gone to St Andrews for the first leg and I remember having things thrown at me in the directors' box - by the fans, not the directors, I hasten to add. So they were not my favourite team.

Of course, when you're Chairman, you always have to be magnanimous and shake the hand of the opponents at the end of the game, even if it's through gritted teeth at times.

It has to be done. You're the host and it's part of your role although at times, circumstances made it awkward.

I always felt sorry for Owen Oyston's family when they came, for example, because obviously the crowd would be singing things and you can hear every word, so you just sit there squirming in embarrassment.

We always tried to show all our visitors respect and, to be fair, at the end of that dramatic Birmingham game, David Gold and David Sullivan wished us all the best in the final. Maybe they were being magnanimous and maybe it was through gritted teeth, but respect to them for doing so in the depths of disappointment.

That had been the most dramatic night of all my time at the club and as a spectacle, it had everything; highs, lows, the last-minute equaliser, penalty misses, penalties scored and ultimately - just pure elation.

You could not ask for more from a night of sporting entertainment.

It was such an emotional night and I think everyone was so caught up in it, we didn't realise the full consequences until later.

We went down to Cardiff the day before the final on a coach for the directors, with Sir Tom and his wife Elsie. It was a magical, memorable experience. Everything was just perfect.

Yet I remember waking up on the day of the Bolton game and being hit by an unexpected wave of sadness. I realised that whatever happened over the next 24 hours - things were going to change. It was inevitable.

I don't know why I'd never thought of it before, but that morning it hit me.

I would either be the Chairman of a Premier League football club . . . or we would still be in the First Division. It sounds obvious, but both outcomes would mean we were not able to carry on as before.

If we *did* go up, I wouldn't have been able to be part-time Chairman of such a big enterprise, as well as being full-time Chief Executive of BAXI. I couldn't have done it and if I'm honest, I hadn't thought through what was going to happen.

If we *didn't* win, keeping everyone together and regrouping the following season would be very difficult. That moment on the morning of the game made me realise that the point we were now at could not be sustained.

Win or lose, things would never be the same again.

We had been on a journey and the Bolton game was the obvious culmination of everything we'd done over the previous seven years.

We'd reached the threshold and the natural progression was for us to win. It sounds simplistic, but because of the trajectory of where we'd come from, we should have won. I remember looking round the changing rooms with David before the game and all the BAXI shirts were hung up ready for the players and that was a very emotional moment for me.

We'd come a long way together, those shirts were symbolic of where we'd been on the journey and there we were . . . we'd got to where we'd set out to be.

We just needed one more step.

There was huge support, amazing scenes from the supporters and in many ways, it was a great day - apart from the result.

I've read accounts from David and players in the previous *North End Souls* books and I think their analysis is right; in a way, that Birmingham game was our final. It took a lot out of us emotionally and perhaps we didn't properly get over that in time.

Of course, if we hadn't had such emotion that night at Deepdale, we might not have made the final anyway. So nothing is set in stone. That's football.

After the game in Cardiff, we had an event with the players but when I looked round the room, I was filled more with sadness for what was to come than for losing the final itself. It felt like the end of an era - and, in reality, it was.

The following season was strange for us because we seemed to be entering it without the clarity and sense of direction that had propelled us in previous years.

There had been interest from other clubs in David, but he remained wholly committed to North End and we managed to retain the squad more or less intact.

But there was an incident that jolted me a bit and told me that the change I feared had imperceptibly begun. I was on holiday in Wales with my family when we popped into Woolworths for a drink and I saw a headline in the Daily Mirror: *'Nightclub shame as Moyes brawls with his players.'*

After spluttering on my coffee, I rang David to ask him about it and his view was that it had been blown out of all proportion, it was a minor thing that happened at every club every now and again.

There had been some hi-jinks involving Paul McKenna. Tepi Moilanen had misread David's response and there had been a bit of 'handbags at dawn' stuff.

I'm sure things like that do happen at football clubs, but I'd never read anything like that involving us. So it was another odd sign that things were changing and maybe my own journey in that role was coming to an end.

However, in hindsight, the BAXI era had ended on that day in Cardiff.

I'd worked hard for seven years and it takes it out of you. Sometimes the most difficult thing is working out when change is needed. I've always believed it's better to change things yourself before people want to change them for you.

I never wanted to overstay my welcome and therefore at the AGM in October 2001 I announced my resignation.

It just seemed like the right time to step down.

I was still very busy with BAXI and was about to become Chairman of the North West Development Agency.

But more than that, I looked at the three new stands at Deepdale, I looked at the position of the club compared to where we'd come from, the playing staff, the facilities, the attendances - we'd achieved what we set out to do.

North End wasn't just a community club, it was now at the heart of its community.

I didn't want to be a back seat driver, so I stepped away completely and passed the baton to other people who have continued to work wholeheartedly for the club. Derek Shaw took over from me and we are two very different characters, but I'd worked with him closely from Day One.

I thought I could negotiate well, but Derek was more of a wheeler-dealer who did a lot of good deals. So he was the continuity ticket and a low risk for the continuation of the work we'd already started.

As for David, the offers started to come thick and fast.

Possibly he had some I wasn't aware of, but those that did come through the club were always passed on to him. He had always been loyal to me personally because I had given him his chance and stood by him.

I never regretted appointing him or Gary and the fact that we only had two managers in that period is a surefire sign of success.

David had turned down many opportunities before the call came from Everton and really, they were a perfect match; a great club, but not a Top Six outfit with those sort of great expectations.

The Chairman Bill Kenwright was an absolute star, who I got to know and he was a true gentleman of the game. I could see David and him having a successful relationship and it was no surprise that he went on to great things.

Me? I have been kept very busy over the years and was Chairman of Liverpool's Capital of Culture celebrations in 2008, which involved a memorable night with Paul McCartney and Ringo Starr at Anfield.

I was chairman of Media City in Salford as well as being the Pro-Chancellor of Lancaster University for 10 years and a few other things as well.

So I've been exceptionally busy down the years and I'm still involved as a trustee with North End's Community and Education Trust, which has done fantastic work during the Coronavirus pandemic.

I'm extremely grateful that the club made me Vice President and that's another source of great pride.

Looking back at my time as Chairman of the club, I've got no regrets at all.

I'm very proud of what we achieved and proud of all the people involved - it was a real team effort on and off the pitch.

The managers, the players and, of course, the supporters all contributed hugely.

But there were so many others who played their part who are little remembered; club doctors, backroom staff, coaches, wives, parents, ground staff, tea ladies and people in the club shop . . . everyone involved.

It was a great time for my family also. We had wonderful times as a family going to away games. My wife was a very loyal supporter - home and away - as was her mother when she visited from Hampshire.

I always remember setting off from Parbold to Rochdale, or somewhere like that, on Boxing Day in the snow.

It was a real family affair. I also had invaluable support from the team at BAXI, especially Ann Edwards, my PA, who acted as gatekeeper, and Laurence King, the BAXI finance director and lifelong PNE supporter.

These are the people that made the machine operate - and still do.

They all deserve a huge amount of credit for their contribution.

I was just the cheerleader really; an unlikely one, a fairly quiet one, but a very proud one and I'm very happy to have played my part.

As a boy, rolling the dice on that Wembley board game, I may have wondered why Preston North End was unique.

As Chairman, I found out for myself.

LIFELONG SUPPORT

St Catherine's Hospice is a local, independent charity which provides highly specialised palliative and end-of-life care for the people of Chorley, Preston and South Ribble.

St Catherine's helps people with all kinds of life-shortening conditions such as cancer, motor neurone disease and heart failure, to experience quality of life to the end of life.

The charity helps keep people out of hospital, providing the specialised, personalised care and support they need to live well with comfort, independence and choice - either at home or in the hospice.

The hospice's diverse teams work with each patient and their loved ones to help them achieve what is important to them at all stages of their condition, from diagnosis to bereavement.

More than 900 incredible volunteers give their time in a variety of roles across the charity. The hospice also depends on the generosity and efforts of its supporters to raise £4m of its annual £5.8m running costs, with £1.8m provided by the NHS.

Funds are raised in a variety of ways including donations in wills; the hospice's weekly lottery; 19 charity shops; events including the popular Moonlight and

Memories Walk; and poignant remembrance campaigns such as Yellow Ribbon and Light Up A Life dedications.

Fundraising activities and charity challenges are also organised by thousands of dedicated supporters, and The Mill café and community hub - set in the hospice grounds of St Catherine's Park - welcomes the local community to enjoy delicious dishes whilst donating proceeds to the charity.

The St Catherine's Support Team not only helps those who have come into contact with the hospice; they're here to help everyone in a range of ways, through drop-in sessions including bereavement and carer support, and hosting a monthly Living Well Hub with guidance about finances, wills, benefits and more.

And the St Catherine's website features a wide selection of helpful resources for everyone – including patients and families, healthcare professionals, and the wider community – covering topics such as bereavement advice, coping with anxiety, guidance about wills, financial wellbeing, and how to support those who are grieving or going through a difficult time.

There are also tips for taking care of your mental and physical health and wellbeing, such as local walking routes, healthy and tasty recipe ideas, relaxation techniques, and home exercise and workout routines.

To find out more about the important work of St Catherine's Hospice and how this much-loved local charity could help you, your family, friends and neighbours; or to discover how you could support this worthy local cause in a range of enjoyable and meaningful ways, visit **www.stcatherines.co.uk** or call 01772 629171. You can also connect with the charity on Facebook and social media via: **@StCatherinesPre @TheMillPre @StCatherinesShops**

St Catherine's
hospice care

PHOTOGRAPHIC CREDITS

All photographs are courtesy of the Lancashire Post, with the exception of the front cover: *Action Images/Ed Sykes Livepic*.

THANK YOU FOR ALL YOUR HELP

Firstly, huge thanks to everyone who agreed to be interviewed and contributed to *North End Souls 3*: Ian Bryson, Mick Rathbone, Jermaine Beckford, Declan Rudd, Tommy Booth, Jonathan Clark, Danny Dichio, Alan Irvine, Darren Ferguson, Phil Brown, Graham Westley, Ricky Heppolette, Jon Parkin, Teuvo Moilanen and Bryan Gray. It was a genuine pleasure and a privilege to speak to so many major figures from the club's past. Thanks also to Dave Seddon and the *Lancashire Post* for their support throughout the production of this series of books.

It would not have been possible without them. Thanks also to Ian Rigby at the PNE Former Players Association, the club shop staff and Hannah Broadley at PNEFC, for their help and efficiency. I'd also like to thank Trevor Johnson *(the original North End Soul!)* John Smith, John Kelly, Andy Murphy, Andy Livingstone, Lee Ashcroft, Kevin Harrison, Michael and Shirley Harrison, Peterborough United FC, West Ham United FC and Toronto FC.

As ever, thanks to my parents and family for their love and support, especially my wife Lisa for her fact-checking skills, unending patience and grammatical brilliance.

Finally, sincere gratitude to all my fellow North Enders out there for buying the first two books, which meant I could finish off the *'Butter Pie Trilogy'* in style. I've dedicated this book to The Gentry, for those who have gone before us, but are always with us.

Their North End souls live on.

ALSO AVAILABLE: HIGHLY RECOMMENDED FOR NORTH END FANS

www.northendsouls.com www.amazon.co.uk